Blessings and Thanksgiving
Reflections on the Siddur and Synagogue

OUPRESS

מגיד
MAGGID

Gladys Neustadter *z"l* Edition

BLESSINGS and THANKSGIVING

Reflections on the Siddur and Synagogue

Rabbi Joseph B. Soloveitchik

Edited by Shalom Carmy and Joel B. Wolowelsky

Maggid Books
OU Press

Blessings and Thanksgiving
Reflections on the Siddur and Synagogue

First Edition, 2019

OU Press
An imprint of the Orthodox Union
11 Broadway, New York, NY 10004
www.oupress.org

Maggid Books
An imprint of Koren Publishers Jerusalem Ltd.

POB 8531, New Milford, CT 06776-8531, USA
& POB 4044, Jerusalem 9104001, Israel
www.maggidbooks.com

Cover Photo: courtesy Yeshiva University

ISBN 978-1-59264-514-5, *hardcover*

A CIP catalogue record for this title is available from the British Library

Printed and bound in the United States

אנו מתכבדים להשתתף ביוזמה להוציא לאור את הספר הזה
לכבוד הורינו

נחם צבי בן מרדכי אברהם וחיה רחל
חוה לאה בת חיים יצחק וחיה גיטל
מרים בת יחיאל וגלי
אהרון אשר זליג בן יעקב יצחק ומיימי
צביה רייצל בת פייבל ומלכה

מאת

משה זאב, מלכה בריינדל
גבריאלה טובה, בצלאל יחיאל, יונתן מנשה ויוסף מרדכי

In Loving Memory of Our Parents

Rabbi Yitzchok and Bluma Singer
הרב יצחק אהרן בן הרב ר׳ אליהו ז״ל
בלומא בת ר׳ ישראל אריה לייב ז״ל
Our Father was Rabbi of the Bialystoker Synagogue and a renowned
תלמיד חכם
Our Mother was a true אשת חיל

In Loving Memory of Our Uncles

Rabbi Dovid Singer and Rabbi Joseph Singer
הרב דוד בן הרב ר׳ אליהו ז״ל
הרב יוסף משה בן הרב ר׳ אליהו ז״ל
Both were scholars of great erudition

Dedicated by
Baruch and Susie Singer   Eli and Rivki Singer
Nussie and Ruchy Singer   Yossi and Suri Singer   Sruly Singer

In Loving Memory of Our Parents

Joseph and Gwendolyn Straus
יוסף שמואל בן בנימין ז״ל
גינדל בת משה יעקב ז״ל

Dedicated by
Moshael and Zahava Straus
Daniel and Joyce Straus

In Loving Memory of Our Parents

ABRAHAM AND SYLVIA WINTMAN
אברהם צבי בן יצחק חיים ז״ל
שרה בלומא בת קלמן מרדכי הכהן ז״ל

Our parents' lives together, devoted to family, community, and Klal Yisrael, and the especially close relationship our parents maintained with the Rav, have been a wellspring of inspiration to our entire family.

Dedicated by
Kenny Wintman and Sandy Welkes

In Honor of

RABBI HASKEL LOOKSTEIN

for his sixty years of dedicated leadership of
and selfless devotion to Congregation Kehilath Jeshurun.

Dedicated by
Raanan and Nicole Agus

In Loving Memory of Our Wife and Mother

GRETA ROSENZWEIG ABELOW

גיטל שרה בת ר׳ זלמן זאב ז״ל

She was a devoted student of the Rav and a dedicated teacher in the Maimonides School for 30 years. Her detailed notes of the Rav's Saturday night shiurim in Brookline
demonstrate her love of learning and still serve us well.
She lived a life dedicated to the Rav's worldview and values.

Dedicated by

Joseph Abelow
Dr. Arthur and Rebecca Abelow
Gerald Abelow
Akiva and Esther Tekuzener

Contents

Editors' Introduction

Although the volume before you is, at one level, a complement and continuation to *Worship of the Heart: Essays on Jewish Prayer* (published by the Toras HoRav Foundation in 2003), in content and form it is a very different kind of book.

Worship of the Heart was intended to provide a comprehensive philosophical framework for prayer and contained an analysis of human nature as it pertains to the experience of prayer. Most of the volume was composed as part of a unified whole. Additional manuscripts incorporated in the book were written during the same period as stand-alone lectures on the same fundamental themes. Much of the book therefore dealt with the ethical, the exalted, and categories of experience related to the human encounter with God. The vocabulary and mode of exposition reflected major trends in European philosophy and theology dominant in the early and mid 20th century. The Rav was concerned with the fundamental building blocks of man's relationship with God and with the prayer experience in particular: such as petition, praise, and commitment (i.e., accepting the yoke of Heaven).

The halakhic and textual analysis in *Worship of the Heart* was devoted almost entirely to the two central institutions of the prayer service, the *Amida* and the *Shema,* with some attention to the prefatory blessings to *Shema.* Halakhically, these subjects are among the most important and they illustrate the rigorous integration of halakhic insight and philosophical anthropology that is one of the hallmarks of the Rav's thought.

Blessings and Thanksgiving, to a large extent, grows out of the analysis in *Worship of the Heart.* The chapter on the Morning Blessings is, in fact, part of the lecture series at the core of the previous book. Other chapters introduce new halakhic and experiential building blocks and concepts essential to Jewish prayer: for example, the distinction between two types of praise in *Pesukei DeZimra* and Hallel, or the concept of divine sovereignty at the root of blessings in general, and the Grace after Meals in particular. Without these essays, the Rav's philosophy of prayer would be drastically incomplete.

At the same time, *Blessings and Thanksgiving* does not repeat the abstract philosophical analysis produced in the earlier book. Despite the significant theoretical contributions referred to in the previous paragraph, it is more concerned with the text and texture of prayer than with its underlying structure. In these lectures the Rav plumbs many of the details of prayer instead of restricting himself to examples that further his systematic argument. He addresses individual prayers and blessings in their particularity, like the blessings recited for physiological functions or upon rising in the morning; he comments on the institution of the synagogue that brings the community together; he considers particular questions that affect prayer, such as praying for the eradication of evil.

The differences in content between the two books are also manifest in their respective style and tone. *Blessings and Thanksgiving,* which makes use of manuscripts and edited transcripts of public lectures, reflects the intimacy of oral discourse where *Worship of the Heart,* for all its searing passion, is very much a book conceived and executed in the solitude of the study. The earlier book presupposes philosophical sophistication. Here, however, Western culture is employed primarily to illustrate and dramatize ideas, rather than to formulate a philosophical case. In *Worship of the Heart,* the Rav hedges his occasional utilization of Aggada with a host of methodological caveats; personal anecdotes are absent. In *Blessings and Thanksgiving* there are no such reservations.

The selections presented in this volume were delivered by the Rav in a variety of circumstances:

The first chapter, "The Morning Blessings," was transcribed by Jonathan Gross, and edited by Rabbi Steven Weil. As noted above, this chapter was part of the Rav's lecture series which formed the basis of *Worship of the Heart*.

The second chapter, "*Pesukei DeZimra* and Kaddish," is a translation of the first two sections of a yahrzeit *shiur* published in Hebrew under the title "*Pesukei DeZimra*" in *Shiurim LeZekher Abba Mari*, volume 2. The translation was prepared by Joel Linsider, *z"l*.

The third chapter, "*Keriat Shema* and the Blessings of Torah," is based on a lecture delivered by the Rav on February 2, 1957, as well as an undated manuscript by the Rav transcribed by Rabbi Dov Karoll.

The fourth chapter, "*Birkat HaMazon*, the 'Grace after Meals,'" conflates a yahrzeit *shiur* delivered by the Rav in 1961, transcribed and translated by Arnold Lustiger, and a 1969 *shiur* transcribed by Ariela Goldsmith.

The fifth chapter, "Grant Us Understanding to Know Your Ways," is a transcription of a lecture delivered by the Rav at the Rabbinical Council of America's Midwinter Conference on February 7, 1968.

The sixth chapter, "Praying for the Defeat of Evil," was a lecture the Rav delivered in Boston on March 7, 1970.

The seventh chapter, "*Berakhot* in Judaism," was the aggadic portion of a yahrzeit *shiur* delivered on January 15, 1956. The Hebrew manuscript of the lecture was published in *Yemei Zikaron*, edited by Rabbi Moshe Krona. The English translation in this volume was prepared by Elli Fischer; the final section of this *shiur*, which does not relate to the subject of this book, was omitted.

The eighth chapter, "Communal Prayer and the Structure of the Synagogue," is a translation of the final section of the yahrzeit *shiur* "*Pesukei DeZimra*" published in *Shiurim LeZekher Abba Mari*, volume 2. This translation too was prepared by Joel Linsider, *z"l*.

The penultimate chapter in this volume, "The Synagogue as an Institution and as an Idea," is the text of a lecture given by the Rav at Kehillath Jeshurun in New York City on December 6, 1972. Originally intended for a volume celebrating Rabbi Joseph H. Lookstein's jubilee year in the rabbinate, his death before publication turned the book into the *Rabbi Joseph H. Lookstein Memorial Volume* (ed. Leo Landman, Ktav 1980).

The Rav's comments regarding Rabbi Lookstein, in which the Rav responded to cries to "modernize" the Orthodox synagogue, can also serve as background for the final chapter in this volume, "Old Prayers and 'New' Jews":

> When I came to the United States so many years ago, Orthodoxy was at low ebb... We were met with laughter and ridicule, not with opposition. The situation is different now. And the change is due to a few people, among whom Rabbi Lookstein is the most outstanding pioneer. He showed the American Jew that it is possible to have a synagogue conform to the *Shulḥan Arukh* both architecturally and ritually...and at the same time, this *Shul* excelled as far as good behavior, cultivated manners, and beautiful sermons were concerned. Rabbi Lookstein contradicted the accusation hurled at us—and I heard this accusation many times—that Orthodoxy is synonymous with slovenliness, vulgarity, ignorance, lack of culture, lack of refinement. I believe we owe Rabbi Lookstein a *yasher koaḥ* for it.

"Old Prayers and 'New' Jews" is a translation of the fifth, sixth, and the first section of the seventh essay, in a ten-part series of articles the Rav wrote for the Yiddish newspaper *Der Tog-Morgn Zhurnal* (40:14,548 [December 13, 1954]: 5–6; 40:14,555 [December 20, 1954]: 5; and 40:14,562 [December 27, 1954]: 5, respectively), originally published with the titles "In What Manner Should a Jew Pray?" "Old Prayers and 'New' Jews," and "Where are the Reform Jews Taking Our Ancient Prayer Book?" Edited versions were reprinted in the Rav's *Droshes un Ksovim*, ed. David E. Fishman (Jersey City, NJ: Published for the Toras Horav Foundation by Ktav Publishing House, 2009), 281–299.

The present translation was prepared by Shaul Seidler-Feller based primarily on the *Der Tog-Morgn Zhurnal* originals, having taken some liberties with respect to both the punctuation of sentences and their division into paragraphs in order to render the pieces more easily understandable for the English reader. References to biblical and rabbinic sources cited did not appear in the original and were added by the translator.

The first of these columns was presented as a response to the following question: "In certain Jewish circles, it has been argued that the manner of prayer in Conservative temples, which feature organ music, mixed choirs, and a good deal of decorum, is more progressive than is the traditional order of worship. Perhaps the service in Orthodox synagogues can also be modernized?" The Rav began his reply as follows: "In order to answer this question, we will need to plumb the depths of how Judaism understands the institution of prayer generally. Once we have clarified that matter, the answer may become self-evident."

While this volume is not a publication of the Toras HoRav Foundation, it is indebted to the work of the Foundation, which was established by family members and former students with the aims of enhancing both our grasp of Rabbi Soloveitchik's philosophy and our understanding of the diverse topics he addressed. Most importantly, we value the work of Rabbi Reuven Ziegler, Director of the *MeOtzar HoRav* Archives, who organized and supervised the transcription of voluminous manuscripts of the Rav, reviewing the material and providing valuable editorial comments and suggestions. *MeOtzar HoRav* has published eleven volumes in English with David Shatz as Series Editor, all made possible by a generous grant from Ruth and Irwin Shapiro.

We thank the OU Press and its General Editor Rabbi Menachem Genack for inviting us to bring these essays of the Rav to publication. We are grateful to Rabbi Simon Posner, Executive Editor, and Rabbi Eliyahu Krakowski, Associate Editor, for their important suggestions and editorial comments throughout the process of publication, and to Rabbi Genack for carefully reviewing the final volume.

* * *

The Rav brought his teachings to a wide range of audiences, committed Jews, *talmidei ḥakhamim*, rabbis and *amkha* who were not fully involved in Torah life. Many personal assessments of the Rav and his legacy attempt to classify him as either the austere Rosh Yeshiva and thinker, ensconced in and intensely preoccupied with the precise analysis of Talmudic law and human experience, on the one hand, or the genial teacher who cast his rhetorical and homiletic spell over thousands, not all of whom were privy to the full range of his religious and intellectual quest, on the other hand. Both aspects were in evidence in his variegated teaching career and both find expression in some of his most memorable literary output. It is fitting that the Rav's teaching in the area of prayer, perhaps the most important interface between halakha, philosophy and daily life, so crucial to the existence of both the sophisticated religious personality and the unlearned practitioner of Judaism, should also exhibit that fruitful mixture of content and style.

Shalom Carmy
Joel B. Wolowelsky

Publisher's Preface

At the beginning of his *Hilkhot Tefilla,* Maimonides establishes his view that *tefilla* constitutes a biblical obligation: "There is a positive commandment to pray each day, as it is written [Deut. 11:13], 'and to worship Him with all your heart.' Said the sages, What is worship of the heart? This is prayer." Likewise, in his *Sefer HaMitzvot,* Maimonides writes: "The fifth mitzva is that which He has commanded us to worship Him… Although this is a general commandment, it has a specific component, which is the commandment to pray…" According to Maimonides, the obligation to pray derives from the Torah, and this obligation applies every day.

Nahmanides, on the other hand, in his glosses to *Sefer HaMitzvot,* disagrees. Basing himself on the Gemara (Berakhot 21a), Nahmanides maintains that prayer is only a rabbinic obligation. In his words, "The concept of prayer is not a [biblical] obligation at all, but rather one of the attributes of kindness the Creator has bestowed upon us—that He listens and responds when we cry out to Him… And if [there is] a Scriptural foundation [for the obligation], we would count it [as a mitzva] as Maimonides does, and explain that it is an obligation for times of distress—that we should believe that God, may He be blessed and exalted, listens to prayer and saves us from distress through our prayers and cries."

According to Nahmanides, there is no biblical obligation to pray every day; at most there is an obligation to pray in times of distress. Maimonides, who maintains there is a biblical obligation to pray every day, counts the obligation to pray in times of distress as an independent mitzva. In the beginning of *Hilkhot Taaniyot,* he states: "There is a positive commandment to cry out and sound an alarm with the trumpets, as it is written [Num. 10:9], '[And when you go to war...] against the adversary that oppresses you, then you shall sound an alarm with the trumpets,' which means that for any issue that distresses you, such as famine, plague, locusts, and the like, cry out and sound an alarm..." According to Maimonides, the prayer of every day and the prayer of times of distress are two distinct obligations, derived from two separate verses. Nahmanides, on the other hand, maintains that there is only one such obligation, prayer in times of distress.

The Rav explained that, in fact, all agree that the obligation of prayer depends upon a feeling of distress—Maimonides too agrees to this principle. The dispute between Maimonides and Nahmanides is about the kind of distress which creates the obligation to pray: According to Nahmanides, the obligation to pray is prompted by the external crises which arise from time to time, but according to Maimonides it is not only the external crises, but the internal, existential crisis which afflicts mortal man throughout his entire life. Man's life in this world is what *Sefer HaYashar* refers to as "*neveh hatelaot,*" the abode of hardships. The foundation of prayer lies in our recognition that without divine assistance we are in a state of constant crisis, that but for God's everlasting kindness we could not survive, as we say in *Modim*: "for Your miracles which are with us every day." Even according to Maimonides, then, prayer emerges from the feeling of distress which man experiences daily.

There is a fundamental link between prayer and distress. The prayers to which we find that God responds are those prompted by inner distress. A prime example of this is Hannah's prayer for a child, which serves as the model of what prayer should be. Yet surely Hannah had been praying for a child for many years—why did God respond to Hannah's prayer only after so long? The Rav explained that in all of Hannah's earlier prayers, her husband Elkanah stood alongside her as a companion in her suffering. Only once her husband said to her, "Hannah, why do you weep and why do you not eat, and why is your heart grieved? Am not I better to you than ten sons?" (I Sam. 1:8) did Hannah realize that her husband had given up on her having children. Now, in her utter loneliness, she recognized that she had no one to rely on but

God. Thus, her prayer at this point was different from all of her previous prayers, and with this prayer she was answered.

Based on this, we can understand the terminology *Ḥazal* use for prayer, "*avoda shebalev*." The "worship of the heart" of prayer refers not merely to intention, but to prayer which emerges from deep within the heart, from the experience of inner turmoil that accompanies man throughout his life, from the internalization of the fact that without God's kindness we are always in a state of despair. Such a prayer is answered by God.

In the passage in *Sefer HaMitzvot* mentioned above, Maimonides cites the *Sifrei* on the verse "to worship Him": "to worship Him, this is prayer; to worship Him, this is study." Likewise, Maimonides cites the midrash *Mishnat Rabbi Eliezer*: "Worship Him with His Torah, worship Him in His Temple." Apparently, both prayer and Torah study constitute the same fulfillment of divine worship. The Rav explained that for this reason, *Keriat HaTorah* was instituted as part of the prayer service. For the same reason, Maimonides combines the laws of prayer with those of the Torah reading in *Hilkhot Tefilla U'Keriat HaTorah*, because both Torah and prayer combine to form one mode of worship.

On the surface, Torah study and *tefilla* are two completely distinct mitzvot. What is the common denominator between them? The answer is that both share the feature of *Amida lifnei Hashem*. Maimonides defines the intention necessary for *tefilla*: "He should clear his mind of all thoughts and see himself as if he is standing before the Divine Presence" (*Hilkhot Tefilla* 4:16). Likewise, the Divine Presence accompanies one who is studying Torah, as we find in the Mishna (Avot 3:7): "Ten who are sitting and studying Torah, the Divine Presence rests among them ... and even one who sits and studies [alone] ..." Both Torah and *tefilla* bring man closer to his Creator, and for this reason, both constitute *avoda shebalev*.

The Rav was a real-life example of Torah study which constituted divine worship. When the Rav taught, it was apparent to all observers that he was standing in God's presence. I remember the Rav's annual "*yahrzeit shiur*" for his father Rav Moshe, during the year in which the Rav had lost his mother, wife and brother. One can readily imagine the impact these losses had on the Rav's state of mind. Yet, despite his grief, as soon as he began the *shiur* it was as if he was a different man. Those present experienced firsthand David HaMelekh's words, "Had Your Torah not been my delight, I should then have perished in my affliction." On this occasion, the Rav commented that when he was preparing a *shiur* alone he could feel a breath at his shoulder, the presence of the Divine, asking him, "*Nu,* Yoshe Ber, what do *you* think about this *sugya*?" Through the example of the Rav, we can understand how Talmud Torah too is a form of *avoda shebalev*.

OU Press is honored to present readers this volume of the Rav's writings on *tefilla,* which represents both of these forms of *avoda shebalev,* and we are grateful to Dr. Atarah Twersky, on behalf of the Toras HoRav Foundation, for allowing us to do so. Many individuals worked assiduously to bring this project to fruition, including Rabbi Shalom Carmy and Dr. Joel B. Wolowelsky, the volume's editors; Rabbi Simon Posner, Rabbi Eliyahu Krakowski and Debra Bree of OU Press; as well as Matthew Miller of Maggid Books and his dedicated staff, with special thanks to Rabbi Reuven Ziegler. Rabbi Shalom Rosner, Ram in Yeshivat Kerem B'Yavneh and Rav of Kehillat Nofei Shemesh, and a close associate of the family that endowed this edition in memory of Gladys Neustadter *z"l,* offered an important perspective from a generation that did not merit knowing the Rav personally. Special thanks go to my colleague Rabbi Steven Weil, Senior Managing Director of the Orthodox Union, who has consistently championed the dissemination of the Rav's works and the preservation of his legacy. This project could not have been realized without the generous support of those who endowed this volume in memory of Gladys Neustadter *z"l,* as well as the Abelow, Agus, Singer, Straus, and Wintman families. All those who participated in this project can be justifiably proud of their contribution to *Klal Yisrael* which this volume represents.

Menachem Dov Genack
General Editor
OU Press

Foreword

The Rav I Never Met

Fifteen years ago, my six-year-old daughter answered the phone in our home. "Is the Rav available?" was the request. Without batting an eyelash, she replied, "The Rav is on the wall, but my father is home." That humorous exchange crystalizes the reality of my generation—the generation for whom the Rav was more of an institution than a personality in our lives.

When I first entered the hallowed hallways of Amsterdam Avenue, the Rav was already ill, and was no longer giving shiur. Our rebbeim are his talmidim, and we are considered *keli sheni,* secondary vessels, in terms of his *mesirat haTorah.* We hear the stories of the yahrzeit *shiurim* and teshuva *derashot,* where thousands of scholars and laymen alike would sit riveted to their seats for hours on end, absorbing the Rav's creative genius in transmitting the secrets of the given *sugya.* We are told of the awe and trepidation, palpably felt, in the hearts of all those who were privileged to sit in the Rav's classroom in the early years. We try to vicariously experience the emotional highs which were felt by those who merited being close to him. And yet, we recognize that we are a distant second generation, that *eino domeh shemia lire'iya*—hearing cannot compare to seeing.

Given this disconnect, I ask what is it about the Rav's Torah that is so powerful, so compelling that even as a *keli sheni,* we feel so influenced, so shaped, so molded by his thinking and teachings? Why, when preparing Shabbat HaGadol and Shabbat Shuva *derashot,* do I always first look into what the Rav has to say on the topic? How is it that when we read his writings, we each feel as if he is talking to each of us personally, spanning the generations and capturing the most modern issues with his perceptive and timeless insights? Maybe by reviewing three of his own thoughts will we be able to better appreciate how his Torah continues to impact and what his Torah symbolizes for all of us.

BAALEI HAMESORA

The Meiri, in his introduction to Pirkei Avot, outlines all of the great Jewish leaders in history, starting with Moshe Rabbeinu and continuing all the way until his own time. Maimonides, in his introduction to Mishneh Torah, also lists the leaders from Moshe Rabbeinu but stops at Ravina and Rav Ashi. Why didn't he continue until himself as the Meiri did? The Rav explained in the name of his father (see R. Hershel Schachter, *Nefesh HaRav,* p. 36) that Maimonides isn't simply informing us of historical facts, but rather is formulating a halakhic principle: Those who came after Ravina and Rav Ashi no longer shared the same status of *ḥakhmei hamesora* as their predecessors, and therefore they could no longer dispute the rulings of the Gemara. After Ravina and Rav Ashi, there was a fundamental change in the nature of the *mesora.*

Our *mesora* is based on the leadership of the *baalei hamesora,* those unique individuals who carry the torch of *Torah Shebe'al Peh* from generation to generation. In the time of Ḥazal, there was one league of *ḥakhmei hamesora,* and that is what Maimonides is emphasizing, but the concept of these cadre of leaders is one that applies for all times. They are people who learn, live, and breathe Torah, and represent our conduit to the true transmission of *Torah Shebe'al Peh.*

The Rav, in *Mah Dodekh MiDod,* his *hesped* for his uncle the Brisker Rav, delineates another inimitable element to our *ḥakhmei hamesora. Ḥazal* (Sanhedrin 59a) tell us that all Jews have *eirusin* with the Torah. The Rav highlights that it's only *eirusin,* the first stage of a Jewish marriage. But there are *yeḥidei segula* in every generation who have *nissuin,* a complete marriage, with the Torah. What does this mean?

> On rare occasions, the Torah weds itself to an individual and becomes his companion. Its marriage to him establishes itself through seclusion (*yiḥud*) which brings togetherness (*yaḥdut*) and which culminates in complete unity (*aḥdut*). The Torah becomes absorbed into the depths of his being and merges with him. One who merits this merits a *neshama yeteira,* the soul of Torah, from which flows the wellspring of blessing…This mysterious intuition is the source of halakhic creativity and *ḥiddush.*

A fully married couple lives as one unified whole, each with an intuition for the other's feelings, desires, and thoughts. That's exactly how the *baal hamesora* merges with the Torah. He merits a halakhic intuition, viewing the Torah from within, as an insider and player, and not just as a viewer and learner. His essence becomes blended with Torah values, and his presentations reflect a true sense of *hashkafat haTorah.* Rashi (Shemot 28:4), after acknowledging his lack of textual knowledge related to the description of the *ephod,* pronounces "*velibbi omer li,* my heart tells me," and proceeds with a lengthy comprehensive discussion of its colors, materials, and weaving. Rashi's heart was one with the Torah, thus giving him a halakhic intuition as to the *ephod*'s description.

The Rav said these words about his uncle, but we can naturally apply them to him as well. He was, and continues to be, the *baal hamesora* for so many of our generation. His Torah reflects an intense *libbi omer li,* which translates for us into an inspirational and universal leader, whose influence has not diminished with the passage of years. In appreciating his *lomdus* of Talmudic texts, his ingenuity in presenting biblical narratives, and his clarity of contemporary issues, we all relive our Har Sinai experience, the experience that started our national *mesora.*

THE CONNECTION OF THE JEW TO TORAH LEARNING

The Gemara (Bava Kama 82a) teaches us the roots of the rabbinic decree of *Keriat HaTorah*:

> For it was taught: "And they went three days in the wilderness and found no water" (Shemot 15:22), upon which those who expound verses metaphorically said: water means nothing but Torah, as it says: "Ho, everyone that thirsts come for water" (Yeshayahu 55:1).

> As they went three days without Torah they immediately became exhausted. The prophets among them thereupon rose and enacted that they should publicly read the Torah on Shabbat… and read again on Monday and on Thursday… so that they should not be kept for three days without Torah.

The Rav (in a *yahrzeit shiur* entitled "*Takanat Moshe,*" *Shiurim LeZekher Abba Mari,* vol. 2) asked a simple question. How is it that they were thirsty for Torah? When did this story take place? In Marah, six weeks before they even received the Torah! What were they thirsty for? They didn't yet have an obligation of Talmud Torah!

The Rav suggested that the *takana* was not enacted to fulfill an obligation, but to quench the natural thirst that every Jew has for Torah:

> It was not concern for lack of fulfillment of the mitzva of Talmud Torah which led to the institution of *Keriat HaTorah* on Monday, Thursday, and Shabbat—for they were not yet obligated in Talmud Torah. Rather, it was the lethargy which possessed them, the fatigue and the discontent which stemmed from lack of Torah study and which brought the congregation to complain and rebel, which prompted the prophets among them to institute *Keriat HaTorah.*

Every Jew, in his heart of hearts, thirsts, pines, yearns for a connection to the Divine through the Torah. The *tzelem Elokim* within us, often subconsciously, is sustained and nourished through our *limmud haTorah,* separate from any divine command. That is why they were thirsty, because their internal Torah compass was pointing them in the Godly direction.

This might also help explain the famous Gemara (Nidda 30a) where we are told that *in utero,* we are taught the entire Torah, and then caused to forget it at the moment of birth. The *mefarshim* are puzzled—what is the purpose of teaching us the entire Torah in the first place, if we will be made to forget it in the very near future? The Rav explained that that learning creates the natural connection, the *pintele Yid,* the spark of holiness, which every Jew has deep within them. Our *avoda* in life is to reconnect to that deep place within us, through our constant dedication and commitment to *limmud haTorah*. [Also see *Eretz HaTzvi, siman* 12, citing the *Baal HaTanya*.]

The Rav taught us, through personal example and through his writings, how each and every Jew has that very special connection to Torah, and thereby to Hashem. He and his Torah were able to connect to both the scholarly Harvard professor and to the elderly survivor from Lodz, to the seasoned rabbinic leaders and to the novice layman just beginning to learn, to students whose native tongue was Yiddish and students whose native tongue was English. He helped American, and really world Jewry, link back to their *pintele Yid* in the deepest way possible. And he did it through a rigorous, honest, and engaging presentation of the halakha and the Talmud. Such an approach to Torah is imbibed voraciously by the student, and has a lasting and permanent effect on his mind and soul.

TEFILLA BE'EIT TZARA

The final element is related to the themes of the present volume. Maimonides (*Hilkhot Tefilla* 1:1) tells that there is a biblical obligation to *daven* each day of our lives. Nahmanides (*Hasagot al Sefer HaMitzvot, aseh* 5) famously argues and holds that there is no biblical daily command to pray (he agrees on a rabbinic level), though he does admit to a biblical obligation under one specific circumstance—*eit tzara*. If there is a national calamity, or even a private time of difficulty, then Nahmanides agrees that one must turn to God in that circumstance. The Rav (*Worship of the Heart*) suggested a deeper understanding of this *maḥloket*.

> The controversy between Nahmanides and Maimonides does not revolve about the conjunction of prayer and *tzarah*. They are in agreement that *tzarah* underlies prayer. They differ, however, about the substance of the experience of *tzarah* itself… [For Maimonides,] the depth crisis addresses metaphysical, unknown, undefined and clandestine personal distress. The crisis is encountered in the strangeness of human destiny… Such a crisis is not brought about by extraneous factors, or precipitated by coincidental entanglements… [Prayer] emerges from seclusion, from out of the loneliness of the individual whom everybody save God has abandoned… Man is always in need because he is always in crisis and distress.

The Rav taught us that prayer in particular, and life in general, is about recognizing our dependence on *HaKadosh Barukh Hu* each moment of our lives. The world is not on autopilot. Mother nature has a Father. He is *meḥadesh bekhol yom uvekhol rega mamash*.

At the end of Masekhet Sota (49a), the Mishna teaches us that when R. Yehuda HaNasi died, the pure unadulterated trait of *anava* died with him. There were no more great rabbinic figures who excelled in humility. Rav Yosef (*ibid.*, 49b) comments, "Do not include [when reciting this Mishna] the word '*anava*,' because I exist." As worded, the Mishna is not true, because I am still alive. The question is obvious. That's not exactly a comment that we would expect from a great *anav*! One answer suggested points us to review who Rav Yosef was, and what happened during his lifetime. Often in Shas (see Rashi, Ketubot 2a), Rav Yosef is reminded by his own students of ideas and messages that he himself had taught them, but had forgotten due to illness. What a tragedy, how awful Rav Yosef must have felt! Rav Yosef exclaims, "If you need a living image to teach you humility, if you need to recognize that you are not the masters in this world, look at my life! My life is a graphic illustration of the vicissitudes and surprises that life might have in store for us. *Anava* didn't die with Rebbe. The message is loud and clear even today."

Life is an *eit tzara*, or at least a potential *eit tzara*, and we need to be connected to and cognizant of Hashem at each stage. The Rav, so often in his writings, not just in the realm of *tefilla*, zeroes in on this central idea to our faith, being God-centric and God-dependent. Be it in context of *simḥat Yom Tov* and *avelut*, of *Beit HaMikdash* and *Beit HaKnesset*, or even the laws of *tefillin* and *mezuza*, he called to our attention the need and privilege to use the religious experience to connect to the *Borei Olam*, which ultimately is the goal of our lives. He deepened our appreciation of all *maasei hamitzvot*, expounding on the hidden *kiyyum*, often found in the accompanying details, while all the while keeping us focused on the goal, to perform the action in a way that brings *naḥat ruaḥ leYotzrenu*.

In summation, then, the Rav, carrying the torch of Torah for our generation, was a living example of one of the *baalei hamesora*. His clear, profound, and compelling presentation of Torah helped so many connect to their "*pintele Yid*," their moment created *in utero* with the angel. And finally, the Rav's *hashkafa* of life being viewed as a continuous *eit tzara* allows us to inject Godliness and God-centrality in everything we do.

The Mishna (Avot 1:2) informs us of the three pillars upon which the world stands. Maybe the Rav was *the* pillar of our generation, carrying us on his shoulders in these three areas. His messages in Torah connected us to our core, his approach to *Avoda* allowed us to gain a God-centric view of the world, and his selfless leadership as one of *baalei hamesora*, representing a role model for the entire generation, was the greatest act of *ḥesed* that he could have bestowed upon us.

So yes, I never met the Rav, he is pictured on the wall in my house, but like many other students of his students, I feel deeply linked and informed by his Torah, shaped by his ideals, and molded by his principles. May we merit to continue in the path of his illustrious tradition, and remain true to his lofty standards of *limmud Torah* and *Avodat Hashem*.

Shalom Rosner

Chapter 1

The Morning Blessings

INTRODUCTION

We begin with three questions about the *Birkhot HaShaḥar,* the Morning Blessings that we say daily. First, why were these particular blessings selected? Each morning a person performs a variety of physiological functions, muscular movements and general activities—for instance, breathing and hearing—that are just as important for his or her survival as the activities to which these Morning Blessings relate. Yet no prayers were formulated in conjunction with these processes. What criterion guided our sages in giving preference to the physiological acts they chose over others?

Our next concern is that the formulation of the blessings seems hard to grasp at first glance. They could have been formulated in a more direct, more expressive and less equivocal way. For instance, the blessing (*berakha*) "Who gives sight to the blind" that we say when we open our eyes implies healing those deprived of vision, not the physiological opening and closing of one's eyelids. Yet it is this physiological function of opening one's eyes in the morning upon awakening that the *berakha* acknowledges.

Third, the meaning of certain blessings is obscure; the ideas expressed are far from being central motifs in Judaism. For instance, the *berakha* "Who gives the rooster understanding to distinguish between the day and the night" is puzzling. A general blessing over light should not have referred to the rooster and should not have been phrased "to discriminate between the day and the night"; it should have been "Who created" or "Who formed" light. Indeed, we have a *berakha* over light—"Who creates the luminaries," the first blessing preceding the reading of *Shema*. Why was the instinct implanted in the cock to crow at daybreak, this mechanical discrimination, isolated by our sages and made the motif of this special blessing?

Similarly, the *berakha* "Who spreads out the earth upon the waters" is enigmatic. Of course, it is related to the primordial creation, the formation of the earth. But the question arises: why was the spreading of the earth upon the waters singled out from the other acts of creation as a specific theme for a blessing?

It is likewise with the blessings "Who girds Israel with strength" and "Who crowns Israel with splendor." According to the Talmud (Berakhot 60b), these blessings are correlated with putting on one's belt or girdle and binding one's turban as part of one's daily routine. But why are they relevant? The relationship of the blessings as formulated to the events mentioned in Talmud is vague and unconvincing.

THE NEED FOR A BIBLICAL MODEL

Before we can answer these questions, let us analyze the phraseology of the blessings. There is no doubt that our sages avoided as much as possible coining new idioms and phrases in the liturgy; they tried to draw upon biblical sources—familiar patterns and structural forms—and borrowed expressions and terms from the prophets when they instituted the Morning Blessings. Sometimes what they found in Tanakh did not meet their liturgical needs—indeed, some paragraphs are original constructions of our sages—but generally, the phrases and idioms have been taken from Tanakh.

The Morning Blessings were not an exception to the general rule adopted by our sages that prayer is something paradoxical bordering almost on the absurd. It is a performance whose meaning and justification transcend the bounds of human intelligence, possible thanks to a specific act of grace on the part of God the Almighty, who allows unworthy human beings to converse with Him. On our own, we do not know how to start the conversation. We are completely ignorant of the basic principles and criteria of prayer. We do not know how to pray, what to say, how to address ourselves to God and how to implore Him, how to invoke His help or His presence. How can the simpleton, whose manners are coarse, whose language is inadequate, and whose appearance is vulgar, appear before the great and august King? We still do not understand why Abel's sacrifice went up in flames toward heaven while Cain, who probably tried his utmost to please the Almighty, received no sign of divine attention to his sacrifice. King Saul's prayers were not answered though his transgression was light (I Sam. 14:37). By contrast, King Manasseh "spilled very much innocent blood" (II Kings 21:16); yet when he was in affliction and prayed to God, God heard his supplication and brought him back to Jerusalem to his kingdom (II Chr. 33:13).

How can we say which prayer is appropriate and which prayer inadequate? It is one of the greatest mysteries in the history of the God-man relationship. Hence, we must not rely too much on our own talents and ingenuity in composing prayers and petitions. We are ignorant as to what pleases God and what is sheer impudence. Therefore, our sages were careful with regard to the composition and formulation of new prayers.

The main function of prayer consists in contacting God, in conversing with Him in dialogue, in establishing a community. The problem of acceptance is irrelevant; indeed, it is almost irrational. No human mind can grasp the criteria or the rules and principles of the Infinite Will, when He accepts prayer or rejects the petition of man. If we are guided in regard to God by rationality or rhetorical criteria or the amenities and rules of courtesy which man has invented, we may actually do something repulsive and our prayers may be rejected. That is why the only ones whose vocabulary and whose structural and idiomatic forms are reliable and authoritative are the prophets who conversed with God and to whom the Infinite Will was revealed. Our sages kept on borrowing expressions, figures of speech and idioms from the Tanakh. They preferred biblical expression to the succinct, direct expression they would have coined had they arrogated the license to introduce their own formulas. Since the prophets spoke of universal phenomena, the blessing that we now recite on performing or witnessing a specific act or a specific phenomenon is pronounced in such general terms taken directly from Tanakh.

This principle of preferring the biblical model may explain the way several of the morning blessings are phrased. "Blessed are You, Hashem, Who opened my eyes," would be closer to the event of daily awakening and the return of his full consciousness. This is not expressed precisely by "Who gives sight to the blind," which denotes a therapeutic miracle: restoring vision to one who has lost this precious sense. What transpires each morning is not miraculous healing but the normal physiological process of rising. The same comment can be made regarding other blessings, for example, "Who straightens the bent ... clothes the naked ... releases the bound." The connotation of these three blessings is a universal one. They do not directly refer to the ordinary performance of particular acts subsequent to rising.

"Who clothes the naked" does not seem to denote the routine ability to put on one's shirt and jacket. It denotes more a deed of charity that consists in providing the needy person with clothes: "When you see a naked person, cover him, and do not hide yourself from your own flesh" (Is. 58:7). Yet when we pronounce it in the morning, the connotation is a not that we thank God that we are not deprived of garments, but for the muscular movements we perform: we are able to put on our garments. It could have been formulated more directly as "Blessed are You Who gives me strength to dress myself."

The blessings "Who straightens the bent" and "Who releases the bound" denote literally elevating those who are downtrodden and liberating prisoners. These attributes refer to God's intervention in man's political community and His intercession on behalf of the weak, imprisoned, downtrodden, and oppressed. The attributes express the idea of divine justice and mercy, echoing Psalms (146:6–9): "Who made heaven and earth, the sea, and all that is in them; Who keeps truth forever. Who executes judgment for the oppressed; Who gives bread to the hungry; God releases the bound. God opens the eyes of the blind; God straightens the bent; God loves the righteous. God watches over the strangers; He relieves the orphan and the widow; the way of the wicked He makes crooked." Little in this text suggests the miracle of ordinary physiological performance such as capability of rising or standing up straight. The blessing in this connection could have been expressed simply and unequivocally: "Blessed are You, Hashem, Who raises me up in the morning."

In summary: because our sages were reluctant to introduce their own phraseology, they had to avail themselves of biblical metaphors and forms of speech. Hence several blessings, referring to restoring the blind, clothing the naked, releasing the imprisoned, straightening the bent, spreading the earth upon the waters, making man's footsteps firm, giving the cock understanding (see Job 38:36), use biblical language.

THE ETHICAL THEME IN THE MORNING BLESSINGS

Perhaps our sages had another reason for following the biblical text when they instituted the Morning Blessings. Perhaps they actually preferred the general to the specific. Even if they could produce from the biblical text a particular alternative, they still might have chosen the general formula because the general idioms have an ethical connotation and a more comprehensive meaning.

Again we are confronted with an old unique Jewish liturgical motif. God in His exaltedness and transcendence is beyond our liturgical impulse. The mere offering of thanks to Him or singing His praise is a paradoxical act that is almost tantamount to arrogance on the part of man. The license to praise God or to offer Him thanks is a unique grant of grace whose prime purpose is to bring man in close contact with his Creator and to elevate him morally by revealing to him the divine attributes as ethical criteria that must guide him. Therefore, each divine attribute should connote an ethical norm.

As human beings extol their Master and Creator, each utterance of praise is filled with an ethical content to be realized later by man. Our sages therefore emphasized the ethical moment in our liturgy. They linked the Morning Blessings with ethical norms and imperatives. If these blessings had tersely described the pertinent physiological activities, the ethical moment would have been lost. The ethical pattern would have been submerged through an overemphasis on the individual private life and on isolated situations and events. Because our sages were more concerned with the moral-ethical aspect than with liturgical specificity, they may have selected prophetic metaphors whose significance transcends the thanksgiving program of the Morning Blessings.

When we pronounce "Who gives sight to the blind, clothes the naked, releases the bound, straightens the bent," we not only thank God for His kindness and benevolence in protecting us against fatal disease or paralysis, but we also assert our credo as to the all-inclusive morality of God which is manifest in His deeds at a natural and an historical level. We also announce publicly our commitment to imitate His ways and to realize this credo. God sets free the prisoners, the captives, the slaves, He lifts up the oppressed, He heals the blind, the unfortunate and helpless, and He clothes the poor and needy ones. The reference to our daily activities is indeed vague, but the link with the ethical norm is pronounced.

We prefer the ethical link between the blessing and the moral-ethical code to the precise description of the particular situation in which we are involved. We sacrifice the minute description of the situation in order to bring to the surface the implicit morality of God and our commitment to follow this moral code. Every morning, while offering thanks to God for some particular deeds or activities, we proclaim the moral code by which God guides the destiny of the world, the code that is the source of our morality.

Thus, according to our interpretation, the series of blessings within the *Birkhot HaShaḥar* beginning with "Who opens the eyes of the blind," followed by "clothes the naked, releases the bound, straightens the bent," contains an ethical message. They were chosen due to some kerygmatic relevance, although their relationship to the particular physical event is a vague one. These blessings can be denominated the ethical group of the Morning Blessings. When one pronounces these *berakhot* he outlines the program for his own life: giving sight to the blind, clothing the naked, freeing the bound, straightening the bent. This accords with the principle of *imitatio Dei*—"as He does, so must I do" (Shabbat 133b).

THE HALAKHIC NATURE OF THE MORNING BLESSINGS

In the Talmud the *berakhot* are mentioned in conjunction with particular events: "When one wakes up in the morning he recites, 'My God, the soul You placed in me'; when he rubs his eyes he says, 'Who gives sight to the blind'; when he stands up, 'Who straightens the bent'; when he puts his feet on the ground, 'Who spreads out the earth upon the waters'; when he puts on his hat, 'Who crowns Israel with splendor'; when he binds his belt, 'Who girds Israel with strength'" (Berakhot 60b). *Prima facie* it would appear as if these blessings are either *birkhot hare'iya* (connected to a particular perception) or *birkhot hameora* (connected to a particular event). As such, they are pronounced whenever the particular event with which the *berakha* is linked takes place. If the occurrence related to the blessing is absent, the blessing is not to be recited at all. This was Maimonides' opinion (*Hilkhot Tefilla* 7:7–9):

> These eighteen blessings have no chronological order, but he says each of them on the matter with which the blessing deals at its time. How? When he puts on his belt while he is on his bed, he says, "Who girds Israel with strength." If he hears the sound of the rooster he says, "Who gives understanding to the cock," and every blessing for which he is not obligated, he does not say. How? If he reclined in his clothing, he does not say "Who clothes the naked." If he walked barefoot, he does not say "Who has provided my every need." On Yom Kippur and the Ninth of Av when there is no washing, he does not say "On the washing of the hands" or "Who removes sleep from my eyes and slumber from my eyelids."

In *Hilkhot Tefilla* 7:9 Maimonides rejects the common practice among Sephardic communities of his time: "Our people had the custom in most of the towns, that they said the blessings one after the other in the synagogue whether or not they are obligated. This is a mistake, and it is not appropriate to do thus; a person should not say a blessing unless he is obligated." Maimonides' premise is that each *berakha* is connected with a certain event, either a sensation or an action; he concludes that if the event is absent the *berakha* is not to be recited. Hence, to recite the blessings in a fixed order is wrong.

Maimonides objects to two practices: first, reciting the blessing even when the event with which it is connected has not occurred; second, the practice of delaying the recital of the blessing and its incorporation into the regular synagogue service. The second objection derives from the first. If the blessings are closely associated with certain actions or experiences in the same manner as other *birkhot hare'iya* (blessings tied to perception), then the *berakha* must be pronounced immediately upon the conclusion of the event. If the blessings are connected to the event, postponing the recital is unwarranted because when the event occurs we have to pronounce the blessing right away. If, however, the blessings are not contingent on the occurrences, then an orderly recital in the synagogue is perhaps preferable. Why postpone reciting a routine blessing, regardless of whether or not the individual has experienced the event to which it corresponds?

The *Geonim* and other early authorities say that we recite the blessings in the synagogue due to considerations of cleanliness (*Seder Rav Amram Gaon, Birkhot HaShaḥar*). The Talmudic discussion confirms Maimonides' view: the *berakha* was connected to the particular event and was recited immediately upon experiencing it. By the time of the *Geonim,* many did not know how to say the blessings; people did not know which event is connected with which blessing. Unlike the blessings for food, where everyone knows that "Who brings forth bread from the ground" is connected with the eating of bread, and so forth, only scholars knew which *berakha* is related to which action. As we have seen, the connection is often, at first glance, a very loose one. That is why they transferred *Birkhot HaShaḥar* from the home to the synagogue.

This historical supposition about the change is confirmed by a certain custom. Even in the synagogue not every individual says the blessings. According to an old custom going back many centuries, to the era of the *Geonim,* the *sheliaḥ tzibbur* is charged with the task of reciting the blessings aloud; when the community answers "*Amen,*" the community discharges its obligation through the principle of "*shome'a ke'oneh,* one who listens is like one who responds" (Sukka 38b). Saying blessings and prayers aloud was originally instituted to enable one who is illiterate to discharge his duty. The earliest example of audible prayer — the public repetition of the *Amida* — developed for the sake of the ignorant: "Why does the emissary of the congregation descend before the table [i.e. repeat his prayer]? ... [It is] to discharge the responsibility of the one who is not erudite" (Rosh HaShana 34b).

The problem of the illiterate person, in my opinion, prompted the *Geonim* to introduce a change in the original ordinance: to transfer the blessings from the home to the synagogue, and to have the *sheliaḥ tzibbur* say them aloud so that everyone could fulfill his obligation. The original institution of the Morning Blessings was connected to events, as Maimonides maintains. The change took place because of the ignorant, although the *Rishonim* explain that it was because of cleanliness.

Nahmanides and other authorities, disagreeing with Maimonides, hold that the *berakhot* are not contingent upon an individual event, but are related to the universal natural routine (their term is *minhago shel olam,* the custom of the world; *Tur* refers to *sidro shel olam,* the order of the world). Rabbeinu Nissim of Gerona (Ran) wrote: "Perhaps we should say that the order for the blessings that we say in the morning in the synagogue is blessings of praise according to the universal natural routine. Even if one did not hear a rooster he says the blessing on it, and the custom of the Jewish people is authoritative; thus Nahmanides wrote in his compilation" (Ran on Rif Pesaḥim 4a and Nahmanides Pesaḥim 7a). This means that the blessings we recite in the morning in synagogue are a hymn of praise related to the cosmic order.

What do Nahmanides and Ran mean by *minhago shel olam*? I translate it as "the universal natural routine." What further meaning does this phrase have? We sometimes employ technical terminology in Hebrew without spelling out the meaning; translating precisely in English might help us understand it better. *Minhago shel olam* means that the blessings are related to the collective experience of mankind, not to the individual experience. The blessings are not bound up with the individual daily sensations of these particular phenomena. In contradistinction to other *birkhot hare'iya,* the Morning Blessings are not bound up with an isolated occurrence but with the human experiential legacy. The blessing is not said over my particular experience but about universal experience. *Birkhot hare'iya* and *birkhot hameora* convey an experiential legacy, which is transmitted from generation to generation. We pronounce the *berakhot* for this accumulation of experience, stretching back to the past, and linking up to the present. For Maimonides the blessing is connected with the individual event while for Nahmanides, by contrast, it is linked with the universal routine of experience.

There is a third opinion, which I don't understand, namely that of Rabbenu Asher (Rosh) and the *Tur*. *Tosafot* say that the blessings are to be recited only when the individual is *neheneh*. (This term should not be given its usual meaning of "deriving pleasure"; here it means "experiencing.") If a person is immobile or in his nightclothes, he should not say the corresponding blessings, since he does not experience them (Berakhot 60b, *s.v. ki paris*). The *Tur* interpreted *Tosafot* as follows: "And all the blessings that are about universal order and routine such as 'My God, the soul that You bestowed upon me…' (*Elokai neshama shenatatta*) and 'Who gives the rooster understanding' and 'Who spreads out the earth upon the water' and 'Who firms man's footsteps'—one should not omit any of them, even if he did not hear the sound of the rooster or did not walk on the ground. But regarding the *berakhot* that are connected with his experiences, he should not say them unless he actually experiences them: for example, if he lies on his bed and does not put on his clothes and does not tie his belt…he should not say the blessing" (*Tur Oraḥ Ḥayyim* 46). This is a third opinion among our medieval sages. The *Tur* and Rosh distinguish between the four blessings pertaining to the collective experience of the natural routine, and the remaining particular blessings that are considered to express the joy of the fresh individual experience that occurs every morning.

What criteria guided them in this distinction is elusive. It is not a grammatical principle, with those in the first person assigned to the concrete experience of the individual, while those in the third person pertain to the collective routine. The Talmud makes no such distinction.

The language of Rosh (Berakhot 9:23) implies that he concurred with *Tur*'s subsequent formulation. Interestingly, however, Rosh apparently modified this position in the direction of Nahmanides in his discussion in Yoma (8:3). There Rosh justifies reciting "*she'asa li kol tzorki*, Who has provided for all my need" on Yom Kippur despite the fact that wearing shoes is forbidden, offering the grounds that this blessing is connected with "the order of the world." Perhaps he revised his opinion after moving from Germany to Spain: in Germany the view of *Tosafot* presumably prevailed; when he reached Spain he was exposed to Nahmanides' position. R. Joseph Karo, in the *Shulḥan Arukh* (*Oraḥ Ḥayyim* 46:8) follows Maimonides; Rama, in his gloss, follows Nahmanides.

Returning to the view of Nahmanides and Ran, the question arises: what category fits these blessings pertaining to the universal daily routine? One may have suggested that these are *birkhot hameora* (blessings on an event) or *birkhot hare'iya* (blessings on seeing or experiencing something). But if the recitation is not contingent on actual experience of the phenomenon, these categories do not apply. Nor are they in the category of *birkhot hanehenin*, blessings preceding enjoyment. Rather, classifying them as *birkhot hashevaḥ* (blessings of praise) or *birkhot hoda'a* (blessings of thanksgiving) is appropriate, as it is applying a modality pertinent to all blessings. Each type of blessing—on an event, on an experience, on pleasure of the senses, or even for the blessing on performing a commandment—is, in effect, a blessing of praise. Our task is to define the specific nature of praise or thanksgiving expressed in these blessings according to Nahmanides.

According to Nahmanides, if the individual does not participate in the experience expressed in the *berakha,* if the *berakha* merely ascertains some natural order of things in which this particular individual is not involved, it would be paradoxical to maintain that the *berakha* is an act of thanksgiving. It is rather a *birkat hashevaḥ,* which glorifies and praises God because of the grandeur of His miraculous deeds, but not on account of His kindnesses. For if one does not experience kindness, there is no reason for giving thanks.

"I have trusted in Your kindness; my heart will rejoice in Your salvation; I will sing to God because He has dealt bountifully with me" (Ps. 13:6). The Psalmist asserts his trust in God's kindness; he anticipates it. He will eventually sing God's praises "because He has dealt bountifully with me"—when the expectation has been fulfilled. I once heard the following comment on this verse from my father in the name of my grandfather, R. Ḥayyim: before the salvation has been realized there is no obligation of thanksgiving; the duty of thanksgiving is linked with the fulfillment of a hope, not with the hope in itself.

Consider the case of a blind person. According to the opinion advanced by Nahmanides, a blind person recites the *Birkhot HaShaḥar.* Since there exists light that is perceived and enjoyed by others, he says, "Who gives the cock understanding to distinguish between day and night" and "Who gives sight to the blind." However, it would be fallacious to assert that the blessing, when pronounced by a person whom God has deprived of the most precious of all senses, vision, expresses thanks to the Creator for the wonderful creation of light. That would fall under the category of "he that utters lies shall not remain before my eyes" (Ps. 101:7). The blind person can praise God for the existence of vision, but he cannot express thanksgiving. Even the most unfortunate person, whom God has denied the basic talents and capacities and the most precious capabilities, may still extol God for His greatness, omnipotence, and wisdom.

Majestas Dei, the majestic manifestation of God, requires praise whether or not one shares the benefits that flow from it. *Caritas Dei,* divine *ḥesed,* must be related to the beneficiary to engender a feeling of indebtedness.

PRAISE AND THANKSGIVING: IMMEDIATE AND REFLECTIVE

Nonetheless there can be a duty of thanksgiving even for the individual who is not immediately involved in the particular event. That is when the historical community which traces back its existence to that event must thank God. That is why we read the Hallel, offering thanksgiving for the Exodus, although we live in circumstances quite different from those under which the Exodus took place. We are a historic community through identification; as we read in the Haggada, "In every generation a person is obligated to see himself as though he went out of Egypt"; and further, "and if the Holy One, Blessed be He, had not brought our fathers out of Egypt, then we, and our children, and our children's children would still be slaves to Pharaoh in Egypt." That sense of identification makes us participants in that particular event.

This is true of historic *ḥesed,* kindness bestowed upon the people in the historical realm. This insight, however, is insufficient to explain Nahmanides' view of *Birkhot HaShaḥar*. If a blind person's ancestors benefited from the light, while he is unfortunately deprived of his optical sense, he cannot thank God for the physical kindness that was bestowed upon his ancestors. In the natural realm one thanks God on one's own behalf, as an individual—not on behalf of one's ancestors.

According to Nahmanides and Ran, the blessings must therefore be "praise" blessings, *birkhot hashevaḥ,* because even one who has been denied the corresponding experience recites them. According to the Maimonidean doctrine, however, the blessings convey personal experience. If we adopt Maimonides' view, the blessings may express gratitude for the kindness God has showered upon us or praise for God's majesty, greatness, infinity, omnipotence and so forth. When witnessing lightning we say the blessing "Who makes the works of creation" (Berakhot 59a). This blessing clearly expresses praise, not gratitude, as there is no personal kindness in this case. In the case of the Morning Blessings, according to Maimonides, there is no obvious criterion that would determine whether they are praise or thanksgiving.

I believe—on halakhic, not philosophical grounds—that Maimonides, like Nahmanides and Ran, regarded the *Birkhot HaShaḥar* as blessings of praise. We have already cited Maimonides' criticism of the custom of reciting the blessings in a definite order as a part of the daily service. His criticism is twofold: first, it is wrong to recite the blessing without personally experiencing the event; second, transferring the recitations from home to synagogue introduces unjustified delay. We noted the linkage between the two objections. From the premise that each blessing is connected with an event, Maimonides concludes that the blessing must be recited immediately upon the occurrence of that particular event.

Ran's discussion starts out with the conventional opinion that the blessings are indeed connected with personal experiences. This led him to ask why we recite the blessing in the synagogue and not immediately on witnessing this particular event. He accepted Maimonides' premise that the blessing is connected with a particular event, but wanted to justify the delay in reciting it. Hence he tried to repudiate Maimonides' opinion by distinguishing between *birkhot hamitzva* (on performing a commandment) and *birkhot hanehenin* (on enjoyment), on the one hand, and *birkhot hare'iya* (on seeing or experiencing), on the other hand. Although the Morning Blessings depend on certain occurrences which constitute the condition *sine qua non* for the pronouncement of the blessing, there is no specific time framework that links the blessing and the event. Thus the blessing need not follow immediately upon witnessing the event.

Still the question about *birkhot hare'iya* lingers in my mind: Must they be said immediately when the event is witnessed or can the recitation be deferred and performed after an intermission? If the former, what is the basis of the requirement? If we maintain that the Morning Blessings according to Maimonides constitute "*birkhot hoda'ah,* thanksgiving blessings," then the whole problem is placed in a new perspective. Whether *birkhot hare'iya* must be recited immediately upon witnessing a particular event or may be postponed for a while would depend on the nature of the *birkat hare'iya* in question. If it is a blessing of praise, it should be recited immediately after the experience. If, however, the *birkat hare'iya* belongs to the "*hoda'a,* thanksgiving" category then the time element is not essential.

If the Morning Blessings are blessings of praise dependent upon events, then Ran and Maimonides are right in saying that they must be recited immediately upon experiencing the event. If they constitute thanksgiving blessings, then the whole problem of immediacy appears in a different light. In *birkhot hoda'a* we express adoration not of *majestas Dei* but of *caritas Dei.* In thanksgiving, it is not the omnipotence, grandeur, exaltedness, artistic and dynamic creativeness that is extolled, but rather the kindness, the ethical deeds, and the infinite morality of God. A person is overwhelmed with gratitude and feels indebted to the Almighty for the great kindness He has bestowed upon him. In the realm of thanks the time element is of no significance.

With praise, however, immediacy is important. The aesthetic experience, when aroused by the sight of the beautiful and lovely, is basically a mood. It is this mood that inspires the song and blessing of praise. Aesthetic experience means an excited state of mind marked by its transience and inconstancy. The soul is stirred by beauty, aroused by great vision, passions flare up, man is enchanted, overwhelmed, and his strong feelings are poured forth into deed and word, into a hymn. This is true whether one experiences strong emotions, a beautiful landscape or the art in a museum. Yet this state of ecstasy is transient and passive in character. It is a short-lived experience that vanishes as suddenly and as instantaneously as it arises. This can be observed in ecstatic gatherings, not only in religious assemblies but in any crowd, since ecstasy is usually generated by a collective experience. When it is time to put out the lights, or if the mood is otherwise dispelled—the excitement dissipates and the turmoil subsides like a geyser that shoots forth to heaven and dries up just as quickly. For this reason the Yerushalmi said that *birkat hashevaḥ,* which is an expression of an ecstatic state, must be said right away, before the excited mind regains its repose and balance. The aesthetic experience can never become a historic experience.

The greatness of the ethical experience consists in its being a long-lived experience, one that can be remembered and relived. That is why a blessing of thanksgiving can be said after the event. Philosophically this is correct because gratitude as a moral experience is not so bounded in by the momentary response. It extends into the future; it is almost a timeless experience.

In Tanakh we see that indebtedness and thankfulness are basically historic and can survive through the ages: "I remember in your favor the devotion of your youth, your love as a bride, when you went after

Me in the wilderness, in a land that was not sown" (Jer. 2:2). Furthermore, this verse implies that counter-experiences cannot extinguish the original experience. Although we have sinned grievously, God Himself, as it were, feels indebted to His people. *Zikkaron,* remembrance, applies to experiences not subject to the curse of forgetfulness.

I do not mean to belittle the aesthetic experience. The aesthetic person is inspired by the completely new, the changeable, surprise, something never experienced before. The religious person sees creation as a continuous process, a perennial renewal. The great sin in Judaism is vulgarity of apprehension and shallowness of mind, not recognizing destruction and re-creation, sacrifice and rehabilitation. Where the aesthetic person seeks the new, the religious person seeks to renew.

Yet unlike the enjoyment of beauty and the appreciation of God's wonders, which is an evanescent experience, the encounter with God's kindnesses engenders a feeling of indebtedness that constitutes a steadfast, durable experience. The feeling of gratitude as a pristine, original experience is a moral one. The normative motif is present in such a state of mind. When I am overcome by beauty, by exaltedness, by might, by grandeur, there is no moral motif. I don't begin to adore beauty because I feel I ought to do so. Beauty is a natural experience, a non-reflective and non-meditative experience, instantaneous and spontaneous. Hence there is no ethical motif involved in it. The artistic experience is not bound up with the moral conscience; there is no normative imperative element.

In the experience of gratitude, of *ḥesed,* by contrast, the normative motif is quite conspicuous. When I feel grateful, it is a reflective experience. I am grateful because I am cognizant of my duty to be grateful, whether or not I am conscious of this motif, whether or not I can spell it out. The function of the ethical conscience in contrast to the aesthetic consciousness is to guide man, to establish permanent standards and criteria by which man must abide. The ethical conscience remembers very well, while the aesthetic experience has a short memory.

I have often cited R. Baḥya's insight that the feeling of gratitude is the basic religious emotion upon which the religious experience in general and the Jewish religious experience in particular are based. Because gratitude is a reflective experience, a meditative experience, in order to be grateful one must be intelligent. The experience of the beautiful has very little to do with intelligence. Since the experience of gratitude is a moral experience it requires reflection. R. Baḥya introduces gratitude in *Sha'ar HaBeḥina* of his *Ḥovot HaLevavot*. The word "*Beḥina*" in the chapter title means analysis, discrimination. If one cannot discriminate, one either cannot be thankful or is thankful for things and goods that don't merit indebtedness. The greatest goods given to them they are not grateful for, because they simply do not understand. The greater the reflection, the more intellectual power brought to bear, the more durable the gratitude, because the intellectual experience is a long-lasting experience.

Moral and intellectual experiences combine to forge an awareness that is not subject to forgetfulness. Quantitative knowledge can be forgotten in whole or in part. Qualitative knowledge, what is experienced methodically, is unforgettable. A moral norm, an experience that prompts us to moral action, can never be forgotten.

THE RELIGIOUS-PHILOSOPHICAL BACKDROP OF BIRKHOT HASHAḤAR

The religious-philosophical backdrop of *Birkhot HaShaḥar* is the consciousness of the impotence and insufficiency of man, his inability to help himself or to protect his existence from extinction or doom. He is helpless and completely dependent upon his Creator.

Friedrich Schleiermacher considered the feeling of absolute dependence upon God as the basic religious emotion. Rudolf Otto remarked (*The Idea of the Holy*) that this feeling is not only a psychological phenomenon in the obvious sense of the term since such a dependent state of mind can also be found in other areas of human experience—economic, political, scientific, etc.; the feeling of not being the master of things and circumstances but, on the contrary, of being determined by them, is a common one. That is why Otto introduces the term of "creature feeling" to indicate that this awareness is of a metaphysical-axiological quality, namely, the feeling of a creature, abused and overwhelmed by "its own nothingness in contrast to that which is supreme above all creatures." As an illustration of this unique feeling he quotes the passage from Genesis (18:27) in which Abraham exclaims, "I am but dust and ashes."

In my opinion, the feeling of dependence is to be understood at two levels: At the level of causal dynamics, man can never free himself from this dependence. He can never gain full mastery over himself or over his environment. He may succeed in attaining some knowledge of and have the opportunity of intervening in certain dynamic processes, but never will he understand nor gain control over creation as such. In short, his dependence is perennial and no rebellion will bring about his freedom. He can never become autonomous, since as a part of creation he cannot completely liberate himself from nature which subjects him to strict and unalterable determination.

In other domains of experience man at least hopes and prays for freedom. He resents his involvement in certain orders which interfere with his individual freedoms and aspires continuously to liberate himself from extraneous causal orders. In the religious realm, man accepts his relatedness to the Creator and his complete submission to the Infinite Will without rebellion and bitterness. He does not try to exempt himself from the transcendental order. He has no hope, nor does he behold any vision of a creature who casts off the yoke of his Creator. In the experience of dependence in the religious area is reflected a feeling of resignation and surrender. No one set himself up against God even in the hidden recesses of one's mind. God has created us and His hand rests heavily upon us.

Second, the feeling of dependence is based not only upon facts of cosmic dynamics, upon the comparative assessment of divine and human power, but upon juridic grounds. I am dependent upon His will, because God is the rightful master and owner of the creation in general and of man in particular. God owns my body and my soul. I am the property of God. I belong to Him, not only metaphysically at the level of origin and emergence, not only dynamically in the sense of cause effect relations, but juridically.

Out of these two basic feelings the awareness of insecurity emerges. Man can never be sure of what will happen the next moment. The morrow is enveloped in mystery. Man can never attain self-sufficiency and security. At any moment, an anomalous physiological process may terminate his life. Any change in his bodily organs may render him a cripple, incapacitate him. Man encounters death continually. Each day must be looked upon as upon the last stretch of time which was allotted to him. "Repent one day before your death," Rabbi Eliezer said. And when his disciples asked him, how could a man know when he should do so, he answered, "Let him repent today for he may die tomorrow" (Shabbat 153a). "Let thy garments be always white; and let thy head lack no oil" (Ecc. 9:8). Not only is God able but He is also entitled to cease sustaining man and bring his existence to a close.

On the other hand, this feeling of insecurity and helplessness is alleviated by the awareness of God's *ḥesed,* His grace. We are confident that God will bestow His kindness upon us and allow us to live and to be able to discharge all life functions and conduct a normal life. He does not owe us anything; He is not obligated to sustain our lives. He does so because He is full of grace and infinite kindness, because He loves His works.

In the awareness of God as King, Creator, Ruler, and Master, man is full of dread of divine omnipotence, and man feels he is nothing but a tiny particle in the order of things. Out of the grace-awareness emerges another idea, namely, the great message of *Eheyeh asher eheyeh, ego sum qui sum,* God is being. He is the very act of existing. There is no multiple existence, a plurality of *modi existentiae*—divine, human, animal, plant, mineral, etc. There is only one form of existence—the absolute being of God. God is existence *per se*. Whatever lays claims to existence and whoever is aware of His being, must *eo ipso* participate in the only form of being that we may speak of—namely the divine. To exist means to be aware of the presence within the finite area of my being of the Absolute Being, the union of relative and absolute existence, the sharing in unconditional being by a conditioned, limited being. God endows the universe with His own existence.

From this awareness of unity of being flows man's confidence in God's love for him. Of course, we are created beings who were placed at an endless distance from their Creator. However, our existence has never been separated from Him. We are drawn into a community of (co-)existence with God. The father and mother are not only the cause of the child but they are bound up with their child existentially in a way that transcends the biological nexus. There is an ontic bond uniting parents with child. If the latter drifts away from this community, it is a drift from his own selfhood and true existence. The same is true of the relationship between man and God—they are irrevocably bound together. The Creator appears as a father, and there is one act of existing on the part of parent and child.

This union experience implies an assurance of perennial love and grace. Not only is the child dependent upon the parent, but the parent needs the child since it is the wish of the parent to share existence with him. Therefore no fear lingers in the heart of the child; he feels secure and certain of himself; God Himself is involved in his existence. This emotional dichotomy finds expression in the blessings. On the one hand, man is never sure at night whether he will wake up the following morning. There is no assurance, no guarantees were granted to him. Waking up the next day is a great, joyful experience; he has found himself healthy and in command of all his faculties. He experiences a rediscovery of a new existence, of which he was not cognizant the night before. There is fear at night and joy in the morning: "Weeping may linger for the night but at dawn there are shouts of joy" (Ps. 30:6). Each day man gives his soul back to the Creator. Each night he offers a sacrifice to his Maker by returning voluntarily to God whatever He, the Creator, has given him—his body and soul. "Into His hand I shall entrust my spirit when I go to sleep—and I shall awaken" (*Adon Olam*).

The prayer preceding one's retirement for the night and the blessing of *Hashkivenu* attest to the willingness of man to entrust his fate to God, to accept God's final edict in full submission and surrender. It is an act of giving up on the part of man, of sacrificing his very flesh and blood, his soul and spirit, of utter resignation and active submission, of offering his existence on the altar of readiness, to promptly pay the great debt to infinity—the extinction of finitude. And each morning, man regaining his awareness suddenly discovers himself—his sacrifice was accepted, God has graciously taken the existential offering and returned it to him. A new man is born, a new existence is created.

THE ROOSTER'S DISTINCTION OF TIME

Let us now focus on some of the specific Morning Blessings. The blessing "Who gave understanding to the rooster to distinguish between day and night" is ancient, going back to the Second Commonwealth. The priests would begin the service in the Temple at the crowing of the cock, which signaled the time for *terumat hadeshen*, the removal of the ashes.

One must understand certain circumstances of olden times in order to realize the significance of the blessing. In antiquity there were no timepieces, no clocks, and no watches. In the daytime it was easy to determine time by the sundial or by observing the position of the sun. People were so trained at it that they determined the hour almost exactly. Nevertheless, they were not immune to mistakes. That is why leavened bread, *ḥametz,* was prohibited beginning with the fourth "hour" of the twelve-hour day on the eve of Passover, two hours before it is biblically prohibited; lacking a mechanical timepiece, relying on the trained eye to assess time and the rotation of the earth around the sun, marginal error cannot be prevented (Pesaḥim 11b).

At night the problem was greater. They used to determine time by the position of the stars and constellations, but this was not easy. In *Eretz Yisrael* where for nine months of the year the days are clear and sunny, almost everyone could determine the time. But determining time by the position of the planets at night was an esoteric skill, not an exoteric method familiar to all. For the farmer, who was neither a scholar nor an astronomer, the only means to determine time at night was the cock. When the rooster crowed, the farmer knew it was close to daybreak. Many aggadot tell of people who took a cock on their journeys: e.g., Rabbi Akiva, who took a candle, a cock, and a donkey (Berakhot 60b). The discussions about the different watches (*ashmorot*) of the night (Berakhot 3a) concern additional methods of determining time. Even in the Temple, the initial service, which used to take place before daybreak, was determined by the crowing of the cock.

In addition to serving as a general blessing over light, the blessing "Who gives the rooster understanding to discriminate between day and night" is an expression of thankfulness to God for the instrument of determining time.

"WHO HAS PROVIDED ALL MY NEED FOR ME": THE SIGNIFICANCE OF THE SHOE

Let us turn to another morning blessing that exhibits an unusual feature: "Who has provided all my need for me." Why does it lack specification and why was it linked with putting on one's shoes?

Our sages instituted *berakhot* for specific realms. They faced the dilemma of classification with regard to blessings. The Greeks also faced the problem of classifying phenomena. For Plato, classification meant abstracting from individual traits, retaining the general features and then creating a species, a genus. In physics one cannot speak about the individual table; gravitation applies not only to the table but to the stone as well. Therefore one speaks of a universal concept—the physical body. Through this process of abstraction, it becomes possible to apply the rule connected with the universal to individual phenomena. This is true for the laws of physics and chemistry and biology.

In history, classification cannot be treated in the same way. How can one write a biography of Napoleon, for instance, about whom we know a great deal? It is impossible to describe every meal he ate, every minor battle, every time he talked to his officers or met with his ministers. Biography requires selection. Selection means dealing with an overabundance of material without leaving out important features that throw light upon the person, the period, or the historical situation. Unlike modern science, history deals with the individual, and so abstraction is not a satisfactory solution to the problem of classification. The same difficulties apply to geography. Epistemological antinomies arise in any science of individual objects. What is important for a scientific description and what is irrelevant?

This problem is very important in studying Jewish law, halakha. We must study the great authorities, the *Rishonim,* but if we are arrested by every sentence we encounter, we will never cover the ground. There is a certain sense of proportion, what the Greeks called *metrion.* It is not a question of classification but a question of measure, a matter of keeping oneself within certain bounds. This intuitive sense is required of the historian and the geographer and of the *rosh yeshiva* as well.

With regard to blessings on food, the sages instituted a parallel general blessing: "*shehakol nihyeh bidvaro,* through whose word everything came to be." Because the sages had no classification principle for other foods and apparently had difficulties with the grouping of the phenomena, they introduced a general *berakha,* "through whose word everything came to be." This avoided the dilemma of classification: when we say *shehakol* we mean that we cannot classify precisely what You have done for us, and so we declare the sanctification of everything You created. The blessing after partaking from these foods is also formulated in general terms: "*borei nefashot rabbot,* who creates numerous living things." ("Fruits of the tree" and "fruits of the earth" lend themselves to classification because they can be classified under one rubric. The principles here are not unlike those that the botanist employs while he classifies the botanic world. Then there are three individual *berakhot* for bread, other grain products, and wine: "Who brings forth bread from the ground," "Who creates kinds of grain," and "Who creates the fruit of the vine.")

Our sages introduced Morning Blessings that are not connected with food, but are as important to the human being as eating and drinking are for the proper sustenance of man's life: "Who clothes the naked"—the fact of clothes; "Who releases the bound"—that a man can move his limbs; "Who firms man's footsteps"—that he can walk. They found many activities in the text of the Bible: "opening the eyes of the blind, clothing the naked, freeing the bound, straightening the bent, spreading the earth upon the water, firming man's footsteps." But the sages knew very well that their list did not exhaust all human activities, including some that are perhaps as vital as those they had specified. Were they to keep on enumerating activities and coining *berakhot* for each activity? The task would go on *ad infinitum*. This is analogous to the problem they had with regard to food: should there be a special *berakha* for eggs, a special *berakha* for meat, a special *berakha* for fish, a special *berakha* for water?

As we have seen, our sages selected the activities they did for the institution of specific *berakhot* because they found them in Tanakh, and they could relate these formulas to daily events, although the connections are sometimes vague. But there are so many activities, just as there are so many kinds of food which man enjoys that were not covered by the specific blessings for food. Many different benedictions were instituted to express thanksgiving for personal enjoyments and benefits. Nevertheless, most activities were still not covered by these *berakhot*. There are so many minor enjoyments in human life. One enjoys company and friendship; he wants to be loved; he enjoys music and books. Does the requirement that we say a blessing on what brings us pleasure apply only to major enjoyments? What really is major and what is minor in one's life? Some enjoyments—breathing, talking with people, associating with people, seeing things, enjoying a landscape, reading books, walking—are not each a discrete activity which can be circumscribed so that you can be required to pronounce the *berakha* before engaging in that activity. The activities are scattered all over the day and are vague in their contours; that is why each individual activity does not require a separate blessing. Since the sages did not want to manufacture *berakhot,* they created one *berakha,* "Who has provided all my need for me," to cover every activity, just as *shehakol* covers diverse foods.

Why then was this blessing connected with putting on shoes? I believe the reason is that in the aggadot of the sages the wearing of the shoe was a mark of distinction. Bondsmen, slaves and servants did not wear shoes; only free men did. In addition to its being a sign of status, the shoe protected its wearer from injury by snakes and other creatures. The shoe is very important, but there is no special *berakha* for it. The shoe is symptomatic of the whole realm of events and experiences that are vital to human happiness, to peace of mind, to enjoyment of life. They provide intangible benefit, and yet have not been marked by specific *berakhot,* as nothing has been mentioned in Tanakh about them. Our sages decided that when a person puts on his shoes he should say, "Who has provided all my need for me" because among all morning activities putting on shoes is the only important one that was not connected with a *berakha.*

We suggested that the enjoyment of the shoe is not the shoe itself; it is the social prestige that it confers on the wearer. Let us examine this idea further. In *ḥalitza* (Deut. 25:7–10), the childless widow removes the shoe of the brother-in-law who does not want to marry her and thus carry on his brother's line. When describing acquisition through *ḥalippin,* in which the acquisition is effected through the handing over of a symbolic object, the verse states, "a man pulled off his shoe and gave it to his neighbor" (Ruth 4:7). According to halakha, any article, not only the shoe, is effective, yet it is the shoe that was regularly employed. *Ḥalippin* is a symbolic exchange. In order to substantiate and validate a promise, removing the shoe and handing it to one's counterpart indicated "upon my honor." The role played by the shoe is connected with the fact that it bestows prestige on a person; much as the coat of arms in medieval times, which served as the mark of aristocracy. At the burning bush, Moses is told, "Remove your shoes from your feet, for the place on which you stand is holy ground" (Ex. 3:5). Since he is standing before God, conversing with Infinity, Moses must humble himself. That is manifested by removing his shoes.

The shoe then signifies social dignity, artificial and conventional dignity. This kind of dignity should be distinguished from the original, primal dignity of man, the *tzelem Elokim* (the image of God). For that original dignity, we have two special blessings, "*Asher yatzar,* Who fashioned man," recited in the morning and throughout the day after natural functions, and "*Elokai, neshama shenatata bi,* My God, the soul You placed in me," which is part of the morning routine. We are not discussing, at this point, our appreciation of the original bodily and spiritual dignity implanted by the Creator, but rather our appreciation of conventional, synthetic dignity, and artificial status; wearing the shoe is taking up one's position in society. What kind of *berakha* is appropriate here? Our sages did not want to compose a blessing thanking God for the fact that we enjoy social success. Therefore, this enjoyment, symptomatic of a multitude of activities that cannot be circumscribed or pinpointed, was subsumed under the general blessing "Who has provided all my need for me."

THANKSGIVING FOR SLEEP AND WAKING

Now let us turn to the last blessing, "Who removes sleep from my eyes and slumber from my eyelids." In Psalm 132, David swears that he will not "give sleep to his eyes nor slumber to his eyelids." Sleeping here is a metaphor: he would not rest until the Temple is constructed. When our sages instituted "clothing the naked, releasing the bound, straightening the bent," they used each phrase in the sense identical with that used in Scripture. But while the vocabulary of the phrase "sleep to my eyes and slumber to my eyelids" coincides with that of the biblical verse, it is semantically different.

The blessing "Who removes sleep from my eyes and slumber from my eyelids" is an obvious parallel to the blessing one recites at night before retiring, "Who casts the bonds of sleep on my eyes and slumber on my eyelids." The only difference between the morning and the night benedictions is that while at night one says *hamappil shena,* "Who casts sleep," in the morning one says *hama'avir shena,* "Who removes sleep." The contrast expresses itself in the verb. God bestowed upon living creatures in general, and humans in particular, the physiological capacity for resting, for refreshing their vigor and relaxing from fatigue. This miracle impressed our sages, who instituted a specific blessing before and after it (*berakha lefaneha, berakha le'aḥareha*). Sleep, like food, is preceded by a *berakha* and followed by a *berakha.* Sleep for the human being is equivalent to food; physiologically it is perhaps more important. The mystery of sleep is already described in the second chapter of Genesis: "*Hashem Elokim* caused a deep sleep to fall upon the man" (verse 21); God granted Adam the ability to sleep, to relax, to rest from fatigue.

Various phenomena are marked with "a blessing preceding and a blessing following": food, Torah (before and after reading the Torah in public), prayer (before and after *Pesukei DeZimra* and *Keriyat Shema*), and sleep. The study of the Torah and prayer represent the heights of our spiritual existence, the most important functions in man's religious ethical life.

As far as corporeal existence is concerned, we have food and rest. Sustaining the world is ascribed to God: "You open Your hand and satisfy the desire of every living thing" (Ps. 145:16). Apparently, the ability to sleep was placed almost on the same level.

This observation goes back to biblical times: God granted Adam the gift of sleeping. Our prophets and David were aware of the precious gift that God gave man by allowing him to retire from his exhausting routine for a night's slumber. The gift is a twofold one. First, there is the physiological phenomenon of falling asleep—the phenomenon of decreasing sensory motor activity of man and diminution of the conscious life. This in itself is a miracle. We adjust to it, although we do not understand it. The second aspect of the gift, of the grace, is the peace of mind and mental tranquility that enable man to enjoy his sleep. One who is overcome by worry cannot rest at night and enjoy sleep. One must feel secure to abandon himself to heavy slumber. For that feeling of satisfaction we thank God. David said, "Tremble and sin not; commune with your heart upon your bed, and be still (Selah). Offer the sacrifices of righteousness, and put your trust in the Lord... You have put more gladness in my heart than they have whose corn and wine increased. I will both lie down and sleep, in peace: for You, Lord, alone, make me to dwell in safety" (Ps. 4:5–9). This refers to the human ability to retire from care.

Let us now examine the blessings that precede and follow retirement for the night. "Who casts the bonds of sleep on my eyes and slumber on my eyelids" refers to the physiological process of sleeping, the diminution of conscious life. We continue at night with a prayer that God may guard and protect us, grant us life and provide us with a sense of security. We express confidence in God and the assurance that we are sufficiently tranquil to abandon ourselves to sleep. "May it be Your will, Hashem, my God and the God of my forefathers, that You lay me down in peace and raise me up in peace. May my imagination, bad dreams, and bad thoughts not confound me"; may sleep not be converted into nightmare.

In the morning, Rabbenu Tam (*Tosafot* Berakhot 46a, *s.v. kol*) held that the blessing "Who removes sleep from my eyes and slumber from my eyelids" is part of a unit that continues with "And may it be Your will...that You accustom us to study Your Torah," such that one does not respond "*Amen*" in the middle. Some scholars separated the blessing from the succeeding prayer. Yet we accept the opinion of Rabbenu Tam. We say "*And* may it be Thy will," with the *vav hameḥabber*, the letter *vav* as a copula, indicating that it continues what came before. We conclude the blessing, "Blessed are You, Hashem, who bestows beneficent kindnesses upon His nation Israel." This implies that it is all one blessing, a *berakha* that starts with *barukh* and concludes with *barukh*.

Thus, the blessing "Who removes sleep from my eyes and slumber from my eyelids" flows into the petition "that You accustom us to study Your Torah and attach us to Your commandments." What is the connection between these two themes? Why do we accept the opinion of Rabbenu Tam and treat it as one unit? *Tosafot* note that the penultimate phrase in the blessing, "*vetigmelenu ḥasadim tovim*, and bestow beneficent kindnesses upon us," reverts to the opening theme: the *ḥesed* connected with sleep and awakening. But there are limitless "beneficent kindnesses" which God can bestow upon us. Why specify the cycle of sleep and awakening? Apparently we must understand sleep not only as a physiological process for which man should be thankful, but also as signifying the conclusion of the satisfactory day, the sequel to a day's accomplishment, a day free from involvement in sin, undisturbed by evil drives and evil instincts, by the so-called Satan. When a human being feels satisfied with the day's work, is not frustrated, insecure, or lonely, then he can sleep and enjoy his sleep. But if he is miserable during the day, if he is frustrated, if he feels that he has failed in his endeavors, he has wasted time and energy, if he is confused, suffers from a feeling of guilt and condemns himself—then sleep is a nightmare.

At night we pray to be spared from disturbed sleep: "May my imagination, bad dreams, and bad thoughts not confound me." In the morning we begin by acknowledging that God removes sleep. I have slept enough, I am awake, refreshed, vigorous, and my day starts again. According to our sages, the ideal day is one in which "You accustom us to study your Torah and attach us to Your commandments. Bring us not to error, nor to transgression and sin, nor into temptation, nor scorn. Let not the evil inclination dominate us. Distance us from an evil person and an evil companion. Attach us to the good inclination and to good deeds and compel our evil inclination to be subservient to You." About such a day one may conclude: "Blessed are You, Hashem, Who bestows beneficent kindnesses."

In Tanakh sleep is understood as a reward for work: "There the weary are at rest" (Job 3:17); "The sleep of a laboring man is sweet" (Ecc. 5:11). Judaism rehabilitated labor in the physical world. Do not forget what work meant to the Greeks, to a slave society. A Greek considered it beneath his dignity to engage in labor. The Greek aristocrat indulged only in higher things, like symposia and the life of the mind. In Judaism, work was the ideal from the very first day of creation. Even God Himself worked. He rested "from all His work which He had done" (Gen. 2:2).

That is why Rabbenu Tam held that "Who bestows beneficent kindnesses upon His nation Israel" is nothing else but a continuation of "Who removes sleep from my eyes and slumber from my eyelids." The common theme of the entire unit is serenity of mind. If this prayer does not come true, sleep is a torture and awakening is a continuation of the torture. If we will read Tanakh carefully we will find that this motif is very popular with the prophets (see Jer. 31:25, Ecc. 5:11, Prov. 3:24).

During the Talmudic period, the *berakhot* had no fixed order; they were pronounced whenever the pertinent activity occurred. If one washed his eyes before dressing, for instance, he said the *berakha* "Who removes sleep from my eyes" on awakening before "Who clothes the naked." When the Morning Blessings were transferred to the synagogue in the geonic era, the blessing we are discussing, which pertains to awakening, was instituted as the last one in the series. The Talmud correlated this blessing with washing the eyes, which refreshes man after slumber. Why this one was placed at the end, now that we have a fixed order for the blessings, is a question in itself.

The order seems to correspond to the chronology of activities. "Who gives the rooster understanding to discriminate between day and night" refers to the first thing a person hears in the morning, even before daybreak, namely the cock crowing. Next should come opening the eyes, then "clothing the naked," which could mean beginning to dress (not necessarily being fully clothed). "Who releases the bound" means stretching one's limbs. "Who straightens the bent" indicates sitting up; "Who spreads the earth upon the water"—putting his feet on the ground; "Who has provided for my every need"—putting on the shoes; "Who firms man's footsteps"—taking the first steps; "Who girds Israel with strength"—putting on the belt; "Who crowns Israel with glory"—binding the turban. These activities follow the usual routine. And the *berakhot* in the synagogue were arranged according to the daily routine in the morning. Washing the face was apparently the last activity; that is why "Who removes sleep from my eyes and slumber from my eyelids" was placed last. (The blessing "Who gives strength to the weary" was not instituted by our sages but was introduced in the middle ages. I have never said this *berakha* and I am not addressing its meaning here.)

But there is another reason: as we have seen, the second half of the blessing is a prayer for the active day. This blessing should be said when a person is ready to begin the working day: "Man goes forth to his work and to his labor until the evening" (Ps. 104:23). Since "Who removes sleep from my eyes and slumber from my eyelids" is a part of this blessing, it is said last before a man actually leaves his home to go out to work. The physiological process of sleep and awakening is less important than the daily routine that warrants sleep and justifies its enjoyment.

TWO BLESSINGS FOR PHYSIOLOGICAL FUNCTIONS

Let us turn to two blessings which are not part of the *Birkhot HaShaḥar* group: *Asher Yatzar* and *Elokai Neshama*. *Asher Yatzar* is said many times a day, whenever a person relieves himself; *Elokai Neshama* is said only once a day, in the morning. According to Rosh (*Responsa* 4:1, cited in *Beit Yosef* to *Oraḥ Ḥayyim* 6:3) the reason why the latter does not open with the word *barukh* is that in the morning, *Elokai Neshama* immediately follows *Asher Yatzar*. These two blessings thus form one continuous whole, one continuum. Let us discuss them as a unit, showing how they express the Jewish philosophy of man.

Judaism regards the human being from under a double aspect. Man is a natural being tied in with vitalistic forms and modes of existence, an animal subject to biological processes and physiological drives.

But Judaism also ascribes to man a metaphysical endowment. He is a unique being different from all other biological creatures, one blessed with a personality. I am speaking now of the duality of man in terms of biological being and spiritual personality, not about the duality of good and evil. Judaism looks with awe at the intricate, organic, biological system, in its complex functioning. It considers the creation of life to be a manifestation of God's infinite wisdom. The creation of man is an artistic, intellectual accomplishment of the highest order, something baffling, transcending all our fantastic conjectures. Judaism thus treats the phenomenon of life as an enigma, a *mysterium magnum*. It is the great mystery of God's creative effort in the physical world. This awe is expressed in the blessing of *Asher Yatzar*.

The text of *Asher Yatzar* draws on ancient sources. Ezekiel 28 refers to the king of Tyre, who considered himself self-sustaining, self-sufficient, secure, impregnable, and invulnerable. The Aramaic Targum to Ezekiel 28:12–13 interprets the prophecy about the king of Tyre as an image of the ideal human being: "You resembled a signet ring formed with wisdom, *di metaken beḥukhmeta*, and perfected in beauty, *umeshukhlal beshufrei*...yet you did not consider your body, made with openings and cavities without which you cannot survive." The Targum thus introduces several formulas belonging to *Asher Yatzar*. It is the greatest vanity to consider oneself secure, merely because we were created with great wisdom and great beauty. We can claim no such accomplishment—we are so full of openings and cavities that we are vulnerable at any moment. In this passage of Targum, the content of *Asher Yatzar*, Judaism presents a philosophy of physical insufficiency and insecurity of man. The human being is a great work but a very frail one; great in that he testifies to his Creator, frail in himself.

Judaism treated the human personality with admiration—not just viewing man as a physical being, but as a spiritual personality, a being with intimate will, the capacity for emotional experiences, freedom of decision and action, creative ability, vision, anticipation, and of course, the ability to rebel, to sin. All these manifestations of human uniqueness fascinated the mind of the Jew from time immemorial. The idea of *tzelem Elokim*, the image of God, stands for the singular role of man. "For You have made him a little lower than the angels, and have crowned him with glory and honor" (Ps. 8:6). Nahmanides (Gen. 1:26

s.v. ve'hineh) coordinates this verse with the idea of *tzelem Elokim.* Indeed the entire Psalm can be read as a commentary on the majesty of man:

> O Lord, our Master, how majestic is Your name in all the earth, Who has set Your glory above the heavens… When I look at Your heavens, the work of Your fingers, the moon and the stars, which You have established. What is man, that You are mindful of him? And the son of man, that You visit him? For You have made him a little lower than the angels, and have crowned him with glory and honor (Ps. 8:2–6).

Both the physical and the spiritual aspects of the human being constitute mysteries. Man as a total psychosomatic personality—because Judaism did not eliminate the body—is the greatest miracle in creation. That is why he merits special liturgical attention.

We may distinguish six ideas in *Asher Yatzar*. First, as already noted, man as a matter of biological fact betrays the inner workings of a hidden intelligence in the cosmos: God created the human being "with wisdom, *beḥokhma*." The human being is the best argument for the existence of God.

Second, the blessing moves from God's creation of man in general (*ha'adam*), to His healing of all flesh (*kol basar*). In other words, we acknowledge the wisdom manifested by universal organic biological life, not only the human world.

Third, we state that our vulnerability is "revealed before God" (*galuy veyadua lifnei khissei khevodekha*). That is because the miracle called life is by far more puzzling than the miracle called death. Man is always exposed to doom; the danger of sudden extinction is imminent: if one aperture is blocked, if one valve is ruptured, we cannot survive for a moment. The mystery of life is known to You: only You understand it; while we live, we don't understand the mystery of life. It is not only death that we do not understand. *Asher Yatzar* conveys to us that we do not understand life. It is important for man to seek a philosophy of life, not only to contemplate death.

Fourth, we speak of life as "standing in God's presence" (*la'amod lefanekha*), joining in the infinite being. God is the only one who can understand life and its purpose. The scientific laws explain only *how* life functions, the functionality of life. We marvel not at the fact of death, but at the fact of life.

Fifth, although we are frail and we have no assurance that our existence will continue, in spite of the absurdity of life, we are still confident that God will sustain us. This is the idea of mercy, or the concept of *Havaya*, Hashem, the Tetragrammaton, the consciousness of *Havaya* that is in the close of the *berakha*. Until now our consciousness is of *Elokim*, the universal God. The personal aspect of God is expressed in "Who heals all flesh" (*Rofei kol basar*). *Rofei* doesn't mean healer; it means protector and sustainer of life. "I will put none of these diseases upon you, which I have brought upon the Egyptians, for I am the God who sustains and protects you" (*ani Hashem rofekha*, Ex. 15:26). In Hebrew, *rofei* does not mean "to heal" in the sense of therapy, of discharging therapeutic functions, but it means more to sustain, to protect. And this is *mafli la'asot*, "acts wondrously"—one's whole life is a mystery. We have unshakable faith in the endless kindness of God.

Sixth, God's mercy is not limited to man; He sustains all organic forms and existences. Particular attention is paid by God to man, but His providence is all-inclusive: it extends to *kol basar. Basar* does not mean man alone; it means actually biological existence.

Let us turn to *Elokai Neshama*, which deals with the spiritual personality of man. We may also discern six motifs in this benediction. First of all, I would place the emphasis on the word *tehora*, pure—the soul is not corrupt, it is innocent and noble; the human personality is sacred. This statement, of course, stands in direct opposition to the Christian interpretation of man advanced by Paul. Perhaps this word *tehora* was introduced against Christian preaching about the corruptibility and impurity of man, which needs redemption. Christians say man is born in sin; his very existence and his spiritual personality are sinful because of the union with flesh. Even an infant one hour old is metaphysically corrupt—not morally corrupt, but metaphysically corrupt. It can be saved only through the act of salvation, by grace. Judaism would not deny the fact that by sinning we corrupt the soul. But metaphysically the soul is not corrupt; it is pure, noble, and sacred. Christianity says the soul becomes corrupt as soon as it joins the body, and Judaism says it remains metaphysically in a state of bliss. Certainly by sinning we contaminate and pollute the soul. But we don't believe in metaphysical *tuma;* we believe in *tuma* which is brought about by sin, by our action, by crimes. Metaphysically, for us the soul is *tehora;* it is still pure.

Second, *teshuva,* repentance, is always possible because the genuine personality is never involved in sin. Sin involves only the pseudo-personality, but not the genuine inner personality; the inner core of the personality remains pure. *Neshama shenatatta bi,* the soul You implanted in me, is always *tehora,* it cannot be stained by any act on the part of man. Sin means destruction and annihilation. Yet something remains within man that motivates him to repent. Call it conscience, call it the voice of God, call it the still, small voice—whatever it is, the feeling of regret and failure flows from within. So even the sinner who is knee-deep in sin and corruption, whose personality has been contaminated and polluted—even such an individual still has something within the deep recesses of his personality that has not been affected by sin. Otherwise *teshuva* would be impossible, because if the total personality would have collapsed then man would not be able to reconstruct it. Man cannot be a creator *ex nihilo;* he can only be a creator *yesh miyesh,* creating out of what has already been given to him.

The third point concerns the old controversy in medieval philosophy about whether the soul was created by God or whether it emanated from Him like light reflected by a great luminary. Rav Sa'adyah Gaon says that the soul was created, and Maimonides joins him. Ibn Gabirol, because he was influenced by the Neo-Platonic school, says that the soul was emanated. Nahmanides also thinks in terms of emanation of the soul: "…and He breathed into his nostrils the breath of life…" (Gen. 2:7). The body was created; but personality was blown in, so to say, was emanated.

In fact, this controversy divided the medieval philosophers and the mystics, the *baalei kabbala.* The *baalei kabbala* believed in emanation of the soul, while the medieval philosophers believed in creation. If the soul is eternal and cannot ever die, the Kabbalists say, it cannot have any beginning in time. If one accepts the immortality of the soul, they say, one must *ipso facto* accept its eternity, so to say, in both directions, in retrospect and prospect. But how can it be that the spiritual existence of the personality can never be terminated—this is the principle of immortality—if man is not eternal? Their answer is that the soul is a reflection of divine light that bestows upon the human being the spiritual endowment that we call personality. For the mystics it was not only man who was emanated by God, but the world as such. Man is the mirror in which the image of God is reflected.

The philosophers, on the other hand, held that the soul is a spiritual creation. It is eternal in anticipation, but not eternal in retrospect. (This entails a philosophical contradiction, but it is not our task to resolve this problem.) *Elokai Neshama* says: "My God, the soul You placed within me is pure. *You created it,* You fashioned it, You breathed it into me." Thus, "He breathed into his nostrils the breath of life" means that the human personality, in pictorial language, is the breath of God. Nahmanides derived from this image the concept of emanation, but apparently our liturgists, the sages who formulated *Elokai Neshama,* saw it differently.

Fourth, spiritual life and personalistic existence are a unique grant of grace by God to man. That is why after saying, "Blessed are You Hashem, who heals all flesh and acts wondrously" in *Asher Yatzar,* we say, "You safeguard it within me" in *Elokai Neshama.* In *Asher Yatzar* we express gratitude to God for our physical existence: *rofei kol basar umafli la'asot.* In contradistinction, *Elokai Neshama* is an expression of thanks for existing not only as a biological being but as a spiritual personality: "*ve'ata meshammerah bekirbi,* You safeguard [the soul] within me." Judaism understood something that is a little alien to us, and Maimonides was also in agreement, namely that it is possible to live physically and not to live a personalistic life. I have thanked God for granting me physical life, for not disturbing the functions of my body, for preserving the media for life pulsation, for protecting me against doom and death, physical death and physical extinction. Now I express thanks for life as personal being and a spiritual personality. Maimonides (*Guide for the Perplexed* II:32) wrote that personalism is not a ready-made possession of man. Personalism is an ideal which man must strive to create. The personality is not created complete. God grants a soul that is the creative ability and capacity for developing a personality. But man can either forfeit or realize it. Special thanks are due to God for allowing man to preserve this position in order to develop and realize it. We believe that anybody, any individual, regardless of his being involved in sin or in crime or in an immoral life, still has developed to some degree his spiritual personality, and that there is at least part realization of this endowment that was given to him.

Fifth, we realize that the awareness of death is implied in the ontic experience. When a man has an ontic experience, he must at the same time also be aware of the fact that he will die. "You safeguard it within me, and eventually You will take it from me..." Man should never forget that he is mortal, that he is doomed to death.

Sixth, of course, is the resurrection of the body—*teḥiyyat hametim*. Death means disintegration of the body but continued existence of the soul (*olam haba*). However, the perfect state of personal existence is not at a transcendental level but at a level of concreteness and in union with the body. Disembodied existence is for an interim period, prior to *teḥiyyat hametim*. Bodily resurrection is the ideal.

Indeed, these two blessings as a whole eloquently express the Jewish philosophy of man.

Chapter 2

Pesukei DeZimra and Kaddish

PESUKEI DEZIMRA

Pesukei DeZimra (lit., "verses of song") refers to a series of psalms and other biblical texts, preceded and followed by a blessing, that are recited before the morning worship service proper. Maimonides' description of the order of public worship strikingly omits the recitation of *Pesukei DeZimra*. Instead, he mentions only their recitation by the individual, in accordance with the Talmudic passage, "R. Yosi said: 'May my lot be with those who recite Hallel daily.' But is that so, for did not Mar say: 'One who recites Hallel daily is insolent and blasphemous'? Rather, this refers to *Pesukei DeZimra*" (Shabbat 118b). Thus Maimonides writes:

> The sages praised one who reads songs from the Book of Psalms each day, from "A Praise-Song of David" (Ps. 145:1) to the end of the book. It has become customary to read [additional] verses before and after them. They instituted a blessing before the songs, i.e., *Barukh SheAmar*, and a blessing after them, i.e., *Yishtabaḥ*. Afterwards, one pronounces the blessings before the reading of the *Shema* and then reads the *Shema* (*Hilkhot Tefilla* 7:12).

Maimonides likewise includes *Pesukei DeZimra* in the order of individual worship presented later: "The order of prayers is as follows. Upon awakening in the morning one pronounces these [early morning] blessings, recites the songs, with blessings before and after them, and then reads the *Shema* …" (*Hilkhot Tefilla* 7:17). By contrast, his account of public worship begins with the *sheliaḥ tzibbur* (prayer leader) leading the congregation by reciting Kaddish and then *Barekhu* (*Hilkhot Tefilla* 9:1). This implies that the recitation of *Pesukei DeZimra* lacks any communal aspect; each individual reads them on his own, concluding with *Yishtabaḥ*. Only when *Barekhu* is reached do the disparate individuals organize themselves within a congregation led by the *sheliaḥ tzibbur*. This demonstrates that *Pesukei DeZimra* was instituted not under the rubric of Hallel but, rather, as a recounting of God's praises through the recitation of scriptural verses or passages. Were the recitation of *Pesukei DeZimra* in fact a form of Hallel—that is, under the rubric of the commandment to praise and thank God—it would be a congregational undertaking as well. Thus, the "Egyptian Hallel" (Ps. 113–118, recited on various festivals), though it was instituted to be recited by an individual, has a public aspect: recitation by the congregation carries added significance as a fulfillment of the obligation to praise and thank God publicly.

PESUKEI DEZIMRA VS. THE FESTIVAL HALLEL

The daily recitation of *Pesukei DeZimra* thus differs from the festival Hallel, which is recited not *qua* Scripture, as reading chapters from the book of Psalms, but *qua* Hallel, that is, as praise and thanksgiving. Hallel, as it happens, is verbally identical with the text in Psalms, but it is recited under the rubric of praise to the Creator of the world. This is evident from the Talmud's comment, in the passage noted above, that one who recites Hallel every day is insolent and blasphemous. Obviously reading the Hallel chapters in Psalms as Scripture entails no prohibition; only reading it daily as a performance of praise and thanksgiving, as we do on festivals, is considered to be insolent and blasphemous.

This point is also implicit in the laws governing the manner of recitation mandated for parts of Hallel. These include repetition of some verses (Sukka 38a; Ps. 118:21–29) and responsive reading of others (Sukka 38b; Ps. 118:1–4, 25). Such rules would in no way apply to a straightforward reading of the Psalms, which must follow the text as written, with no repetitions or responses. As noted above, however,

Pesukei DeZimra are recited not as Hallel itself but as a reading of Scripture, hence there are no particular rules referring to the congregation.

Furthermore, it is noteworthy that the praises read each morning are called *Pesukei DeZimra* (verses of song) rather than *parashot dezimra* (chapters of song), although the texts include six consecutive psalms (from 145:1 to the end of the book) and a complete section from I Chronicles (16:8–36). The reason for this terminology is that these passages are not recited as chapters but as a series of verses. By contrast, the norm governing Hallel mandates the recitation of complete chapters, as was also the case regarding the singing of the Levites in Temple, who chanted entire chapters.

The reading of the song of *Parashat Haazinu* (Deut. 32) in the Temple likewise illustrates the principle that song is defined in terms of units of text ("chapters"). The Talmud (Rosh HaShana 31a) mandates a specific division of the verses into sections. This division defines distinct units for the oral reading of the Torah: the Talmud states that the division followed by the Levites when they chanted *Haazinu* to accompany the Sabbath *musaf* sacrifice in the Temple is to be followed when the section is read in the synagogue. That is because this division designates not only the units of song in the Temple, but also the division for purposes of public reading. If the reader pauses within those units, he violates the halakhic principle that states: "We do not divide into sections other than those into which Moses divided it" (Berakhot 12b).

The term *Pesukei DeZimra* implies a contrast with our practice regarding Hallel and *Haazinu*, emphasizing that we are reading a series of biblical verses, where the unit is the verse rather than the section or chapter. When Maimonides (*Hilkhot Tefilla* 7:13) mentions the custom of including in *Pesukei DeZimra* a collage of verses from various chapters, he implies that we are not reciting Hallel but are merely engaged in reading Scripture.

To explain the existence, structure, and content of *Pesukei DeZimra*, it is necessary to consider two enduring principles in Judaism—principles that at first appear mutually contradictory but are both true. Indeed, both resonate in the praises sung by Israel. One principle declares: "Praise the Lord; servants of the Lord give praise, praise the Lord's name, may the name of the Lord be praised…" (Ps. 113:1). In other words, there is a commandment to praise and extol the Creator of the world for His wonders and great kindness. That commandment, moreover, is well suited to man's character and will; for man by his nature feels gratitude and wants to express his thoughts and feelings about the Holy One Blessed be He through poetry and song, however incapable one is of recounting all of God's praise.

The second element, however, counters: "Who can recount the Lord's mighty acts, proclaim all His praise?" (Ps. 106:2). Expressing the perpetual mighty acts and kindnesses of the Holy One Blessed be He is impossible. On the contrary, "To You, silence is praise" (Ps. 65:1), for it is inconceivable and incomprehensible that mortal man, lacking in strength and dwelling in materiality, can render praise to the King of Kings (Megilla 18a; Berakhot 33b).

Both of these principles appear at the beginning of the Song at the Sea (Ex. 15:1): "I will sing to the Lord"—I am obligated to thank and praise the Holy One Blessed be He for the wonders He has done for us—yet "He is highly exalted," elevated far beyond any song or praise. David, the sweet singer of Israel, proclaims (I Chron. 29:13): "And now, our God, we acknowledge You and praise Your glorious name"; yet the Levites, directed by Nehemiah (Neh. 9:5), affirm that He who abides forever is elevated "and lifted up beyond all blessing and praise." Here we have two opposing views which together express a single complete and perfect truth. For man is obligated to bless his Creator and praise Him; yet he is also prevented from reciting words of exaltation and praise.

PRAISE AS A MITZVA AND PRAISE AS READING FROM SCRIPTURE

How did the halakha sustain this contradiction? It declared that exaltation and praise are permitted—indeed, required—in either of two situations. The first is where exaltation and praise are themselves a commandment (mitzva) or derive from some other commandment, such as on Ḥanukka, Purim, or festivals. There, the commandment to publicize the miracle or to be joyful requires one to recount the praises of God through the recitation of Hallel, as is explained by Nahmanides (see his comments on Maimonides' *Sefer HaMitzvot*, toward the end of *Shoresh* 1). In such instances, the Torah demands that man conduct himself in accordance with the first principle, "Servants of the Lord give praise, may the name of the Lord be praised now and forevermore," setting aside the second principle. In such instances, it is clearly man's privilege and duty to offer pleasing and deferential words in accord with the will of the Holy One Blessed be He. All the verses encouraging man to exalt, praise, and glorify apply in these circumstances.

The second situation in which praise and thanksgiving to the Holy One Blessed be He is permitted is in the manner of one reading from the Torah, in which case the authorization to present pleasing words flows from the commandment to study Torah. The person reading the words of Hallel is studying the ways and deeds of the Holy One Blessed be He. The Prophets and the Hagiographa teach us the ways of God, which constitute an entire realm of Torah and which we are obligated to study so that we may follow them and imitate God. While a prophet has no authority to innovate with respect to halakhic matters, he is summoned by the Holy One Blessed be He and authorized by Him to reveal to and teach His people the actions and ways of the Creator that they must strive to emulate. Reading the words of Hallel affirms this commitment.

These two situations correspond to Hallel and *Pesukei DeZimra,* respectively. We recite Hallel because it is our obligation to do so; this obligation, incumbent upon the individual, authorizes the recitation of God's praises. In acknowledgement of that obligation and of our intention to render praise, we recite a *birkat hamitzva* (blessing for performance of a commandment) before commencing Hallel. When we recite *Pesukei DeZimra,* by contrast, we are engaged in the recitation of scriptural passages, and the principal obligation discharged is that of studying Torah, examining and understanding God's word so that we may thereby gain the wisdom to live and act properly.

Accordingly, there is no separate *birkat hamitzva* for *Pesukei DeZimra,* for we do not recite a blessing each time we engage in Torah study. Instead, the blessing of *Barukh SheAmar* is a kind of declaration of what we are about to do. In that declaration, we invoke the name of David: "and through the songs of David Your servant we praise You, O Lord our God; with praises and songs we magnify and praise You, give prominence to Your name, and proclaim You King." Why do we not similarly state, in our blessing over Hallel, "to recite Hallel from among the songs of David Your servant"? The answer is obvious. In Hallel, the essential concept being fulfilled is expressed by the recitation of these chapters not *qua* scriptural passages or songs of David but *qua* praise in and of itself. Our purpose in reading these selections from the Book of Psalms is not identical with that of simply reading scriptural passages. In the case of *Pesukei DeZimra,* however, the entire purpose fulfilled consists in reading from the Book of Psalms. Therefore, we explicitly state that we are praising Him through the songs of David His servant.

THE BLESSINGS FOLLOWING HALLEL AND PESUKEI DEZIMRA

There is a similar distinction in content between the blessing that follows Hallel (*Yehallelukha*) and the blessing after *Pesukei DeZimra* (*Yishtabaḥ*). Note the following textual differences: (1) *Yehallelukha* concludes "the King extolled (*mehullal*) through praises"; the conclusion of *Yishtabaḥ* refers to "a King great (*gadol*) in praises." (2) *Yehallelukha* has a brief conclusion, while the conclusion of *Yishtabaḥ* is prolonged: "God of thanksgivings, Lord of wonders, Who chooses melodious songs, King, God, Who lives eternally." (3) *Yehallelukha* uses verbs: "For it is good to thank You, and to Your name it is appropriate to sing"; *Yishtabaḥ* relates to God through nouns: "For to You, Lord our God, it is proper to render song and praise, exaltation and melody, power, governance, eternity, greatness, might, renown, glory, sanctity and kingship, blessings and thanksgivings now and forevermore." (4) In *Yishtabaḥ,* we refer twice to His Godliness and Kingship: "God, King, great in praises, God of thanksgivings... King, God, Who lives eternally." (5) *Yehallelukha* uses the verb *lehallel* in an active (*pi'el*) form, "we will praise You"; *Yishtabaḥ* resorts to the reflexive (*hitpael*): "May Your name extol itself (*yishtabaḥ*) forever, our King."

On Sabbath and festivals, *Yishtabaḥ* is preceded by additional words of praise (*Nishmat kol ḥai*). Attending to these will shed light on the significance of the distinctions we cited above. We recite:

> And amidst the assemblies of the myriads of Your people, the House of Israel, Your name, our King, will be glorified in song through every generation. For thus is the duty of all creatures before You, Lord our God and God of our fathers, to thank, praise, extol, glorify, elevate, honor, bless, exalt, and acclaim You, beyond all the words of song and praise of Your anointed servant, David son of Jesse.

That is to say: our obligation to praise God is not exhausted by these passages, nor by reciting the Book of Psalms *in toto*; our obligation goes far beyond that. It is simply impossible for a human being to discharge his obligation to recite the praises of God, and one might claim that it is therefore preferable not even to try, for "Who can tell of the Lord's mighty acts, proclaim all His praise" and "To You, silence is praise." Indeed, that tension between our attempt to praise God and our utter inability to do so is manifest in the *Nishmat* prayer that ends *Pesukei DeZimra* on Sabbath and festivals:

> Even were our mouths filled with song like the sea, and our tongues as vocal as its mighty waves, and our lips filled with praise like the expanses of Heaven, and our eyes as luminous as the sun and moon and our hands outstretched like the eagles of the sky and our feet as swift as a deer's, we could not adequately thank You, O Lord our God and God of our fathers for even one of the thousands and myriads of kindnesses that You performed for our fathers and for us…

In other words, it is futile to attempt to thank You, for how can the mere mortal, dwelling in darkness and shadows, glorify God on high? All of David's Psalms would fail to discharge even a fraction of our obligation. The necessary conclusion, then—made explicit in the Sephardic rite, which adds the explanatory word "accordingly" (*lefikhakh*) at the beginning of the *Yishtabaḥ* blessing—is that since we cannot properly praise God, we pray that His name extol itself forever. The praise flows from God Himself, as it were; it is You who dwell in praise, for to You, Lord, song and praise are fitting—in other words, as the hymn *HaAderet VeHaEmuna* puts it: "The song and the praise are of the One who endures forever." This hymn can be understood to mean not only that song and praise should be directed to the Holy One Blessed be He, but also that they belong to Him. All is His: "exaltation and melody, power, governance, eternity, greatness, might, renown, and glory, sanctity and kingship."

One who recites *Yishtabaḥ* thus enumerates the attributes in which God is revealed and His ways of acting, which we are commanded to follow. He tells the Creator of the world: All is Yours and is given by Your hand. God has no need for our words and praises, for He is God in heaven and on earth, hidden and concealed from all ("The God who conceals Himself in a hidden canopy" (R. Avraham Meimin, *E-l Mistater BeShafrir Ḥevyon*); all is His. It is not fitting for us to praise, for we cannot articulate what we wish to express, but to You, Lord our God, all is fitting, and all praises flow from Your essence. In Your name we conclude, "King, great (*gadol*) in praises," the King who is beyond ("great" implying "infinite"), even when He is extolled with praises; "God of thanksgivings," the God who conceals Himself in a hidden canopy, to whom thanks are due; "Lord of wonders"—You, who in Your great kindness and mercy, nonetheless chose melodies of song and permitted us to recite them so that we might learn how to live and how to conduct ourselves. We refer to God as "King," who needs us as a king needs his people (for "without a nation, there is no king"—*Tanya, Shaar HaYiḥud VeHaEmuna,* Ch. 7); yet, primarily, He is the "ever-living God," concealed and hidden from all.

In summary: at the conclusion of *Pesukei DeZimra,* after reciting the praises of the Holy One Blessed be He, we proclaim the vanity of all our effort. The goal is beyond our reach; the name of the Holy One Blessed be He extols and glorifies itself on its own. We start from the principle "Give praise, servants of the Lord" only to conclude with the principle "To You, silence is praise."

In Hallel, by contrast, we also start with the principle affirming human praise, but we remain with this principle until the end. As we approach the conclusion, we say, "All Your creatures will praise You, Lord our God, and Your pious and righteous ones who carry out Your will, and all Your nation, the House of Israel, will melodiously thank, bless…" We have assembled His praises and thanked Him for His wonders, and we will continue to do so, for we are so commanded to thank Him and render praise by His Torah, "for it is good to thank You and it is fitting for us to sing to Your name." It is fitting for us to praise and bless Your name, for we are commanded to do so. We conclude, "King extolled in praises," for He accepts our worship with satisfaction and love, and He is extolled by service in praise and song. Because we are rendering praise consequent upon and in reliance on the commandment to do so, there is no need for us to reflect on the problematic nature of the entire enterprise.

By the same token, however, we may not consider broadening the scope of Hallel, even by adding more of David's songs and praises. The Torah and halakha set the limits, which may not be breached. The commandment and its embodiment are bounded; and praise of God consists in extolling Him in accordance with the law, adding nothing to what is commanded. In *Pesukei DeZimra,* however, because the recitation of praise is rooted in and authorized as the study of Torah, the examination of God's attributes for the purpose of emulating Him and walking in His ways, the recitation has no prescribed limits.

And yet, one might still ask, how indeed can we persist in speaking of "the King extolled in praises" at the conclusion of Hallel? Can the King of all kings be elevated by flesh and blood singing His praises? Our answer, consistent with the Jewish perspective, is that we can, for so He has decreed. Do we not present a royal crown to the Holy One Blessed be He on Rosh HaShana? It is the request of the Holy One Blessed be He that we crown Him as our King. That flesh and blood present a royal crown to the Eternal One is an enormous paradox, yet Judaism has made it an underpinning of halakha.

KADDISH AFTER PESUKEI DEZIMRA

According to Maimonides' view that there is no congregational aspect to *Pesukei DeZimra,* individuals may recite them, each on his own, and only afterward does the congregation assemble for *Barekhu,* the *Shema* and its blessings, and the *Amida*. But that approach seems to make the recitation of Kaddish following *Pesukei DeZimra* problematic. On its face, that Kaddish seems to be intended as a demarcation between *Pesukei DeZimra* and the blessings of the *Shema*. But if *Pesukei DeZimra* are recited by individuals as individuals, why should the prayer leader recite Kaddish?

Apparently, Maimonides takes the view that the Kaddish is required not as a pause between *Pesukei DeZimra* and the blessings of the *Shema* but as a preface to reciting *Barekhu* and beginning the blessings of the *Shema*. Note also the "Order of Prayers for the Entire Year," at the end of *Mishneh Torah, Sefer Ahava,* where Maimonides determines, before presenting the text of the Kaddish, that "the prayer leader always says Kaddish before each prayer and after each prayer." Maimonides makes the recitation of Kaddish before each prayer part of an introductory assembling of praises, such as the recitation of *Ashrei* and so forth.

The point may be further clarified on the basis of an observation by *Tosafot* (Berakhot 49b, s.v. *amar*) on a dispute between R. Akiva and R. Yosi HaGalili regarding the formulation of the *zimmun* (the introductory call to recite *Birkat HaMazon,* the Grace after Meals). R. Yosi HaGalili was of the view that "they formulated the blessing in accordance with the size of the assembly, as Scripture says (Ps. 68:27), 'In assemblies bless God; the Lord, from the source of Israel.'" R. Akiva, who took the view that the *zimmun* formula did not vary with the number of participants (above ten), responded: "We find that in the synagogue, regardless of whether there are many or few, he says 'Bless the Lord.'" Similarly, in his view, once ten are present, the *zimmun* blessing is not adjusted in accordance with the size of the assembly. *Tosafot* comment as follows:

> We can infer that R. Yosi HaGalili concedes in the synagogue [that the formulation does not vary], for [R. Akiva] said, "We find," that is, you concede to me. And why do they disagree regarding *Birkat HaMazon* yet agree with regard to the synagogue? And the answer is that they certainly drew no distinction between ten and one hundred with respect to prayer [in the synagogue], for some enter and some leave without the prayer leader being aware of it, but in the case of *Birkat HaMazon,* where they have convened and come together [for a meal], there can be no error, for no one will leave until after *Birkat HaMazon* is recited.

The essence of *Tosafot*'s position is that in the synagogue, there is nothing to bind a group greater than ten, and one accordingly cannot speak of "assemblies"; they simply do not merge to form a distinctive unit of more than ten. In the case of *Birkat HaMazon,* however, the meal bonds them, for there is a halakhic category of gathering at a table (*heseba*) that establishes and unites all the participants into a single group, and in fact one person cannot say the blessing before the meal to discharge the obligation of all unless that group is established. Accordingly, in R. Yosi HaGalili's view, the formulation of the *zimmun* also varies with the size of the group, for they are united by the meal itself, and the person reciting it must invite the entire group to say *Birkat HaMazon*—"let us bless Him of whose food we have eaten"—and all the diners are thereby united into a single group.

On this theory, it appears that a *minyan* of ten also requires some amalgamating factor, even in the synagogue, for without such a factor, they do not form a unit. That amalgamating factor, therefore, must be identified; and it appears that the performance of any activity requiring a congregation unites the individuals into a congregational unit.

But an activity that can be performed either individually or communally, even if additional significance attaches to its communal performance, lacks the power to generate a congregational unit; for who can say that the activity is being performed communally? It is entirely possible that the individuals are carrying it out as individuals, and that the activity—prayer, for example—does not demonstrate the formation of an entity with the status of "congregation." Simply gathering in one place does not in itself clearly prove the formation of a group, and the congregation, before praying, must formally come together as a single unit, through the mechanism of an amalgamating factor. The prayer itself, again, cannot forge the congregation into a unit, for prayer can be recited by individuals as well; and though communal prayer is in a category of its own, simply rising in prayer does not necessarily attest to the formation of a congregational unit. We therefore must recite Kaddish, a *davar shebikedusha* (a "sacred public utterance") that cannot at all be regarded as the action of individuals and that is recited only as a public sanctification of God's name. That recitation invokes the concept of the community and forges the assembled individuals into a congregation. At the morning service, therefore, where it is impossible to recite Kaddish between the reading of *Shema* and the *Amida* (because of the need to juxtapose the *Amida* with the blessing of redemption that follows the *Shema*), Kaddish is recited before *Barekhu.* At the evening service, where Kaddish is inserted before the *Amida,* it is not recited before *Barekhu.*

But further inquiry is needed, for praying is preceded not only by Kaddish but also by *Barekhu.* Why, then, introduce Kaddish as the amalgamating factor, and why not regard the congregational unit as being formed through the recitation of *Barekhu*? The answer is plain, for *Barekhu,* in reality, forms an integral part of the blessings accompanying the Shema; it is an element of that corpus. This is proven by Rashi's view (Megilla 23b) that when the *sheliaḥ tzibbur* calls on the assembly to bless, they are obligated not only to respond "Blessed is the Lord Who is to be blessed for ever and ever"; they must also recite in full the ensuing first blessing preceding the *Shema* (even where the practice seems to have been that one individual recites the blessing on behalf of all of the assembled). But the call to bless does not pertain to the blessings of the *Amida*, to which it is unconnected, for the *Amida* prayer is an independent act of entreaty, not subordinate to the demand of *Barekhu*. More generally, the individual blessings in the *Amida* lack independent standing, differing thereby from those of the *Shema*. Each of the latter is a distinct entity, as appears from the deliberation over whether the validity of reciting one of the blessings depends on the recitation of all. (See Berakhot 11b-12a; Yerushalmi Berakhot 2:1. It should be noted that even if we regard the blessings of the *Shema* as dependent on one another, that is in regard to fulfilling the obligation of reciting the *Shema* with its blessings, but reciting one of the blessings alone would not be considered a blessing in vain.)

The situation with respect to Kaddish is radically different. Kaddish and *Barekhu* alike are *devarim shebikedusha*, yet they differ in an important respect. *Barekhu* is a *davar shebikedusha* within the rubric of praise for the Creator of the world; the *Kedusha* recited during the repetition of the *Amida* partakes of the same quality. By reciting *Barekhu*, we bless the Holy One Blessed be He, in accordance with the first principle outlined above, "Servants of the Lord give praise," because it is proper for us to thank and exalt God, and He lovingly and mercifully accepts our praises, just as He accepts the *Kedusha* recited by the angels. In Kaddish, however, we do not declare that we are magnifying and sanctifying the Holy One Blessed be He (as we do in *Kedusha*); rather, we say that He will be magnified and sanctified of His own accord, and, in a series of reflexive verbs, that He will be blessed, praised, glorified, exalted, raised on high, adored, and elevated. The entire Kaddish is grounded in the second principle, "To You, silence is praise." Its recitation provides a means of declaring to the Holy One Blessed be He that we are not permitted to utter even one word of praise and exaltation; instead we pray to Him that His holy name will be magnified and sanctified in accordance with the verse (Ez. 38:23) "and I will be magnified and sanctified and be known in the eyes of many nations."

In fact, Kaddish is the only *davar shebikedusha* that is based on the principle of "To You, silence is praise" and "Who can tell of the

Lord's mighty acts?" and that comprises prayer, rather than praise and exaltation. Accordingly, it is distinct from *Barekhu*; and though *Barekhu* generates the congregational unit needed for the recitation of the *Shema* and its blessings, it does not generate the congregational unit with respect to prayer, i.e., the *Amida*. That function is served by the Kaddish, for Kaddish itself is prayer. And that is why it seems that according to Maimonides the *Amida* requires Kaddish both before and after it, as an introduction and a conclusion. Accordingly, in the evening service we begin with *Barekhu* to form a congregational unit for the recitation of the *Shema* and its blessings; for that recitation, when done in a congregational unit, partakes of an added special quality of publicly acknowledging God's dominion. In that vein, Maimonides wrote (*Hilkhot Tefilla* 8:4), "And how is congregational worship [conducted]? One person should pray aloud as the others listen... and, similarly, one person should recite the blessing[s] for the *Shema* aloud, with the others answering 'Amen' after him only in the presence of ten." Meanwhile, Kaddish is recited before the *Amida*, in order to renew the congregational unit before recitation of the prayer. At the morning service, where one may not separate the *Amida* from the redemption blessing that precedes it, Kaddish is recited before the blessings for the *Shema*, but its efficacy pertains to the formation of a congregational unit for the *Amida* prayer.

Chapter 3

Keriat Shema and the Blessings of Torah

THE OBLIGATION OF KERIAT SHEMA

The *kiyum,* fulfillment, of *Keriat Shema* expresses itself in a state of mind, in a thought, in a feeling. Like *tefilla,* it is a subjective experience of the heart, a *kiyum* of *avoda shebalev.* The universal *kavvana* of mitzvot denotes an action in response to a divine norm which one feels binding: "I am prepared and ready to fulfill the commandment of my Creator." But the *kavvana* required of *Keriat Shema* is *kabbalat ol malkhut shamayim,* accepting the yoke of Heaven.

The first two sections of *Keriat Shema* demonstrate unqualified surrender to God's ethical will: *Kabbalat ol malkhut shamayim* in the first, and *kabbalat ol mitzvot,* accepting the yoke of mitzvot, in the second. The third section mentions the Exodus and concludes with the covenantal phrase, "I am the Lord your God, who brought you out of the land of Egypt, to be your God"; this is a phrase that reflects establishing a *brit*—"and I will take you to Me for a people, and I will be to you a God" (Ex. 6:7)—that expresses the great vision and hope that the covenant will sometime come true. You will always be helped and saved by Me, God says, because I once demonstrated My faithfulness to the promise I made to the patriarchs. Thus *Keriat Shema* contains two themes of sanctification: first, commitment to a great normative message, an absolute imperative norm; second, faith in a messianic and eschatological promise. The declaration of faith in the final realization of the historical cause is found in *zekhirat yetziat mitzrayim,* remembering the Exodus, and this comes to expression in the third section of *Keriat Shema.*

Actually, *kabbalat ol malkhut shamayim* consists of three media: first of all, *yiḥud Hashem,* acknowledging the unity of God, to which the first section of *shema* is dedicated; second, *kabbalat ol mitzvot,* which is found in *vahayah im shamo'a;* third, *zekhirat yetziat mitzrayim.* The Gemara says, "I am the Lord your God ... this indicates kingship" (Rosh HaShana 32a).

There are several views regarding the biblical obligation of *Keriat Shema.* According to one, it is only the first verse that is obligatory; a second view requires the whole first section, as the first verse is part of that section. Another opinion—that of *Peri Ḥadash* (*Oraḥ Ḥayyim* 67)—is that both *ve'ahavta* and *vehaya im shamoa* are obligatory, because in both sections the Torah says "when you go to sleep and rise up." And then Maimonides holds that all three sections are *mideoraita.* In the *Mishneh Torah* (*Hilkhot Keriat Shema* 1:3), Maimonides states that there is a commandment pertaining to *zekhirat yetziat mitzrayim,* remembering the Exodus, in the morning and the evening (in accordance with the view of Ben Zoma [*Berakhot* 12b]: "'all the days of your life' includes the nights as well"). However, he does not count remembering the Exodus as a separate mitzva among the 613 commandments. My grandfather Rav Ḥayyim Soloveitchik explained that *zekhirat yetziat mitzrayim* is not a separate mitzva; it is but one facet of *kabbalat ol malkhut shamayim.* Whenever there is a performance of *kabbalat ol malkhut shamayim,* one must mention the Exodus. This is just one of the ways that *kabbalat ol malkhut shamayim* expresses itself. Maimonides thinks that the section of "*vayomer*" is *mideoraita,* because *kabbalat ol malkhut shamayim* is incomplete as long as a section which is dedicated to the Exodus has not been recited.

Even though *yiḥud Hashem* and *ahavat Hashem,* the obligations of unifying God and loving Him, are included in *kabbalat ol malkhut shamayim,* they are also counted as separate mitzvot. Maimonides counts them as permanent mitzvot which refer to no specific experience; in other words, they are not bound by some physical performance or confined to some time period. They are to be observed all the time, like the obligations of knowing God and fearing Him. In contrast, the *yiḥud* and *ahava* of *Keriat Shema* are dynamic, short-term, great experiences.

THE BLESSINGS OF KERIAT SHEMA

Keriat Shema has three blessings, two preceding it and one following. Each *berakha* corresponds, as to content and theme, to one of the three sections of the *Shema*. In the first *berakha, Yotzer Or,* the verse "*Kadosh, kadosh, kadosh Hashem Tzeva-ot melo khol ha'aretz kevodo*" corresponds to "*Shema Yisrael, Hashem Elokeinu Hashem eḥad.*" *Ahava Rabba,* the second *berakha,* corresponds to *vehayah im shamo'a*—the *kabbalat ol mitzvot* of this section parallels "*lishmoa lilmod ulelamed lishmor velaasot,* to listen, learn and teach, guard and observe" of the blessing. The last *berakha, Emet VeYatziv,* corresponds to *zekhirat yetziat mitzrayim.* The section *ezrat avoteinu* of the blessing deals with the *geula* theme, the divine intervention in the historic occurrence which took place thousands of years ago and which we expect to occur in the near future, when the final *geula* of Israel will be realized: "Our Redeemer, the Lord of hosts is His name, the Holy One of Israel. Blessed are You, Lord, who redeemed Israel." The Exodus motif is intertwined with the motif of the future redemption.

Ahava Rabba consists of two different motifs. First, it contains a prayer for a pure heart and concentration of the mind in order to be able to understand and realize God's Word.

> Our Father, compassionate Father, ever compassionate, have compassion on us. Instill in our hearts the desire to understand and discern, to listen, learn and teach, to observe, perform and fulfill all the teachings of Your Torah in love. Enlighten our eyes in Your Torah and let our hearts cling to Your commandments. Unite our hearts to love and revere Your name.

Commitment to God is not only a question of resolve, of a decision to want it. It is also a question of courage, ability and having the willpower to do so. So we are praying for the intellectual ability to be able to understand and the moral ability to be courageous.

The second motif of *Ahava Rabba* is a petition for salvation and redemption, that God's promise may be fulfilled, that the people of Israel be rehabilitated, that history should not disappoint and humiliate us.

Not being humiliated by history is a very popular motif in our liturgy. This fear of humiliation can be traced to Moses: "Wherefore should the Egyptians speak, saying: For evil did He bring them forth?" (Ex. 32:12). The charismatic community should not be put to shame and the great expectations of countless generations must not be classified by history as a tragic illusion, as a mockery, an anticipation of something absurd which has never been realized. "And because we have trusted in Your holy, great and revered name, may we be glad and rejoice in Your salvation. Bring us back in peace from the four quarters of the earth and lead us upright to our land, for You are a God who performs acts of salvation…"

Ahava Rabba thus asserts the categorical validity of the divine norm to which the covenantal community is committed, and the truthfulness of the divine promise whose fulfillment that same community anticipates. It is basically a thanksgiving prayer, which expresses gratitude to God for His mercy, love and benevolence, in giving us His living laws, *ḥukei ḥayyim*.

This blessing is of a very ancient origin. The Mishna (Tamid 4:3, 5:1), which is a very old Mishna preceding the codification of the Mishna by Rebbe and which can be traced back to the *Bayit Sheini*, the Second Commonwealth, says that during the *Bayit Sheini*, after completing the morning service, the *tamid shel shaḥar*, the *Kohanim* would assemble in the *Lishkat HaGazit*, where they would "say one *berakha*" and read the *Shema*. *Ḥazal* (Berakhot 11a) were not sure if this *berakha* was *Yotzer Or* or *Ahava Rabba*, showing that both can be traced back to the Second Commonwealth.

AHAVA RABBA AND BIRKHOT HATORAH

There is no doubt that following in chronological order, the liturgy first evolved the sanctification of the Lord before reading a portion of the Law in public. As ancient as *Ahava Rabba* is, it is of a much later period than *Birkat HaTorah betzibbur*, the blessing said when the Torah is read publicly. The practice of praising God before the reading of the law to the congregation is considered a part of *Keriat HaTorah* itself. As a matter of fact, I once heard from my father, in the name of my grandfather, that if one should enter the synagogue after the *oleh* had pronounced the *berakha*, but before the *baal korei* began to read the portion, the individual did not discharge the duty of hearing *Keriat HaTorah*, because the duty of listening to *Keriat HaTorah* implies the answering of *Barukh Hashem hamevorakh le'olam va'ed* before the reading of the portion. The *berakha* is a part of the *ḥiyuv* of *Keriat HaTorah*. "And Ezra opened the book in the sight of all the people... And Ezra blessed the Lord, the great God. And all the people answered, Amen, Amen... So they read in the book in the Torah of God" (Nehemiah 8:5–6). The duty to hear *Keriat HaTorah betzibbur* implies not only the intellectual engagement, but more than that—it includes offering of praise and thanksgiving to God for giving us the law. The whole *tzibbur* participates in that by responding *Barukh Hashem hamevorakh le'olam va'ed*.

Birkat HaTorah betzibbur is actually derived from the verse "When I proclaim the name of the Lord; ascribe greatness to our God" (Deut. 32:3). Then *Ahava Rabba* was introduced, incorporating a twofold idea: commitment and expectation.

Finally, the *Birkhot HaTorah* preceding private study were developed. It is difficult to ascertain the exact date of the ordinance pertaining to *Birkhot HaTorah*. However, there is no doubt that they belong to the post-Mishnaic period. The Talmud (Berakhot 11b) quotes Rav Yehuda in the name of Shmuel or Rav Hamnuna as the scholars who emphasized the importance of *Birkhot HaTorah*, and most probably the first generation of *Amoraim* introduced them.

THE INDIVIDUAL'S BIRKHOT HATORAH AND THE EMOTIONAL COMPONENT OF TORAH STUDY

The first blessing of the individual on Torah study, which consists of *la'asok* and *veha'arev*, is an abbreviated version of *Ahava Rabba* (of course, the second motif of God's fulfillment of the promise of redemption was left out) and the second blessing for an individual on Torah study was borrowed from the communal service, *asher baḥar banu*.

There are two versions of the first *berakha*: "*la'asok bedivrei Torah*" is the version of the *Ḥakhmei Ashkenaz*; "*al divrei Torah*" is the version which was quoted by Rif, Maimonides, and most *Ḥakhmei Sepharad*. I cannot see any basic difference as to the motif and theme between the Ashkenazic version and the Sephardic version. *Birkhot HaTorah* are not related to the cognitive act of Talmud Torah, but rather are associated with the axiological involvement and consecration to Torah. Whether the version of "*la'asok*" or "*al divrei Torah*" is adopted is of no relevance; the net result is that we do not pronounce a blessing concerning the actual study of Torah—"*lilmod divrei Torah*" is not mentioned. What is emphasized is the fascination which *divrei Torah* possess. "*La'asok bedivrei Torah*" means to occupy ourselves, to devote ourselves, to be fascinated. "*Al divrei Torah*" means to be emotionally involved in it, not merely "*lilmod divrei Torah*," the intellectual act of study.

Veha'arev na means the Torah should fascinate us, it should allure us, it should become sweet in our mouths. In "*veha'arev na*" we spell out the ideal of *mesora*, of continuity—"so that we, our descendants, and the descendants of Your people, the house of Israel, may all know Your name and study Your Torah for its own sake." The idea of passing on, of transmitting, of perpetuating *divrei Torah*, of what I call belonging to the *mesora* community, is not realized through an intellectual act, but through emotional involvement. You can pass on mathematics because it is very useful for your child to know mathematics or physics. But when it is not a question of usefulness, it is impossible to pass on an axiological system without loving it, without being dedicated and devoted to it.

As a matter of fact, the intellectual genius cannot be creative unless he is emotionally involved. It is the intuitive feeling which is the source of creativity; creativity does not come from having a certain discipline at one's fingertips, it does not come simply from accumulated knowledge. Of course, it is impossible to develop intuition unless you know your astronomy, or chemistry, or physics, or philosophy. But it is a great love which generates intuition, an involvement which reveals new horizons. Creativity comes from total involvement in a discipline.

We have to distinguish between cognitive pluralism and axiological monism. A man can know many things, but one can live only in one value system. Intellectually, man is basically a pluralist. There is no competition within the intellect, no envy or jealousy. I can know many things. However, there is great competition among values in the axiological world. I can cherish one value; I cannot cherish five values, because values are basically competitive; they are jealous of each other, if I may use this expression. Since intellectual commitment is not total commitment, I can commit myself to different fields of knowledge. But axiological commitment is a total commitment that requires full devotion. Love has the element of jealousy, like a husband jealous of his wife.

It demands full attention, like a child who wants the full attention of the mother. Intellectually, we can be engaged in many things but one cannot be involved emotionally in two worlds. We cannot worship two gods. We cannot divide our emotions, our love, our sympathy, our appreciation, between two fields. Axiologically, we require a monistic attitude, and that means to be devoted to Torah alone.

HALAKHIC PROOFS THAT BIRKHOT HATORAH RELATE TO THE EMOTIONAL COMPONENT

If we should scrutinize the halakhot pertaining to *Birkhot HaTorah,* we would find a few laws which are peculiar to *Birkhot HaTorah,* in contrast to other *birkhot hamitzvot,* which will corroborate our thesis that this *berakha* relates to the emotional component in Talmud Torah.

The recital of the *berakha* in the morning suffices for the whole day and also for the night study, whereas other *birkhot hamitzvot* are canceled by *hese'aḥ hadaat* (distraction from the act at hand). If I should take off my *tefillin* for a while not intending to put them back soon, and then I change my mind and I want to put the *tefillin* on, it requires another *berakha*. However, reciting *Birkhot HaTorah* in the morning relieves me of the duty of reciting the *berakha* for twenty-four hours.

Tosafot (Berakhot 11b) note this difficulty and explain that there is *hese'aḥ hadaat* with regard to other mitzvot but not with regard to Torah for we are duty bound to study all the time. It is difficult to understand the answer. Whether or not one is permitted to interrupt the study is irrelevant concerning the problem of *hese'aḥ hadaat,* as the whole problem revolves around a factual, not an ideal, situation. It is not a question of what he is supposed to do, the question is what is he doing. We have to reckon with the fact that many people interrupt their studies with no intent of resuming them after a short while. This means there is *hese'aḥ hadaat*. Why shouldn't they recite the *Birkat HaTorah* if they are ready to read the Torah after a long intermission during which they haven't even thought of engaging in the study of the Torah? The fact that those people acted not in accordance with the law that requires that a man should never have *hese'aḥ hadaat* should not change the fact the *berakha* has been canceled for reason of *hese'aḥ hadaat.*

However, we understand the answer of *Tosafot* when we realize that *Birkat HaTorah* is related not to the explicit intellectual preoccupation, which is not continuous, but to the emotional consecration and involvement associated with a state of mind, with love for and devotion to the Word—and this involvement is a permanent, continuous experience which cannot be interrupted or canceled. Of course, emotional involvement sometimes is an acute experience, an explosive experience—I think of my great treasure and my heart overflows with love—and sometimes it is a latent experience; however, this love can never be extinguished.

Let us take our relationship to children. There is certainly emotional involvement with children, devotion, but you cannot say the experience is at all times identical. Sometimes it is an acute experience, when I play with the child, when my heart overflows with love for the child, I experience an explosive feeling which demonstrates itself in some external traits, like an expression on my face and so forth. It is an acute experience. And frequently, when the father is in his office or in his shop and his mind is occupied with other matters, it loses its acuteness and explosiveness and turns into a latent feeling. Yet he can never forfeit its greatness and depth.

This is exactly my relationship to Torah. The emotional involvement is a continuous experience, sometimes in an acute stage, sometimes in a latent stage, in an inactive stage. Yes, sometimes the acute experience is sharp with passion, and overabundant feelings, and sometimes, under other circumstances, it is a quiet experience; when the mind is occupied with other matters it loses its acuteness and explosiveness and turns into latent feeling. Yet the father can never forget the child and can never stop loving the child, and this is exactly valid with reference to Torah. The emotional attachment is never broken.

Maimonides actually says that the *Birkhot HaTorah* every day are part of *Birkhot HaShaḥar*. *Birkhot HaTorah* are a *birkat hodaya*—just as every day one has to recite a *berakha* of "who gives the rooster understanding," every day man has to praise God that He actually involved him and entitled him in this great experience.

Second, many *Rishonim* hold the view that there is no need to recite any passages from the Torah after reciting *Birkhot HaTorah*. *Tosafot* (Berakhot 11b, s.v. *shekvar*) quote the French sages who say there is no need to study *Torah Shebikhtav* or *Torah Shebe'al Peh* following the pronouncement of *Birkhot HaTorah,* in contrast to other *birkhot hamitzvot* which are necessarily related to the subsequent action. For example, if I should say *al netilat lulav* without holding the *lulav,* that would be a *berakha levatala,* blessing in vain. But most of the *Rishonim* think there is no need for *limud haTorah* following *Birkhot HaTorah.* The *berakhot* refer not to the actual performance but to a value judgement, emotional assessment, a mood, a world perspective and the actual study is of no significance and has no bearing upon the validity of *Birkhot HaTorah.*

Third, the *Shulḥan Arukh* (*Oraḥ Ḥayyim* 47:14) ruled that women must say *Birkhot HaTorah.* With regard to *mitzvot aseh shehazman grama,* time-bound commandments, there is a controversy between Maimonides (*Hilkhot Tzitzit* 3:9) and Rabbenu Tam (*Tosafot, Rosh Hashana* 33a) as to whether women should say a *berakha* or not. Ashkenazim have accepted the viewpoint of Rabbenu Tam and the Rema that women pronounce a *berakha* on all *mitzvot aseh shehazman grama* like *lulav, shofar, sukka* and so forth. The *Meḥaber,* R. Yosef Karo, however, does not accept the viewpoint of Rabbenu Tam but Maimonides' viewpoint that women must not say a *berakha* over *mitzvot aseh shehazman grama* (*Oraḥ Ḥayyim* 589:6). If they are relieved of the duty, they cannot say "*vetzivanu,* who has obligated us" because there is no "*vetzivanu.*" The Vilna Gaon asks why the *Meḥaber* rules that women recite *Birkhot HaTorah,* since women are actually relieved of the duty of Talmud Torah. If the *Meḥaber* is of the Maimonidean opinion that whenever there is no duty, the *berakha* is out of place, women should not recite *Birkhot HaTorah* either. The answer is that women recite *Birkhot HaTorah* because women have also witnessed *Ma'amad Har Sinai,* and the Torah says "Assemble the people, the men and the women and the little ones" (Deut. 31:12). Women are duty bound to attend *hakhel* because *hakhel* is not intellectual *limud;* it is more a demonstration of our total commitment to the Torah. Men and women might differ in their respective obligations in intellectual *limud,* but there is no difference between men and women regarding emotional involvement, and that is why women recite *Birkhot HaTorah.*

A total commitment is at first an emotional commitment. The objective which is anticipated is an ideal; the objective which is attained is a value. Torah is a great ideal and a great value. Whatever is realized is a value; whatever I haven't attained is an ideal which has unlimited fascination for me. Torah exerts some supernatural power of fascination upon the human personality in the same manner as God fascinates me and captivates my imagination. I yearn for Him, "As the hart pants after the water brooks, so my soul pants after Thee, O God" (Ps. 42:2). This great, total involvement involves not only the study of Torah but for its ideals to be integrated in my existence and my personality as a value. *Limud Torah* expresses intellectual engagement; *esek bedivrei Torah* expresses emotional involvement or the axiological relationship. *Birkhot HaTorah* are related not to the first aspect but to the second aspect.

A PERSONAL COMMENT

I can speak of my own experience. Axiologically, I belong totally to one mother, and this is the Torah. One uses his knowledge not only for pragmatic purposes; he lives in his knowledge. Somehow, he finds and cherishes an enclave for all his drives and cravings and yearnings. It gives him comfort, peace of mind, consolation, and some self-assurance or security. I can't find that in any discipline. I can read and understand books of philosophy, but this doesn't reassure me emotionally. I don't find my equilibrium. When I open up the Gemara, I feel the sailor is back home. In my moments of stress, when I am downhearted and dejected, when I feel that I failed, have gone bankrupt—the only remedy for me is to open up the Gemara. If I am able to engage in a *sugya* or in a problem, a Gemara, an Aggada or Midrash, something which is connected to this great *mesora* community, little by little I find that somehow my fear has been alleviated, I am relieved of this burden and I find repose and peace. I can't do it through reading a philosophical book. For instance, I know Kant almost by heart. But I know Kant is still a Prussian and I have no relationship with him. But when I engage in the Gemara, I have Rava on my left, Abaye on my right, and Maimonides in front of me. I argue with each, I quote him, I agree with him, I say he's wrong, he tells me I'm wrong. It's a conversation, it's a dialogue. And this living experience of contacting the *ḥakhmei hamesora*, of living with them completely, this is the emotional involvement in Torah, and this is exactly what *Birkhot HaTorah* spell out. The words "*la'asok bedivrei Torah*" relate to the verse "*ki hit'asku imo*, they contended with him" (Gen. 26:20)—it is about people dealing with people. So it means by dealing with Torah I deal not only with Torah, but I deal with the entire community, with the *mesora* community. The past reemerges. *La'asok bedivrei Torah* is the quickening of the past, the past which appears to be dead.

This is the meaning of the prayer "Please, Lord our God, make the words of Your Torah sweet in our mouths ... so that we, our descendants, and the descendants of Your people, the house of Israel, may all know Your name and study Your Torah for its own sake. Blessed are You, Lord, who teaches Torah to His people Israel." It might have said, "who taught Torah to His people," in the past tense. But this fellowship with God is realized through integration and involvement in the *mesora* community in the present. This is what is important in Torah—otherwise our intellectual studies, however good and important they may be, are actually of no value, are worthless in the long run.

Torah cannot be taught at a low temperature: "Is not My word like fire? says the Lord" (Jer. 23:29). Fire symbolizes passion, emotional excitement, involvement, dedication and consecration. "And the mountain burned with fire unto the heart of heaven" (Deut. 4:11). Why did Mount Sinai burn with a great fire? Why did God want to demonstrate that the Torah was given, the Law was given, through the flame? It symbolizes the eternal dedication and consecration, the emotional outburst, the emotional upheaval, the great love—"For love is strong as death, jealousy is cruel as the grave; the flashes thereof are flashes of fire, a very flame of the Lord" (Song 8:6), a great love burning like a flame which keeps on burning and spreading warmth and heat. You not only know it, you feel it. This is exactly what it means, "*la'asok bedivrei Torah*."

Talmud Torah embraces both the intellectual engagement and the commitment to comply with the norm, a decision to make oneself ready to carry this particular burden. But for the decision to be dynamic and powerful, for it to actually become a reality, a volitional act does not suffice; one must get entangled in it emotionally. God's Word becomes a precious treasure, something which lends meaning and purposefulness to one's existence, a great vision which captivates the imagination, that stirs the soul, that gives a feeling of happiness and pleasure, and actually fills me with ecstasy when I think that I will realize the great goal. One not only abides by the Word and the norm, but loves it; he is not only committed to it but also devoted and passionately affected. In a word, the kerygma becomes the central value around which one's axiological system revolves, the focus of all emotions and sentiments, that highest good after which one feels a deep yearning and a great longing. It is an ecstatic involvement in God's Word.

Emotional involvement always expresses itself in assessment, in evaluation, in the formation of an axiological relationship. It is an aesthetic involvement in God's Word; I cherish study of the law because it is precious to me. This almost mystical yearning for the Word or for the Torah asserts itself in my longing to find God, to establish fellowship with Him by studying His Word. I cherish His Word because it is the only contact I have with Him. The contact is an intellectual one which expresses itself not only in abiding by the norm and the message, but in loving and cherishing it.

Halakhically, there are two fundamentals: First, "and you shall teach them diligently unto your children, and shall speak of them when you sit in your house, and when you walk by the way, and when you lie down, and when you rise up" (Deut. 6:7), which expresses the propriety and significance of the cognitive approach to the word. The Torah must be studied, understood, analyzed, broadened and deepened. Under this aspect, the intellectual venture must meet the highest standards of logical thinking: abstraction, definition, analysis, classification must be flawless, consistent with our great tradition of halakhic research. The methods must be exact, the thinking clear, the approach objective and faithful, the formulation unequivocal, the premises consistent, etc. These attributes are a result and consequence of unlimited curiosity. This is Talmud Torah.

Second, "And these words, which I command you this day, shall be upon thy heart, *al levavekha*" (Deut. 6:6)—a total involvement with particular emphasis upon emotional attachment and assessment, complete identification with the word, getting totally entangled and involved, experiencing the word as an aspect of my own existence, as the substance and meaningfulness of inner personality which one cannot disclaim or forget. Knowledge alone does not suffice. The words should be implanted in thy heart, become one with thy very essence.

THE QUEST FOR TRUTH AND THE YEARNING FOR ḤESED

These two precepts of Talmud Torah express two basic metaphysical drives: one, the quest for truth, and two, the yearning for *ḥesed*. The longing for truth, for knowledge, for enlightenment stems from the fear of insensateness and absurdity. Man in his naturalness and full primitive immediacy, part and parcel of a brute, mechanical senseless nature tries to rise above a compulsive existence to freedom and self-knowledge, and therefore wants to interpret reality in general and himself in particular. The fear of a mute, non-intelligent and meaningless existence within an almost absurd universe, driven by uncontrollable forces nowhere drives him to self-interpretation or self-definition. Of course, if he wants to define himself or interpret himself, the first thing he must do is interpret his environment. In his potent desire to face the order of thinghood on the outside as an observer and onlooker who does not drift along with the overwhelming tide of events, he must form a new approach to this order, namely, a subject-object relationship.

The first step in man's great endeavor to redeem himself from brute existence and to raise himself to an intelligent, individualistic, personalistic existence, to not be one within nature, to not be included and swallowed by nature but to play the role of the outsider who observes and watches and understands nature, and who wants to gain control over nature, the first step in knowledge, in the cognitive process of man, the first beginning is classification, descriptive understanding. Man is not an object anymore; he is a subject who studies the world of objects. This drive is responsible for the great strides man has made in harnessing various forces in nature, in mastering his environment. This mastery over nature inspires him with self-confidence and gives him assurance that his status is unique in the universe. This rise above blind obedience and total integration into nature is corroborated by the technological achievement of man; this is the drive, the quest for truth. The quest of truth is out to redeem man from his bondage, from his unity with nature, and places him outside of the universe in the role of the knower, of the viewer, of the observer.

Now comes the great quest for *ḥesed*, for sharing his ontic experience with others, the powerful longing for love. This is due to the fear of loneliness which overcomes man as a direct result of man's triumph over the immediate, instinctive, brute existence and his rise to independence and personality. The so-called primitive human being has never felt lonely because he saw himself as part of his environment. He was in communication with the animal in the field and with the bird in the forest. He was not aware of his distinctness, had no capacity for self-recognition and his existence consisted completely in this non-reflective, instinctive union with nature. When man tore himself loose, at least partially, from the mechanical order of things and became aware of his own selfhood as something peculiar and singular, he suddenly discovered that he is the loneliest being on earth. He broke with his environment, he emancipated himself from their state of mind, and, so to say, betrayed his old "friends." Hence he is impelled to look for new companionship, for someone with whom he could share his existence, since he cannot address himself to Mother Nature anymore. There is no bond between the victor and the vanquished enemy.

Man is not part of nature, so he has to look for companionship with someone who is as lonely as he is. God called in all the animals and told man to give them names, "but for Adam there was not found a help meet for him" (Gen. 2:20). After man has torn himself loose from nature, after man recognized and had become aware of the incommensurability between him and nature, that he has no fellowship with the animal and with the bird—it was then that Eve was created.

This longing for giving love, for uniting destinies, for sympathetic understanding, is the basis of all social institutions. Marriage is typical of that metaphysical will in man. "It is not good for man to be alone" (Gen. 2:18). Judaism has never considered the marriage institution as a mere result of the physiological-sexual drive but of man's desire to live a life of love, to be in a community, to address oneself to a thou. Only then is the individual redeemed from his loneliness and the I suddenly finds common interests with a strange thou of whose existence he was hardly aware a while ago. This is the metaphysical drive for *ḥesed*—to share one's existence with others.

However, this craving for love is not confined to human companionship. It reaches a much higher level of fellowship, namely, that of ideas-ideals and values. In order to save oneself from the curse of loneliness, the I who was dedicated to himself, to his selfish interests, must transcend his hemmed-in selfhood and experience something else which lies outside of his individual realm—and this mysterious something is to be found in the world of ideas which form values. One associates not only with people but with values and ideals as well and perhaps human fellowship is warranted only by the common involvement in a higher order of ideas. Loneliness which is ameliorated and alleviated by friendship and love must actually be redeemed not just by friendship for a human being, but by commitment to an ideal, by involvement in some value that is cherished. When the ideal breaks through to the within-himself-arrested-I, then the I liberates himself from his absurd egocentricity and accepts the thou.

While the world of theoretical ideas sprang from man who rebels against the absolute dominion of nature over him, the order of ideals flows from man's flight from himself to others, to an existence much broader than his own.

The intellectual engagement we term *limmud Torah*; the total involvement—*esek bedivrei Torah*. While the first act is representative of man's quest for knowledge and self-interpretation, the second is typical of his yearning for community existence which sees the other person or the ideal not from a pragmatic but from a metaphysical viewpoint. I regard the other not as useful to my egotistic petty utilitarian self but as something essential to my very existence.

Halakhically, both aspects constitute one whole which is called Talmud Torah. When the Pentateuch speaks of the severe sin of forgetting the word of God: "Only take heed to thyself, and keep thy soul diligently, lest thou forget the things which thine eyes saw, and lest they depart from thy heart all the days of thy life" (Deut. 4:9), it intends not to emphasize that one must not forget a single detail of the Torah insofar as accumulation of quantitative knowledge is concerned, but the qualitative approach, the loss of interest, the estrangement from the Torah as a great ideal and value which must be cherished forever. The same is true of the saying in Avot (3:10): "One who forgets even one thing of his Torah learning, Scripture regards him as if he had endangered his soul… One does not endanger his soul unless he deliberately removes teachings from his heart." Forgetfulness signifies emotional alienation and transvaluation of the worth of the Torah and the development of personal neutrality toward the word of God. The phrase in the Aggada (Pesaḥim 49b), "He who has studied and then abandoned, is worse than all of them," refers not to one who does not devote full time to Talmud Torah but to the apostate who separated himself emotionally, axiologically from the Torah, who has suddenly reassessed his own axiological consciousness.

In light of this premise, we may safely venture to say that *Birkhot HaTorah* are not related to the cognitive act of Talmud Torah. They rather are associated with the axiological involvement and consecration. Whether the version of *la'asok* or the one of *al divrei Torah* is true, the net result is that we do not pronounce a blessing concerning *limmud Torah*, the spelling out of Torah; the actual study is not mentioned, what is emphasized is the worth, the fascination, which *divrei Torah* possess.

Chapter 4

Birkat HaMazon, the "Grace after Meals"

PERMISSION TO BLESS GOD

Maimonides' *Hilkhot Berakhot* (ch. 1) includes the laws pertaining to *Birkat HaMazon*, the "Grace after Meals," and also classifies, defines and explains the laws pertaining to a variety of *berakhot*. A *berakha* is due to some experience; sometimes it is eating, sometimes it is observing or witnessing something. It is the basic unit of all of our prayers, all of which have been formulated and standardized within the framework of *berakhot*. The *Amida*, for example, consists of eighteen or nineteen *berakhot*, and the recital of *Shema* is placed within the context of *Birkhot Keriat Shema* (blessings upon the recital of *Shema*). Indeed, each *tefilla* finds its expression within the frame of reference of a *berakha*.

As was his method, Maimonides indicated at the beginning of *Hilkhot Berakhot* the biblical source for *berakhot*. "*Uveirakhta et Hashem Elokekha*, And you shall bless the Lord your God" (Deut. 8:10) is the only place where the Torah tells us that it is our duty, that it is incumbent upon us, to bless God. Actually, the semantic of *uveirakhta* is not clear; it can be interpreted in two ways. First, it might mean to praise Him for the good He has bestowed upon us. Second, *barukh* can also mean be blessed. "*Barukh ata ba'ir uvarukh ata basadeh*" (Deut. 28:3) cannot mean "You should be praised in the city and in the field." It clearly means blessed.

Most *Rishonim* and mystics translated *barukh* as blessed. We do not praise God; we bless Him. But how can a human being bless God? We can understand God blessing a human being, but how is it possible to do the reverse? For a human being, a mortal, a frail being to bless God would be close to blasphemy.

Thus, we derive two principles from this biblical verse: a commandment and a concept. The commandment is that following a meal we have to recite *Birkat HaMazon*. The concept we derive is that man is granted a license to bless God—a prerogative and privilege indicative of the high and exalted station of man within creation.

BLESSING THE "GREAT AND HOLY NAME" AFTER EATING

In his introduction to *Hilkhot Berakhot*, Maimonides writes: "There is one positive commandment [in this section], which is to bless the great and holy name (*hashem hagadol vehakadosh*) after eating; and the explanation of this commandment appears in the following chapters." Maimonides does not list attributes for God at random. He selects attributes related to the nature of the subject discussed. For instance, in *Hilkhot Yesodei HaTorah* 2:1, he calls God *nikhbad venora* (honored and feared), while in *Hilkhot Yesodei HaTorah* 6:1, referring to the prohibition of erasing the name of God, he writes that these names are *kedoshim* and *tehorim* (holy and pure). Why, in reference to *Birkat HaMazon*, does he use the two attributes *gadol* and *kadosh*?

In Kabbalistic terminology, the word *gedula* is replaced with the word *ḥesed* (loving-kindness), which is apparently its synonym. *Gadol* does not mean might; that is *gevura*. *Ḥazal* understood greatness, at least in some respects, not in actual physical terms, but in terms of morality. *Kadosh* refers to a gesture of retreat, *tzimtzum*; God is in hiding and needs to be found in transcendental recesses. With regard to man, *tzimtzum* means the ability to withdraw when one expects to derive pleasure and happiness but knows that by engaging in this action he will violate an ethical principle. The ability to retreat, withdraw, and restrain himself is *kedusha*.

The Jewish concept of having a meal was determined by these two ethical principles. The first is the principle of *ḥesed*. There is no *seuda* without breaking bread with someone else. The Gemara (Taanit 20b) tells us that Rav Huna would open the door at every meal and say, "Whoever is in need, come and eat." What we say in the Haggada on Pesaḥ used to be the motto of our sages every day. Maimonides says that whoever closes or locks his door and rejoices on the holidays, it is not a *simḥa shel mitzva,* the kind of joy that the Torah commanded us to engage in, but *simḥat kereso,* the joy of his belly (*Hilkhot Yom Tov* 6:18). This is emphasized on Yom Tov because then one engages in a sumptuous meal, but it is applicable to any meal. Every meal should be an act of *ḥesed.* "Let the poor be members of your household" (Avot 1:5).

The second principle which guides us in enjoying food is *kedusha,* sacrificial action, the ability to withdraw from forbidden food, to discriminate and resist temptation. Man is elevated by the ability to withdraw at the moment when withdrawal is not desirous and not very pleasant. One expects to derive pleasure and happiness from something but at the same moment reminds himself that engaging in this action would violate an ethical principle. There is a clash between desire for success and expansion and the moral law. *Kedusha* represents the ability to resist temptation.

It is interesting how with only two words, *gadol* and *kadosh,* Maimonides formulates a whole philosophy of eating. To a Jew, a meal is not just eating, responding to some physiological drive. It is more than that. It is an ethical performance which must be based upon the two basic principles of *ḥesed* and *kedusha.*

A HUMAN RESPONSE

Maimonides (*Hilkhot Berakhot* 1:1) states: "It is a positive commandment from the Torah to bless after eating food (*mazon*) as it is written (Deut. 8:10): 'And you will eat and be satisfied, then you shall bless the Lord your God…'" He goes on to say that one is duty bound under Torah law only if he has satisfied his hunger, as the verse states, "And you will eat and be satisfied (*vesavata*)." By rabbinic ordinance (*divrei sofrim*) even eating the size of an olive requires a blessing afterwards.

Strangely, Maimonides' source for qualifying the biblical commandment of *Birkat HaMazon* to a case in which one is satisfied is found in an aggadic source, not a halakhic one. The Mishna (Berakhot 45a) mentions only a dispute regarding whether the minimum amount obligating *Birkat HaMazon* is the size of an olive or the size of an egg.

The Mishna does not mention that these amounts are merely rabbinic, and that the biblical commandment requires *kedei sevia* (complete satisfaction). In fact, the Gemara derives the *kezayit* and *kebeitza* from words in the Torah (Berakhot 49b).

There is an aggadic statement (Berakhot 20b), however, that comments on these rabbinic amounts:

> Rav Avira said: The ministering angels said before the Holy One: Master of the world, in Your Torah it is written "who shows favor to no one and takes no bribe" (Deut. 10:17), yet You show favor to Israel, as it is written "The Lord shall show favor to you" (Num. 6:26)? He replied to them: Should I not show favor to Israel? For I wrote in the Torah that one should recite *Birkat HaMazon* if one has eaten and been satisfied, but they are meticulous [to recite it] even for the size of an olive."

Though such a meal does not provide satiety, the Jew will nevertheless recite *Birkat HaMazon*. Rabad (*Hilkhot Berakhot* 5:15) rejects R. Avira's statement. According to his view, the dispute about *kezayit* and *kebeitza* pertains to the biblical obligation. Maimonides, however, translated this aggada into halakhic terms.

Rav Avira said that the angels complained to God. How did he know—did he hear them? But when *Ḥazal* tell a story they have each word in the proper place; each word represents an idea. He quoted angels because angels are perfect beings, who completely carry out the assignment which is given to them by God. There is no failure or omission, violation or rebellion on their part. An angel ministers to God and fulfills the divine will to the last iota. There is never failure because they are perfect beings

Human beings are weak and frail creatures; guilty of sins of omission and commission. Many times man is corrupt and dishonest; he doesn't understand himself or his duty. The assignment which is given to man has never been fulfilled fully. Every human being has an assignment to carry out. No one can succeed fully; the human being must fail. Failure is characteristic of the human being. Complete success and compliance is characteristic only of the angel.

But despite the angel's superiority, there is one thing the human being can manifest that the angel cannot—sacrificial action. The angel is not exposed to the vicissitudes of life and encounters no opposing forces. The human being is surrounded by nature, which is indifferent and sometimes even vicious, hostile, and violent. Natural law is sometimes cruel. Man is also exposed to temptation and to a variety of impulses that induce him sometimes to violate a commandment. So when a human being carries out his assignment, even in an imperfect manner, he pays a high price for it. The implementation of an assignment given to the human being is always a sacrificial action. He cannot accomplish anything in this world without sacrificing. To build or do anything for *Yahadut*, or even to bring up his children properly and to live a decent life, spells sacrifice. Without sacrificial action there is no service of God.

The angels, those perfect beings, complained to God because perfection to them was simple. They don't know what it means to abide by God's will in a society which may be completely secular, agnostic, cynical, and sarcastic. They don't know what it means to meet opposition or to be in a dilemma where they don't know how to act. They have never had a test or temptation; all is simple, direct, automatic. There is no opposition, no evil instinct or good instinct for an angel. But man is sometimes shaken by conflicts and struggles.

So the angels complained to God: why is He so forgiving and so tolerant toward the human being? They said, God does not bear special regard for anyone; justice must prevail. He who sins must be punished. Why forgiveness, tolerance, perseverance, and patience, why the bestowal of *ḥesed* on the human being, on the Jew?

God's argument about *Birkat HaMazon* is metaphorical. What it signifies is that it is easy for angels to sing the praise of God. They are never sick or hungry; they have never been in exile. They don't know what death is, or loneliness or solitude or despair. It is not difficult for them to chant "Holy, holy, holy."

Sometimes it is very hard for man to say it. It is hard for man to say the benediction *Barukh Dayan HaEmet* ("Blessed is the faithful Judge") at a funeral. Such a *berakha* tears the human being apart. How much discipline the halakha demands of us! Discipline in matters of food, as far as our physical actions are concerned, is not as strict or demanding or difficult as the discipline that the Torah requires of us with regard to our emotional life. There are laws that require one to be superhuman in order to properly fulfill and implement them. If, to take an example I often offer, one buries a member of his family, who was very dear to him, and he feels as if he were burying a part of himself, and then an hour later it is Passover or another holiday. Having just witnessed the complete absurdity and nonsense of human life, he must now lift the cup of wine and recite the Kiddush or the Haggada, including the verses from Hallel (Ps. 118:18, 24): "The Lord has chastised me severely but he has not given me up to death ... This is the day which the Lord has made we will rejoice and be glad in it."

This is a strange experience, but the halakha demands it. Many have done it; not only exceptional individuals. A Jew could say *Birkat HaMazon* in the concentration camp, the same *Birkat HaMazon* with the same dedication and devotion as if he had eaten a sumptuous meal and as if he were completely satisfied. A human being will never be perfect. But this attempt on his part to be perfect involves the sacrifice of giving away, withdrawal, accepting defeat. God did not demand that we say *Birkat HaMazon* when we are hungry; we have taken this duty upon ourselves.

THE SCOPE OF THE BIBLICAL COMMANDMENT

Maimonides' source for the biblical commandment of *Birkat HaMazon* is Berakhot 21a: "Where do we find that *Birkat HaMazon* is ordained in the Torah? Because it says: 'And you will eat and be satisfied, then you shall bless.'" In this respect, *Birkat HaMazon* occupies a privileged position. The *Rishonim* disagree as to whether the requirement of prayer is derived from the Torah or from rabbinical law. Maimonides (*Hilkhot Tefilla* 1:1) writes that it is derived from the Torah, while virtually all *Ḥakhmei Ashkenaz* maintain that it is a rabbinic obligation. There is an opinion in the Gemara (Berakhot 21a; *Tosafot*, Menaḥot 43b *s.v. ve'eizo*) that *Shema* is rabbinically ordained, and when one is in doubt about whether or not he has recited the *Shema*, he need not recite it again. There is no such question about *Birkat HaMazon*: the only dispute (Berakhot 46a) is whether the fourth blessing, *HaTov VeHaMeitiv* ("He who is good and does good"), is part of the biblical commandment. Regarding the first three blessings of *Birkat HaMazon*, it is universally maintained that they constitute a fulfillment of Torah law.

Although the basic obligation is biblical, it is unclear which elements in each blessing derive from the Torah. The situation here is analogous to the one addressed by Nahmanides (*Hasagot al Sefer HaMitzvot,* first *shoresh*) regarding the obligation of Hallel. The *Halakhot Gedolot* (*Behag*) counts the mitzva of Hallel among the 613 commandments. Maimonides asks how this can be when the text of Hallel (Ps. 113–118) was composed later. Nahmanides responds that the obligation is from the Torah, but the determination of a specific text is not. And he offers *Birkat HaMazon* as another instance of this phenomenon: "The prophets instituted a set wording... and the text is recited according to the times."

Nahmanides' last statement means that in the time of the Temple, when phrases such as "Rebuild Jerusalem, the Holy City" did not apply, they were not included. Nahmanides does not offer an alternative wording. Very likely, in the Temple era, they said "May He sustain the Temple on its foundation," along the lines of the prayer of the *Kohen Gadol* on Yom Kippur (Maimonides, *Hilkhot Avodat Yom HaKippurim* 3:11), after he read the Torah publicly. Or they offered a blessing of thanks that the Temple existed and the service was in place. In any event, according to Nahmanides, the Torah law requires no more than minimal praise—"like Benjamin the Shepherd's blessing" ("Blessed is the Master of this bread"; Berakhot 40b). This suggests that according to Torah law, the obligation depends on the individual's intelligence and understanding.

Kesef Mishneh (*Hilkhot Berakhot* 2:1 *s.v. berakha*) and others interpret Maimonides in harmony with Nahmanides. In this respect, Maimonides' exposition of *Birkat HaMazon* differs from that of *tefilla*. In *Hilkhot Tefilla* (1:1–4) too, Maimonides rules that the specific text of the blessings derives from rabbinic law. There, however, he maintains that the threefold structure of prayer (praise followed by petition and then thanksgiving) is mandatory (1:2) even though the specific wording is not. For *Birkat HaMazon,* however, Maimonides does not require specific motifs. On this interpretation, Maimonides presents the biblical commandment in chapter 1 of *Hilkhot Berakhot*. In the second chapter, he goes on to the rabbinic law, which details the specific blessings.

A second opinion among the *Rishonim,* by contrast, identifies mandatory themes in *Birkat HaMazon,* beyond minimal words of praise. The way one formulates these motifs is not important, but the motifs themselves—thanksgiving for food, for the land, and for the Temple—derive from the Torah. This is the view of Rashba (Berakhot 48b): "Moses, Joshua, and David instituted a formula for each blessing in their time..." Of course, before the conquest of the land and the building of Jerusalem they did not recite the same formula as that recited after the conquest and building. Similarly, we do not recite the same formula that David and Solomon instituted. Whereas we request the return of the kingdom and building of the Temple, they requested maintenance of the kingdom and of the Temple and continuation of peace in the land." *Shita Mekubetzet* holds the same opinion.

The difference of opinion between Nahmanides and the other *Rishonim* about whether the Torah requires only minimal praise or the specific motifs for *Birkat HaMazon* depends on the scope of the verse "And you will eat and be satisfied, then you shall bless the Lord your God for the good land which He has given you" (Deut. 8:10). Does this verse mandate praise for the land as well as the food?

The Talmud (Berakhot 48b) derives the individual blessings of *Birkat HaMazon* from this verse: "'And you will eat and be satisfied, then you shall bless'—this signifies *Birkat HaZan* [the first blessing]; ... 'for the land'—this signifies *Birkat HaAretz* [the second blessing]; 'the good'—this signifies *Boneh Yerushalayim* [the third blessing]." The "goodness" of the land is interpreted not in the sense of beauty or good, but in the sense of the land's perfection. The Land of Israel cannot be perfect unless it includes the element of holiness of Jerusalem.

According to Nahmanides, the derivations from each phrase are only *asmakhtot,* enactments attached by the Rabbis to these phrases, rather than derivations of Torah teachings. Indeed, the interpretation of the adjective "the good" can be viewed as an *asmakhta*. But the blessing of the land seems to be explicit in the verse: "then you shall bless the Lord your God for the good land which He has given you." Should not the mention of the land engender a biblical obligation? The solution is that according to Nahmanides, "land" is an elliptical way of referring to the "fruit of the land." Thus, according to Torah law, we bless Him not for the land but for the food that the land produced. Indeed, while Onkelos translates the verse verbatim, the Aramaic translation attributed to Yonatan ben Uziel expands the word "land" to "fruit of the land." Thus, the halakhic disagreement about inclusion of the land in *Birkat*

HaMazon depends on the correct translation of the verse. [It should be noted that Nahmanides on the Torah (Deut. 8:6) does include reference to the land, and not only to its fruits, in the commandment of *Birkat HaMazon*. Here, unlike in *Sefer HaMitzvot*, Nahmanides seems to adopt the view associated with his student, Rashba.]

CHARACTERIZING THE BLESSING

Another issue is how to characterize *Birkat HaMazon*. Yonatan translates the word "*uveirakhta*, then you shall bless" as *modin umevarekhin*, thank and bless. The obligation of blessing thus includes a mitzva of *hoda'a*, giving thanks. Let us contrast this with Nahmanides' position in *Sefer HaMitzvot*. Nahmanides cited the simple formula of Benjamin the Shepherd for *Birkat HaMazon*, "Blessed is the Master of this bread," which has no element of thanksgiving. *Birkat HaAretz*, the second blessing in our Grace, starts with "*Nodeh lekha*, We thank you." Yet Benjamin does not utter words of thanks. He only blesses God for the bread (that is the meaning of *barukh*), recognizing God's mastery. *Sefer HaḤinnukh* (§430, dealing with *Birkat HaMazon*), in the course of explaining the meaning of *berakha*, paraphrases as follows: "May it be Your will that all people of the world relate the blessing to You and confess [*modim*] that all emanates from You." Here the word *modim* does not mean thank but acknowledge. We are to recognize God as the source of all blessing. The *Sefer HaḤinnukh* thus conforms to Nahmanides' view, that *Birkat HaMazon*, in its original form, is simply a declaration of His mastery and kingship—that God created everything, renews everything, and sustains everything—and contains no expression of thanks, against the view found in the Targum Yonatan, who would require both thanksgiving and blessing.

Nahmanides' view is almost explicit in the Torah's words. Immediately following the commandment of *Birkat HaMazon*, the very next verses warn us, "Beware lest you forget the Lord your God ... Lest you eat and be satisfied ... and your heart will grow haughty and you will forget the Lord your God who led you through that great and terrible wilderness ... who fed you in the wilderness with manna ..." (Deut. 8:11–12, 14–16). The Torah does not here command an act of thanksgiving on the part of man, but rather warns man against forgetting that He is the Creator of everything, lest "you say in your heart, my power and the might of my hand has gotten me this wealth" (8:17). *Birkat HaMazon* forestalls this type of human arrogance: "And you shall remember the Lord your God, for it is He who gives you power to succeed" (8:18). Through *Birkat HaMazon*, man recognizes God not merely as "He who provides you with bread," but as "He who gives you power to succeed."

According to one Tannaitic view (Berakhot 48b), the obligation to bless God before eating (*berakha rishona*) can be derived from a *kal vaḥomer* argument: If one blesses when he is satiated, *a fortiori* he should bless when he is hungry. If *Birkat HaMazon* expresses thanks, as implied by Targum Yonatan, we cannot understand the argument, since before eating, when the person is not satisfied, there can be no thanks. According to Nahmanides, the *kal vaḥomer* is appropriate. If recognition of God's mastery is mandated when one is satiated and tempted to brag, "My power and the might of my hand has gotten me this wealth," then such a recognition is certainly in place when the person is still hungry. According to Nahmanides in *Sefer HaMitvzot*, as we have seen, *Birkat HaMazon* and the blessing before eating, which is derived through rabbinical law, are essentially the same. For the blessing before eating, too, is not considered thanksgiving, insofar as there is not yet anything for which to offer thanks.

My grandfather R. Ḥayyim Brisker *zt"l* remarked: "Of course a Jew must have *bittaḥon* (trust) in God, but there is no obligation to give thanks for *bittaḥon*. The obligation of thanks only applies when the trust has been realized." The psalmist (Ps. 13:6) says: "But I have trusted in Your loving-kindness, my heart shall rejoice in Your salvation. I will sing to the Lord, because He has dealt bountifully with me." The psalmist asserts that his faith in God's loving-kindness is such that he rejoices in the anticipation, yet he does not burst into song until he can acknowledge what God has already done for him. This comment illustrates the principle we have articulated regarding Nahmanides' approach in *Sefer HaMitzvot*.

This theme is similar to that of the standard formulas of the blessings recited before eating, such as "Creator of the fruit of the vine," "Creator of the fruit of the tree," "By whose word all things came to be." All these blessings emphasize the act of creation. They are blessings of recognition, not of thanks. He is the Creator of everything and, because He is the Creator, He is the owner; it is all His. The Gemara says: "Whoever derives benefit from this world without reciting a blessing has made unauthorized use of God's property (*ma'al*)" (Berakhot 35a), meaning that the act of recognition allows the human being to exercise the right of enjoyment. This theme pertaining to the blessing before eating, that recognition of God's mastery must precede benefit from this world, is essentially the same as the fundamental idea of *Birkat HaMazon* according to Nahmanides. One might recognize God when hungry and forget Him when full. That is why the Torah warns us against this self-satisfied forgetfulness.

Maimonides (*Hilkhot Berakhot* 1:3–4) writes that "the sages instituted many blessings of praise and thanks and many petitions so as to remember the Creator always and fear Him." Maimonides enumerates three types of blessings: blessings linked to enjoyment, blessings of commandments, and blessings of thanks (*birkhot hahanaya, birkhot hamitzva* and *birkhot hahoda'a*). Praise and thanksgiving, in themselves, have nothing to do with fear. They are connected to fear through the idea of remembering God, and this again highlights that it is the recognition of divine mastery that is the root of all blessings.

Note that Maimonides includes both the blessings before eating and *Birkat HaMazon* in the category of blessings linked to enjoyment. If Maimonides considered *Birkat HaMazon* as fundamentally an act of giving thanks, he could not have included it in the same category, since the defining quality of the blessings before eating is recognition of God, not thanksgiving. We infer from Maimonides' categorization that conceptually *Birkat HaMazon* shares the same primary theme with *birkhot hanehenin*: *Birkat HaMazon*, according to its origin in Torah law, is not defined as thanksgiving but as recognition of His mastery.

Maimonides introduces the laws of *berakhot* with the Talmudic statement that one who derives benefit from this world without reciting a blessing has made unauthorized use of God's property (*Hilkhot Berakhot* 1:2). By quoting this statement before introducing the general concept of *berakha* Maimonides seems to apply this principle not only to enjoyment but to blessings over mitzvot as well. Here too the blessing is recognition that God is the giver of the mitzva: "Who has sanctified us with His commandments" is recognition of His dominion, which extends beyond nature to include moral dominion as well; God is the origin of the moral norm, the religious law. This is also recognition of

His mastery—it is an acceptance of the yoke of the kingdom of heaven. The main element in every blessing is not thanks or praise, but rather it is remembering God: "Beware lest you forget the Lord your God" (Deut. 8:11).

From the standpoint of the psychology of the religious person, this recognition is a primary element in one's religious experience. The basic religious experience is to remember God, to ascribe everything to Him, to attribute the whole cosmic process of creation to Him, and to always be aware that He is the Master, the Lord and the Owner of everything. In order to gives thanks, sentiment is sufficient. Remembering to constantly ascribe everything to Him requires a mental discipline of the highest order. All blessings, then, are subsumed under the obligation "to remember the Creator always and fear Him." The emphasis must be placed on the word "always": always to be conscious of His presence and His mastery over the universe.

The Talmud (Berakhot 35a-b) contrasts two verses: "It is written, 'The earth is the Lord's and the fullness thereof' (Ps. 24:1) but it is also written, 'The heavens are the heavens of the Lord, but the earth He has given to the children of men' (Ps. 115:16)." The Talmud resolves the contradiction: "In the one case it is before a blessing has been said, in the other case after." Whatever belongs to God is *kadosh* (sanctified), and therefore the whole world is sacred. Since one must not enjoy or embezzle anything which belongs to God, how is one entitled to enjoy the world? The answer is that he has to pay a price. If an object is *hekdesh* (consecrated property) and I want this particular object, I have to offer *pidyon*, I have to redeem it. I redeem it by giving the equivalent value to *hekdesh* and I say *zeh taḥat zeh* (this is in place of that). The equivalent value becomes endowed with *kedusha* (holiness) and the object that I am interested in becomes redeemed. I acquire the object in exchange for an equivalent value, which I gave to *hekdesh*. The Jerusalem Talmud (Berakhot 6:1) says, "The entire world is like a [holy] vineyard. How is it redeemed? With a blessing." This means that before one pronounces the blessing he is not supposed to even consider the food on the table to be his; the table is set, and the food on the table was bought with his money. But until he says "Blessed are You, Lord our God, King of the Universe, who brings forth bread from the earth," the food on the table doesn't belong to him; it belongs to God. The blessing of *HaMotzi leḥem min haaretz* is a legal act of acquisition. It is like buying something from someone and paying the price.

Let us note in this context a disagreement between Beit Hillel and Beit Shammai about Kiddush (Mishna Berakhot 8:1). Beit Shammai says that one recites the blessing of Kiddush pertaining to Sabbath or the holiday, and then the blessing over the wine. Beit Hillel says, and this is our practice, that one begins with the wine and concludes with Kiddush. Logically, Beit Shammai is right: Before Kiddush, one is not ready to drink the wine, and *birkat hanehenin* must be pronounced at the moment that one is prepared to drink the wine. The time of drinking will arrive only after the Kiddush.

What then is the reasoning of Beit Hillel? In addition to the explanations of the Gemara (Berakhot 51b), we can note that before saying *borei pri hagafen* the wine belongs to *hekdesh*. It is as if one were to steal a cup of wine and recite Kiddush on it, which would be an act of blasphemy (Sanhedrin 6b). That is why Beit Hillel insists that he must first acquire the wine by reciting *borei pri hagafen*, and only then may he recite the Kiddush.

ZIMMUN – THE INTRODUCTION TO BIRKAT HAMAZON

Zimmun, the introduction to *Birkat HaMazon*, requires a group. Giving thanks does not require a group. For example, Hallel may be said both privately by an individual praying alone and in public. Maimonides, to be sure, holds that on Rosh Ḥodesh, the custom is to say it only in public; however, we maintain that even an individual may say Hallel with a blessing on Rosh Ḥodesh, because there is no reason to limit praise and thanksgiving to communal performance (Maimonides and Rabad to *Hilkhot Ḥanukka* 3:7, and *Hilkhot Berakhot* 11:16).

By contrast, the recognition of God's mastery is what the sages called a *davar shebikedusha*. This halakhic category is defined not by the appearance of the word *kadosh* (holy)—it is rather recognition of His mastery and kingship. Acceptance of the yoke of the kingdom of heaven involves sanctifying God in public: "I will be hallowed among the people of Israel" (Lev. 22:32), so that "all of the world's inhabitants will recognize and know" (*Aleinu*). Recognition of His kingship entails not only the individual's acknowledgement but also proclaiming our commitment to the whole world. Acts of sanctifying God are meant to publicize that no power in the world can break our desire to follow God. This mitzva is not a matter of praise and thanks; it is the mitzva of recognizing His mastery.

A *davar shebikedusha* ordinarily requires a quorum of ten people. In *Birkat HaMazon, zimmun* requires only three. While ten are required to create a community for purposes of prayer, three who eat together suffice to define a meal as communal because, unlike the situation of communal prayer, participants do not enter and exit without the leader knowing; they remain until *Birkat HaMazon* (see *Tosafot* Berakhot 49b *s.v. Amar Rabbi Akiva*).

The institution of *zimmun* is that when three eat, their performance of *Birkat HaMazon* should not be merely a private affair. They are to sanctify God and recognize His mastery and kingdom in public. This is true whether the fulfillment of *zimmun* is only on the level of rabbinic law or whether it is also obligatory according to Torah law. The performance follows the standard paradigm of a *davar shebikedusha,* in which the leader calls out and the others respond to his invitation. The element of dialogue is a very important characteristic of a *davar shebikedusha,* as witnessed by *Kaddish* and *Kedusha,* for example.

There is a disagreement in the Gemara (Berakhot 45a) regarding two people who ate together: "One says: If they want to, they may make a *zimmun*…The other says: Even if they want to, they cannot make a *zimmun.*" The Yerushalmi (Berakhot 7:1) connects this disagreement about *zimmun* to another disagreement concerning two judges who judged a case, instead of the standard court of three. Shmuel, who maintains that when two judges judge a case their ruling stands, also holds that if two want to make a *zimmun,* they may. The opposing opinion, which states that the judgment of two judges does not stand as law, maintains that two people who ate together who want to make a *zimmun* may not do so. Commentaries on the Yerushalmi wonder about the connection of *zimmun* and the question about the status of two judges. The simple explanation is as follows: Shmuel holds that the decision of two judges is valid because judgment requires the possibility of balanced consideration (*shikkul hadaat*), which is impossible when there is only one judge. Three judges represent not only balanced consideration but also the possibility of an authoritative decision. The leader's declaration, "*Nevarekh,* Let us say Grace" during the *zimmun,* followed by the participants' response, "Blessed is He whose food we have eaten," is compared by the Yerushalmi to a judge pronouncing the verdict and the other judges affirming that their balanced consideration is in accord. The implications of this Yerushalmi are amazing. *Zimmun* is not merely a call and response. It is a judicial verdict.

This confirms our explanation that the *zimmun*-leader's invitation, "*Nevarekh*," is analogous to a definitive halakhic decision; that, having eaten, we must offer recognition of His mastery and kingship. And the response, "Blessed is He whose food we have eaten and through whose goodness we live," affirms the authoritative decision.

The obligation of *Birkat HaTorah* (the blessing over the study of Torah) is also derived from *Birkat HaMazon*: "If one blesses for finite life in this world, should one not bless on life in the World-to-Come all the more so?" (Berakhot 48b). Interestingly, *Birkat HaTorah* also has a concept of *zimmun*, an invitation to bless. When the Torah is read in public, the person called up to read says, "*Barekhu et Hashem hamevorakh*, Let us bless the Lord, the blessed One," and the congregation answers, "*Barukh Hashem hamevorakh le'olam va'ed*, Bless the Lord, the blessed One, for all eternity." According to the Yerushalmi (Berakhot 7:1), the requirement of *Birkat HaTorah* mandated by Torah law is limited to the *Birkat HaTorah* said in this public forum. The *Birkat HaTorah* recited by the individual is not derived from the individual's obligation of *Birkat HaMazon*. The Yerushalmi made the inference to *Birkat HaTorah* only from *zimmun*, because *zimmun* expresses a group recognition of His mastery; unlike praise, which is an individual act, recognition of God's mastery has an added dimension which can only be fulfilled in a group.

THE THEMES OF THE INDIVIDUAL BLESSINGS

The Talmud (Berakhot 48b) derives the obligation to recite *Birkat HaZan* from the word "*uveirakhta*, then you shall bless"; the next phrase, "the Lord your God," is the source for *birkat hazimmun*. When some members of the group want to say *Birkat HaMazon*, the others answer the *zimmun* and must wait until they can resume eating. Rama (*Oraḥ Ḥayyim* 200:2) rules in accordance with Rav Sheshet (Berakhot 46a) that the others must wait until the conclusion of the first blessing, *Birkat HaZan*. This implies that *Birkat HaZan* and *zimmun*, although they are two blessings, form one conceptual unit.

The common denominator of these two blessings is recognition of God's mastery. In the *zimmun* we do not thank God; we bless Him. That is, we do not say: "Let us thank God"; we say: "Blessed is He whose food we have eaten and through whose goodness we live." Hence, *Birkat HaZan* elaborates the motif that was introduced in the *zimmun*. For this reason, the Talmud cites the phrase "then you shall bless the Lord your God" to derive these two blessings; it is not simply fracturing the phrase in order to derive two separate *halakhot*. Both blessings express the same motif of recognizing His mastery.

If one recites *Birkat HaMazon* over a cup of wine, Rav Sheshet rules (Berakhot 51a; Maimonides, *Hilkhot Berakhot* 7:15) that the leader begins with undiluted wine, and adds water so that it will be suitable for drinking only when he reaches the second *berakha*. Why is this not done from the outset? The answer is that *Birkat HaMazon* has two parts. The first blessing is recognition of God's mastery. During the act of recognizing God's kingship, it is not necessary for the wine to be drinkable. However, the moment that one arrives at the second blessing, to the *hoda'a* aspect of *Birkat HaMazon*, the wine must be made drinkable.

In the opening blessing of *Birkat HaMazon* the individual himself is not mentioned, nor is the nation of Israel or even mankind as such. That God "gives bread to all flesh" means the animal kingdom as such, without any distinction (see Ps. 136:25 and 145:16). This is not giving thanks; it is recognizing God's kingship and His mastery. God "nourishes the entire world with His goodness, favor, kindness, and mercy. He provides food for all flesh." This includes the zoological kingdom as well. When we are satiated we praise God for feeding everybody, the beasts of the field and the fowl, every reptile and every insect.

God is *zan umefarnes lakol. Zan* refers to *mazon,* that is, food. *Mefarnes* refers the whole chemistry of the body, which is dependent upon taking in food, digesting and assimilating it. *Parnassa* includes not food alone but also clothing and a roof over one's head, shelter. We acknowledge God as being the caretaker and manager of all flesh.

In the second *berakha,* food and sustenance are peripheral. The universal aspect in the first blessing is important; yet if there is no particularistic aspect then all universal philosophy is meaningless. In the second blessing we thank God because He established us as a unique, singular Jewish community and charged us with a certain mission. He gave us commandments, a covenant sealed into our flesh, and a Torah which He taught to us. We thank God not only for the land but for the singularity of the Jewish people. *Eretz Yisrael* must be associated with the uniqueness of the Jewish people and the fact that God has chosen the Jewish people as His own.

We thank God for the "*eretz ḥemda tova ureḥava,* lovely, good and spacious land." These are not just three synonyms, which the Men of the Great Assembly chose at random. The root *ḥ-m-d* appears in the Torah not as a noun but as an adjective. The tree of knowledge is called *neḥmad* (Genesis 2:9 and 3:6). In this connection the word *neḥmad* does not mean simply beautiful or pleasant, for something may be pleasant without exercising a power of attraction. In fact, some forms of beauty may even repel a person or inspire fear in him. *Neḥmad* refers to fascinating beauty that draws like a magnet. One becomes intoxicated by such beauty and succumbs to it; it is irresistible. When the woman saw that the tree of knowledge was to be desired, it means not merely that she chose to pick the fruit from the tree but that she went under the spell of the tree; she acted like a sleepwalker. As if involuntarily she reached for its fruit. This is *ḥemda. Eretz Yisrael* attracts the Jewish people. Judaism is identified with Zionism. That is because Jews have loyalty to *Eretz Yisrael.* If *Eretz Yisrael* were not *eretz ḥemda* we would have forgotten it long ago. Instead, we take absurd, almost suicidal risks for *Eretz Yisrael.*

The word *reḥava* derives from Nehemiah (9:35). The Vilna Gaon (*Kol HaTor,* Ch. 5) says that the idea of spaciousness means that *Eretz Yisrael* will always be capable of accommodating, sustaining and feeding the entire Jewish people. Finally, *Eretz Yisrael* is "*tova,* good." The Talmud (Berakhot 48b) understands this as a reference to Jerusalem, as it says "the goodly mountain and the Levanon" (Deut. 3:25). *Tova* means a land endowed with *kedusha*—and the emblem of *kedusha* in *Eretz Yisrael* is Jerusalem. Without *kedusha* the best of all lands is not *haaretz hatova.* The finest feature of *Eretz Yisrael*—Jerusalem—has its own *berakha, Boneh Yerushalayim.* Thus, the theme of *haaretz hatova* takes up two *berakhot.*

The third blessing, *Boneh Yerushalayim,* does not express thanks; it is a *tefilla,* a supplication. "*Raḥem na,* Have mercy, please, Lord our God…on the great and holy House that bears Your name…Our God, our Father, tend us, nourish us, sustain us, and support us." If giving thanks is required by Torah law, as Targum Yonatan maintains, and this obligation includes thanksgiving not only for the food, but for the land and for Jerusalem as well, as is the position of Rashba and others, then the absence of thanksgiving in this blessing is puzzling.

However, it seems to me that the explanation is simple. Following the discussion about the derivation of the blessings, the Gemara (Berakhot 48b) cites a statement of Rabbi Meir who derives the principle that we are to bless God under all circumstances from the continuation of the verse in Deuteronomy: "For the good land which He has given you" means that we are to bless God no matter what judgment He has given us. R. Akiva (Berakhot 54a) had learned this idea from the *Shema*, which speaks of loving God "with all your resources, *bekhol me'odekha*" (Deut. 6:5). What does R. Meir add to R. Akiva's derivation?

The *Rishonim* (Rashba, Berakhot 48b *s.v. ha*; Rosh, Berakhot 7:22) note that the blessing of *Boneh Yerushalayim* was different in the period in which Jerusalem and the Temple were standing. Then they expressed thanksgiving for Jerusalem and for Zion, and for the royal house of David, and for the great and holy (*hagadol vehakadosh*) House which bears God's name, together with prayer for its continued existence. Thus, when the Temple stood, the third blessing contained thanks for God's beneficence. But now Jerusalem is destroyed, the Temple is destroyed, and the monarchy of David is destroyed. Alas, the blessing cannot now be one of thanks for benefits granted; instead we must offer thanks for adversity. *Birkat HaMazon* requires not only thanks for "the good land which He has given" but also thanks for adversity. This is what R. Meir instituted in *Birkat HaMazon*. On the basis of R. Akiva's derivation alone we would not know that *Birkat HaMazon* requires thanksgiving for adversity, in addition to recognition of God's mastery. According to R. Meir, the verse is to be interpreted as: "then you shall bless the Lord your God for the good land [and for all] which He gave you." The words "which He gave you" do not merely describe "the good land," according to R. Meir's reading of the verse; rather they define the way we experience that which God has given us—the fact that we experience both good and bad at His hand.

Upon hearing of the recent death of a close person, one is required to recite "*Barukh Dayyan HaEmet*, Blessed is the true Judge." Mourning for Jerusalem, by contrast, is analogous to a death that is no longer new to us. How shall we, generations later, offer God thanks for an ancient adversity in the absence of the immediate *Dayyan HaEmet* formula? We justify God's judgment and thank Him for it within the request to rebuild Jerusalem and the Temple. Therefore, the blessing of *Boneh Yerushalayim* was instituted using the language of petition, but expressing the idea of thanksgiving in adversity. When the event mourned is ancient, thanksgiving can only be expressed through request. *Raḥem* is not a blessing of prayer; it is basically a blessing of thanks, albeit in a situation where there is no benefit to be thankful for.

The theme of thanksgiving for adversity, expressed through the blessing of request, is not limited to the restoration of Jerusalem and the Temple. Often, when a Jew gives thanks to God for food, he lacks food. Often he is unhappy, and it appears as if God has not provided sufficiently for him. Often the Jew, unfortunately, requires the "gifts from the hands of flesh and blood" referred to in this blessing. We must thank God not only for life, grace, and kindness granted us; we must thank Him for adversity as well. In *Raḥem,* even as one thanks God for the adversity of the destruction of the Land and of Jerusalem, he can also thank Him for his need and not only for his satiation. Thus in this blessing we say, "Sustain us, support us, relieve us; Lord our God, grant us speedy relief from all of our troubles. And please, Lord our God, do not render us needful of gifts from the hands of flesh and blood … so that we will not feel inner shame, nor be humiliated for all of eternity."

Chapter 5

"Grant Us Understanding to Know Your Ways"

HAVINEINU

Prayer is a total gesture of man that embraces body, mind, and soul—our most hidden desires, feelings, and emotions. Thus an insight into prayer means insight into our destiny as Jews who are part of modern society and at the same time are totally and unqualifiedly committed to another great society. Here, I would like to share some personal thoughts, and I have organized these insights around the *Havineinu* prayer in order to have a frame of reference.

The *Shemoneh Esreh* consists of eighteen or nineteen blessings. However, if one is upset or is in distress, has no patience, or is confused, then instead of reciting the *Shemoneh Esreh in toto,* he may recite the first three *berakhot* and then give a synopsis, a digest, of the thirteen middle *berakhot,* which represent the petitional prayer.

The author of *Havineinu* was Shmuel (Berakhot 29a). Rav and Shmuel were the authors of the finest parts of our liturgy. The Yerushalmi (Rosh HaShana 1:3) called *Malkhuyot, Zikhronot,* and *Shofarot* the "*Tekiata DeRav.*" *Tekiata* has the connotation of prayers, not *tekia* of sounds of a *shofar*. Rav was the author. The Gemara (Berakhot 33b) tells us that "*VaTodi'enu,*" the *havdala* that we recite on *Motzaei Shabbat* which coincides with *Yom Tov,* is a *marganita,* a beautiful gem which was composed by Rav and Shmuel. And Shmuel is the author of *Havineinu*. He was also probably the author of "*Vekhen ten paḥdekha*," the exalted prayer of the High Holy Day liturgy which even the Christian theologian Rudolf Otto called "wonderful" (*The Idea of the Holy*, Appendix I). In practice, we don't ordinarily recite *Havineinu* anymore because Abaye (Berakhot 29a) said that one should try and make an effort to recite the full *Shemoneh Esreh* instead of substituting *Havineinu* for the full text. But it is important to us because it is a synopsis, and the digest reflects the central motifs of the *Shemoneh Esreh*.

The opening line of the prayer—"*Havineinu Hashem lada'at derakhekha*, Grant us understanding to know Your ways"—is the digest and synopsis of "*Ata ḥonen le'adam daat*, You grace man with knowledge." To understand it fully we must know an important historical point.

The first Torah scholar who came to Poland from Germany and who was responsible for the development and the rise of Torah institutions in Poland was Rav Yaakov Pollack. He was the *rebbe* of Rav Shalom Shakhna, who was the *rebbe* of the Rama. He left no *sefarim* or *ḥiddushei Torah*, and we know very little about him. But we know his opinion about the blessing *Ata ḥonen*. On weekdays, we say "*Ata ḥonen le'adam daat*, You grace man with knowledge." On Saturday night we insert additional words pertaining to the end of Shabbat into the middle of this blessing, beginning "*Ata ḥonantanu lemada Toratekha*, You have graced us with intelligence to study Your Torah." Rav Yaakov Pollack maintained that we should begin the blessing immediately with the words "*Ata ḥonantanu lemada Toratekha*"; if one recites the "*Ata ḥonen*" opening, the phrase "*Ata ḥonantanu*" would be redundant (see *Baḥ* and *Taz*, *Oraḥ Ḥayyim* 294). We have not accepted this position.

To be frank, I cannot see how reciting both statements is repetitive. In my opinion, the statements refer to different objectives and different ideas. In fact, it is impossible to start with "*Ata ḥonantanu lemada Toratekha*" before we have stated clearly and unequivocally "*Ata ḥonen le'adam daat umelamed le'enosh bina*." The thesis of "*Ata ḥonen*" refers to a universal situation and stresses the fact that a human being is endowed by his Maker with intelligence and the ability to observe, to judge, to interpret, to infer, to comprehend, to anticipate, and to plan for the future.

Man differs from the beasts or the brute in the field only because of his intellectual endowment. However, what we add on *Motzaei*

Shabbat is that there is a specific private, particularistic endowment superimposed upon the universal dimension in which every human being shares, a *havdala bein Yisrael la'amim* that expresses itself in both a theoretical and practical gesture, in the understanding of the Torah and the norms of mitzvot.

It would be impossible to speak of a chosen charismatic community without setting this community in the proper perspective and within the proper frame of reference. "*Ata ḥonen*" refers to general intelligence, scientific knowledge, practical prudence, theoretical wisdom, and it includes all the aspects and all the facets of the human intellectual gesture. Within this frame of reference, we state that there is a second endowment of Torah which is sensible only within the general perspective of man as an intelligent being. To leave out the universal theme on *Motzaei Shabbat* would affect the whole idea of *havdala*, of discernment and discrimination.

The premise of "*Ata ḥonen*" is that human intelligence is the source of man's greatest pride and bliss, the source of his greatness and uniqueness. Without intelligence, man would be a brute in the field, and progress would be impossible. It is only through intellectual powers that man distinguishes himself as an independent and powerful being who can free himself from his environment and gain control over it. At the same time, human intelligence is also the source of man's misery and suffering. Because of his intellect, man realizes his own tragic destiny and the distressful and sorrowful state of being in which he finds himself. So before we are ready to present God with our petitions, we have to state why we pray. We are thankful to God for our intellectual talents and the powers He has bestowed upon us. However, at the same time, we must come before Him and pray for our salvation, for our survival, for our peace of mind, for our happiness, for our success. Prayer is the result of human perennial distress, of man living constantly in the state of tension, of fearing something, of not being secure. We say "You grace man with knowledge and teach mortals understanding." By so doing, You have raised man to lofty ontological heights; You made him great. However, at the same time, You made man a tragic figure, one involved in a perennial conflict with his environment, with himself, with his future, with death. He is intertwined with something which is beyond and above his control.

Our petition is not that God should take our intelligence away or simply make us less intelligent, even though "*yosif daat yosif makhov*, increasing knowledge increases pain" (Ecc. 1:18), the more understanding, the more profound the tragedy; the more perceptiveness, the greater the conflict. The intelligent person is never satisfied with himself.

Every life is a failure for a simple reason: the last battle is always lost by man, and the last battle is for immortality. (When I say immortality, I mean carnal, bodily immortality, without extinction of the biological life.) There are no successful men. If we survey the story of the heroes of our history, the towering personalities, those responsible for the existence of the *Knesset Yisrael*, God's messengers and apostles, His prophets, we find that each one of them, despite his greatness, lost the final battle. Abraham lost Ishmael his son. Jacob lost Rachel, and he remembered this loss many years later, even when he was on his deathbed: "And I, when I was coming from Padan Aram, Rachel died" (Gen. 48:7). With the death of Rachel, Jacob had to make his exit from the historical arena. After her death, Jacob appears only in the context of the story of another hero, Joseph, and on his deathbed, when he parts from his household and tells them about the future. Moses was engaged in a battle to enter the Land of Israel, and he lost. It was almost a petty request, but it meant everything to Moses, and it was denied to him and he lost. And so forth and so on. This is the destiny of man: to lose and to fail. It only depends how one fails and what one loses. This is exactly what we mean when we say "*ḥoneinu me'itkha deia bina vehaskel*." Despite the fact that knowledge and intelligence are responsible for our failures, for our misery, for our sorrow; because we are intelligent, because we understand; because we can think of the future and reminisce about the past; because there is sometimes a feeling of consuming nostalgia in a person who has wasted so many opportunities and sees in retrospect; despite it all, this is no reason to pray that our intelligence should be at a lower grade. We want as much knowledge as possible, as much intelligence as He sees fit to bestow upon us, as much understanding and discernment and insight into the future as He feels we are qualified for. Yes, our tragic role will be proportionate to the amount of knowledge we possess, but we are ready to accept the burden. That's what a Jew says in "*Ata ḥonen le'adam daat*." We are ready, in spite of everything, to accept the burden and to carry it.

And the same is true not only of general knowledge; the same is true of Torah knowledge. Here too, "*yosif daat yosif makhov,* increasing knowledge increases pain." After all, the Torah is a source of inspiration and joy, but also a source of suffering. The Torah's demands require sacrificial action, movements of retreat and recoil. Sometimes man wants to surge forward, to grab, to stretch out, to reach out. Modern man particularly is aggressive and covetous, and very desirous almost of infinity, of boundlessness, of vastness as far as property, as far as power, as far as intelligence, as far as control of his environment is concerned. And the Torah many times tries to limit man, to fence him in, taming man who is in the quest for acquisition and power. And still we say, "*Ata ḥonantanu lemada Toratekha,* You have graced us with intelligence to study Your Torah." We still hope that God will make it possible for us to study and to acquire as much knowledge as possible. We are ready to accept the burden which knowledge carries, at a universal level, and at a private charismatic level as well. This exactly is "*Ata ḥonantanu*" and "*Ata ḥonen le'adam daat.*"

THE TELEOLOGY OF KNOWLEDGE

In "*Havineinu Hashem ladaat derakhekha*" we find a very succinct and clear definition of the teleology of knowledge. In one sentence, not only was the request for knowledge formulated, but its purpose and teleology was stated. It is "*ladaat derakhekha,* to know Your ways."

No one was as enthusiastic about the human intellect as was Maimonides. In any book of history or philosophy we find that Maimonides belonged to the school of rationalism. But such a viewpoint actually distorts the image of Maimonides, and results from the fact that the last part of his *Guide* has been neglected. It is here that he becomes less philosophical and more inspirational, more of a religious personality. The mind relinquishes its role to the heart. In the last part of the *Guide,* Maimonides begins to confide in us about his own private religious experiences. I wish he would have done it in the *Mishneh Torah.*

True, there is no doubt that there was no greater enthusiast vis-à-vis the lovers of the intellect than Maimonides. He considered the intellectual gesture as the highest and most exalted human achievement. Conceptual thinking and the comprehension of ideas is, according to Maimonides, the noblest and worthiest act in which man can engage.

Modern man is also a great enthusiast of the human intellect. He is an admirer, indeed, a worshipper of the human intellect. What then is the difference between Maimonides and modern man, between the Maimonidean apotheosis of science and the modern apotheosis of science? The difference is in the purpose, not in the method. Modern man considers the intellectual gesture as the prologue to technological achievements. He knows that with scientific progress he will impose his will upon his environment. He is utilitarian. The greatest impetus to scientific research and scientific advancement is given by the search for a more comfortable life, the desire to rule the environment, to rule natural forces. This is a very honorable undertaking and a very honorable desire. But there is no other goal, no other telos as far as the intellectual gesture is concerned.

Maimonides' commitment to the intellectual gesture was not motivated by pragmatism. Indeed, if there was a thinker who was an opponent of pragmatism and utilitarianism it was Maimonides. Knowledge must lead, according to Maimonides, to *daat Hashem,* the knowledge of God, *ve'al pi hadei'a tihyeh ha'ahava*" (*Hilkhot Teshuva* 10:6); the "*ahava,*" the love of God, will be proportionate to the depth of knowledge. Maimonides was not satisfied with this. This was not the highest purpose, the ultimate goal of knowledge. In the last chapter of the *Guide* where he spoke about the teleology of human existence, he quoted Jeremiah: "Thus says the Lord, Let not the wise man glory in his wisdom, neither let the mighty man glory in his might, let not the rich man glory in his riches: but let him that glories glory in this, that he understands and knows Me, that I am the Lord who exercises faithful love, justice, and righteousness in the earth, for in these things I delight, says the Lord" (Jer. 9:22–23). If the knowledge of God is the highest kind of perfection he would have stopped after "but let him that glories glory in this, that he understands and knows Me." The knowledge of God must lead to something else, to doing *ḥesed, mishpat,* and *tzedaka.* We cannot be moral unless we understand the ways and the actions of God. The divine acts which ought to be known and ought to serve as a guide for our actions are *ḥesed, mishpat,* and *tzedaka.* These should serve as the ethical norms by which we should be guided in our lives. We cannot fulfill our obligation "*lalekhet biderakhav,* to walk in His ways," unless we understand His ways. Shmuel captured this idea in four words: "*Havineinu Hashem,*" please give us understanding, reason, discernment, depth, the power to discriminate, for one purpose only "*ladaat derakhekha,* to know Your ways."

The brand of *lomdus* which my family represented is impersonal, formal, and abstract, with strict concepts that appear to have absolutely no relationship to ethics and morality. How can a person sensitize his soul, grow as a moral personality, and develop finesse and refinement of spiritual perceptions through this study? Yet *Gedolei Yisrael* represented spirit, spirituality, refinement, sensitivity, sympathy and compassion. In Rav Ḥayyim's house one could not find a *Ḥovot HaLevavot,* or a *Mesilat Yesharim,* or Reb Yisrael Salanter's *sefarim.* He had a *Shas,* the four volumes of the Rambam, *Shitta Mekubetzet, Ḥiddushei Rabbi Akiva Eiger,* and a *Shulḥan Arukh* with the *Biur HaGra*—that's all. Yet there was no greater *baal ḥesed* than Rav Ḥayyim Brisker *zt"l.* He had ordered that no attributes be inscribed on his tombstone, but my father and my uncle *zt"l* insisted that one attribute be mentioned. Not *gaon,* but *rav ḥesed*: Rav Ḥayyim ben Rav Yosef Dov HaLevi, *rav ḥesed.* In my opinion his *ḥesed* personality towered above his intellectual personality. He understood God's ways.

When we study *Sefer Ḥiddushei Rabbeinu Ḥayyim HaLevi,* the substance is so dry, so formal, so impersonal. So many of the *halakhot* discussed have no relevance, *prima facie,* to our lives. But still, this kind of *lomdus,* this knowledge, this training, extended not only to the mind but to the heart as well. Somehow in Torah knowledge, no matter what the substance, is reflected Shmuel's prayer, "*Havineinu,* grant us understanding to know Your ways."

On the other hand, I knew really great philosophers of international renown. I heard Heidegger lecture and I heard him speak about human destiny, spiritual perceptions, and the consciousness of time. Sometimes it was a genuine spiritual pastime to listen to him. Still, when Hitler rose to power, the first one to join the Nazi ranks was Heidegger, and he was joined by many more philosophers whose job was to teach ethics. Only a few of the German professors stood firm and resisted the Nazi onslaught; most of them succumbed. Indeed, the best ones succumbed; I knew some of them personally. Apparently, *lomdus* enhances the human ethical personality, elevating the human mind and human heart to dizzying heights. Kant's categorical imperative, which is a very strict one, cannot accomplish this job, and makes no contribution to the emergence of the human personality. The word of God ennobles one's character; it redeems a person from frivolity, vulgarity and cruelty. It elevates us and gives meaningfulness to our life. Secular ethics, secular morality, and philosophical morality cannot achieve this purpose. To me it's a puzzle, but it is a fact.

CIRCUMCISE OUR HEARTS

In the second benediction we plead with God for our *teshuva,* our repentance. In summarizing it, Shmuel could have used any sentence from the *berakha* itself—"*hashivenu avinu letoratekha,*" or "*karveinu malkeinu la'avodatekha.*" Instead, he introduced new phrasing, "*umol et levavenu leyiratekha,* circumcise our hearts so that we may fear You," paraphrasing Deuteronomy (30:6), "*Umal Hashem Elokekha et levavekha ve'et levav zarekha le'ahava et Hashem Elokekha bekhol levavekha uvekhol nafshekha lemaan ḥayekha,* And the Lord your God will circumcise your heart, and the heart of your seed, to love the Lord your God with all your heart, and with all your soul, that you may live." What motivated Shmuel?

To understand this, we recall that the Torah uses two different verbs with regards to Pharaoh's stubbornness: "*Veḥizakti et lev Paro,* I will strengthen Pharaoh's heart" (Ex. 14:4), and "*Kaved lev Paro,* Pharaoh's heart is heavy" (Ex. 7:14). I believe these two terms are not strict synonyms but represent two different ideas. "*Ḥazak*" denotes strength, vigor, firmness, or in this context, the ability to resist and not yield. A person who can resist an onslaught of an enemy is considered *ḥazak. Ḥazak* can be applied not only to physical vigor but to spiritual vigor as well. *Kaved* does not represent vigor or firmness. A man can be ponderous on the scales, but very weak morally, mentally, emotionally. *Kaved* is weighty as a stone is weighty. "*Kaved lev Paro*" does not mean a heavy, sad heart as in colloquial English. It means a "heart of stone," as in "I will take away the stony heart out of your flesh, and I will give you a heart of flesh" (Ez. 36:26). In other words, an insensitive heart, a heart which is not responsive to the call of the conscience or to the divine moral challenge, a heart that does not understand the moral law, the heart of a person to whom moral categories are alien, who doesn't feel the need for an apology for his criminal act.

On the other hand, "*Veḥizakti et lev Paro*" means that the heart is sensitive, that Pharaoh was open to change; his heart is a human heart, but it resists the onslaught of a moral challenge. A firm heart is capable of spiritual perceptions and delicate understanding, but it is also "realistic," overly cognizant of social and economic interests which clash with the moral law, too concerned with the impracticability of conforming to the moral issue.

Let us understand Pharaoh. The Jews formed many brigades of slave labor. Slave labor is a gold mine. Pharaoh understood that it was unethical and immoral to oppress innocent people. He was aware of the challenge but unyielding because the decision in favor of morality would have had adverse effects on his self-interest. Such a person lacks the raw quality of the moral personality. He is too much enmeshed in the life of pleasure-loving, pragmatically conscious society which lets comfort, economic welfare, and prosperity take precedence over the word of God.

In Shmuel's prayer we plead with God for a circumcised heart. The contrast to a circumcised heart is "*orlat halev.*" *Orla* means closed, covered (Rashi, Lev. 19:23). *Orlat halev* has the connotation of being closed, surrounded by something unapproachable which prevents the heart from communing with others—a selfish heart remote from everything but its own pleasure. "*Milat halev*" entails purging one's personality, opening it up to the outside, sensitizing the heart, exposing it to spiritual stimuli and actually making it perceptible. We do not ask God to make our decisions, to give us a moral life. That is our decision; God will not intervene. We have free will. We ask only that He enable us to understand the two alternatives, the moral one and the practical one. Many a time the two alternatives are locked in battle and are mutually exclusive. Then the decision is up to us. "*Hashivenu avinu letoratekha, vekarvenu malkeinu la'avodatekha*" means that we should understand the value of Torah, what it means for our children, what it means to us. The decision between the moral alternative and the practical alternative, between the social alternative and the ethical alternative, or the Torah alternative and the so-called non-Jewish alternative, is up to us. We ask that our heart, which is many times insensitive, should be exposed to the moral norm. Circumcising the heart is a bloodless operation in contrast to "*milat basar.*" By exposing the heart to the word of God, we can choose a moral life. When we meet people whose life is far from Torah life, we should not sermonize or exclude them. In fact, preaching will many times do the reverse of what we want. We should expose them to Torah and thereby sensitize and circumcise their hearts.

FORGIVENESS THROUGH SEEKING GOD

Shmuel continues, "*vetislaḥ lanu lihyot geulim,* forgive us so we may be redeemed." Rabbeinu Manoaḥ (to *Mishneh Torah, Hilkhot Tefilla* 2:3) interprets this as "*tehei nimtza lisloaḥ lanu uvazeh nihyeh geulim,* be present to forgive us, and with this we shall be redeemed." We ask not only for forgiveness but for the presence of the Almighty in our midst. Forgiveness is equated with the awareness of the presence of the Almighty.

There is a precept which is perhaps the focal point in our hierarchy of mitzvot. The Torah requires of every Jew to seek God until he finds Him. One must not say, I have been seeking Him and I couldn't find Him, because this would contradict the verse, "But from thence you will seek the Lord your God; and you shall find Him, if you search after Him with all your heart and with all your soul" (Deut. 4:29). If one can't find God, there is one explanation: it was not a total search. If the quest is total, all-embracing, all-inclusive, body, mind and soul, then God is surely found. A conditional search will never discover God.

Not only should one be aware of God, not only should one have faith in Him, not only should one abide by His will. More is required of the Jew. To find Him means to experience His presence, to feel His proximity, to have our faith in God becoming a perception, a sensation, like the sensation of light or sound.

A THREEFOLD TRADITION

Judaism has a threefold *mesora,* a triple tradition. One part is purely intellectual, consisting in what we call "*lomdus*": understanding, analyzing and classifying, discriminating and discerning and inferring. It is the logic of Torah, its epistemology, methodology and the way it has been passed on to us from generation to generation. This is the *mesorat hamaḥshava,* the tradition of Torah thought.

Then there is the practical *mesora,* the tradition of action. It is not enough to know the Torah; we have to observe and implement it. We have a tradition about how one should observe Shabbat, how one should celebrate Rosh HaShana, how one should lay *tefillin,* how one should recite his or her prayers. This is the *mesorat hayad,* the tradition of the hand.

And then there is a third *mesora* which unfortunately was neglected by many Jews, and it is of utmost importance. It is *mesorat halev,* the tradition of the heart, the inner experience of the Jew.

Speaking as someone who has been in contact with American youth for these past decades, I can say that *mesorat hamaḥshava* is the least difficult to transmit. If the teacher is a good pedagogue and knows what he is supposed to teach, he will find the mind of the American student far superior to the mind of the Lithuanian and the Polish student of the last generation. The American's comprehension is by far quicker and his mode of thinking more precise. Of course, this is due to secular training since early youth. Our problem here is one of numbers, of attracting more students to our *yeshivot.*

Regarding the *mesora* of *mitzvot,* we are certainly a small minority, very far from dominating the American scene. But we are a strong minority, a minority with the power of resistance. We resist pressures, we resist temptations, we resist ridicule, we resist enmity and opposition. Moses called the Jews "*keshei oref,* stiff necked." He said it in a negative sense, but we experience it now in the positive sense.

The tradition most difficult to transmit is that of experiencing God, of meeting Him, of searching for Him, of questing for Him, of feeling His presence, of embracing Him, of feeling as if we were embraced by Him. The highest religious experience is to feel as if one were in the embrace of God, in the embrace of infinity. Without this *mesora,* the other two cannot be sustained for too long. Modern man is intellectually oriented. But at the same time he quests for something meaningful, for something great, for an ideal, for grandeur of living. He wants no less than to cross the borderline of finitude. Somehow there is in him a drive for infinity that can be comprehended and experienced only with the heart.

For thousands of years, we were very reluctant to discuss in public our intimate relationship with the Creator, our great romance with the Master of the Universe. True, *Shir HaShirim* is the story of the great reciprocal love affair between finitude and infinity, between man and God, between little man and the Almighty, between mortal man and the Eternal God. But it is couched in the symbolism of earthly love to portray the heavenly love of God and *Knesset Yisrael.*

When we read the writings of Christian mystics, we hear of their confessions, and their meetings with God. However, a Jewish mystic doesn't write in personal terms; he doesn't confide in us his stories about his rendezvous with God. The Kabbalistic mystics were great, rich, colorful personalities who were intoxicated with love for God. If any of them had only confided in us and told us what he had experienced, our minds would have been richer. A Jew confesses from time to time, and not only on Yom Kippur, but confession is a private affair between him and *Borei Olam*. Others cannot overhear this confession. This is, in my opinion, typical of the modesty and shyness of a Jew. Our noblest and most exalted feelings should remain like the Ark of the Covenant, concealed behind the curtain. "*Vehivdila haparokhet lakhem bein hakodesh uvein kodesh hakodashim,* and the veil shall divide unto you between the holy place and the most holy" (Ex. 26:33). In the human personality, the sanctuary is one's emotional and not logical life. The Ark is hidden, concealed behind the curtain, protected from the eye of the cynic, the glance of the skeptic, and the ridicule of the so-called practical, realistic man. We have no means for verbalization, externalization, and objectification of our inner feelings. We can't pronounce them or spell them out. Our *Kodesh Kodashim* is enveloped in a cloud of holiness and privacy.

The same method is applied to our relationship with the Creator. We have never written about our great romance, what our love for and dedication to God means to us. This great experience of *mesorat halev* was handed down from generation to generation, through silent osmosis. However I don't believe that we can afford to be as reluctant, as modest and as shy at this time as we have been generations before.

I observed my father *davening* on Rosh HaShana, and it is an experience that I will never forget. I once as a child saw my grandfather Rav Ḥayyim saying "*VehaKohanim veha'am ha'omdim ba'azara*" on Yom Kippur. If on Yom Kippur I feel that I lack in dedication, in pietistic devotion or enthusiasm and I want to inspire myself, no philosophical ideas help me at such a time. I just visualize Rav Ḥayyim saying "*VehaKohanim veha'am.*" The memory is pale and vague but what I see is a man completely consumed by nostalgia and yearning. This *mesora* has been passed on from generation to generation through a tune, simply through observance of the conduct of the parent and so forth and so on. Now, if I want to transmit my experience to my students, I will have to transmit my soul, my own heart—and no transplant will help as far as this is concerned. I must somehow merge with them in one existential awareness, merge our souls and personalities. It is very difficult, but this is exactly what we must do. We should not only learn Torah but actually experience Talmud Torah as a great drama, as a great redeeming act which purges the personality. This is exactly what is necessary for *geula*, redemption, to follow.

REDEEMER OF ISRAEL

When we speak about the blessing of "*Goel Yisrael*, Redeemer of Israel," we usually relate it to the redemption of the Jewish community as a whole, to the Messianic era. However, just as the preceding blessings all relate to the individual's needs, even though we use the plural form, so too does the prayer for redemption. It does not allude to the Jewish community which is oppressed or is in exile and which needs Messianic redemption. Rather, it refers to the individual who needs redemption; he is always in trouble and wants God to redeem him. But one can be redeemed only if he has the receptivity and the sensitivity for the presence of God. If one does not experience the actual presence of God near him, if he doesn't feel that he is in the embrace of God, then there is no redemption. Perhaps I am now breaking the rule which I formulated before about Jewish shyness by revealing something personal, but sometimes it is very hard to be silent when the heart is full and the mind carries a heavy burden. Let me tell you, if there is someone who is in need of *geula*, I am the individual. When my wife died, I went through what the mystics call a dark night of the soul, a night of desolation and loneliness and complete desertion, a night of *hester panim*, of God's hiddenness. My life had been destroyed and shattered, and it completely lost its meaning; it became an absurd nonsensical affair. What saved me? Two things: Torah and *tefilla*.

When I sit down and I begin to say a *shiur*, somehow I move in a beautiful world which is so peaceful, so serene and so neatly arranged, as if I hadn't lost anything. The very moment I close the Gemara, I awaken to reality, to an ugly, lonely, indifferent and cruel world. Torah is an island of serenity, a place of peace and equilibrium of sanity. I achieved this only because I try very hard not only to study with my mind, but to experience the Torah with my heart. Many times when I say a *shiur,* when I succeed in disentangling a *sugya* and defining and formulating concepts with which I am satisfied, I would like to take the Gemara in my embrace, hug it and kiss it. But the kiss actually is not addressed to the Gemara; the Gemara is just paper and print. The kiss is addressed to *Borei Olam,* the Creator. The same is true of *tefilla.* When praying, I feel that I am not alone, that there is someone with me. *Tefilla* somehow purges my mind; it has a redemptive quality for me. This is applicable to everyone, but it cannot be attained merely by listening to a lecture or to a *shiur.* It can be attained only if a person commits himself to that goal and works on it.

WHO GATHERS THE DISPERSED OF ISRAEL

When Shmuel summarized the *berakha* of *Teka beshofar,* the prayer for the ingathering of exiles, he avoided the term *nidḥei Yisrael* mentioned in the closing sentence of the blessing in the *Shemoneh Esreh, "Barukh ata Hashem mekabetz nidḥei amo Yisrael."* Instead he said *"unefutzoteinu me'arba tekabetz,"* using the word *nefutzot.* Apparently Shmuel has equated *nefutzot* with *galuyot* which is used in the body of the *berakha* of *Teka beshofar, "vesa nes lekabetz galuyoteinu." Havineinu* is a prayer and it has to reflect not the praise of the *berakha*'s closing, but the petition, which is simply *"vesa nes lekabetz galuyoteinu."*

The basic difference between *nefutzot* and *nidaḥim* is as follows: *Nefutzot* means dispersal and has the connotation of division. It means the historical reality of the Diaspora, the fact that the Jewish people are dispersed all over the earth, and has the same connotation as *galuyot. "Nefutzot Yisrael"* means communities which live abroad in foreign lands, and it has no connotation of disorganization, anarchy, or the absence of communal life or discipline. Nor does it allude to any spiritual breakdown or disintegration. Jewish communities may live in various parts of the world, but each community can be highly organized. We know that the communities in Babylonia or Poland actually were little states with almost unlimited powers in internal matters. Surely we cannot say that spiritual life in Babylonia was on the decline during the period of Rav and Shmuel, Rava and Abaye. It flourished, it blossomed, and still Babylonia was called *nefutzot.*

The term *nidaḥim,* in contrast to *nefutzot,* is related not to large segments of population, to entire communities or considerable aggregates of Jews, but to a few individuals limited in number. "*Im yihyeh nidaḥakha biketzei hashamayim misham yekabetzkha*" (Deut. 30:4) means if a single Jew will be isolated at the outskirts of the world, God will bring him back. A *nidaḥ* is isolated from the *klal* and in danger of complete alienation. The *nidaḥ* lacks communication with the centers of Judaism and lives on the very periphery, surrounded by an alien environment, missing the facilities indispensable for the perpetuation of the Jewish heritage. The "*ir hanidaḥat*" is geographically isolated and also spiritually exposed, rejected, cast away.

Throughout our two millennia of exile, the phenomenon of *nefutzot Yisrael* was a big problem—Jews were divided and dispersed all over the world—but the problem of *nidḥei Yisrael* hardly existed. Very seldom did a Jew live in a place which was remote from centers of Torah and *Yahadut.* They always tried to join the *klal.*

Of course, God refuses to give up on any single Jew. Not one soul should be eliminated. "*Im yihyeh nidaḥakha biketzei hashamayim misham yekabetzkha Hashem Elokekha umisham yikaḥekha,* If your dispersed be in the uttermost parts of heaven, from there will the Lord your God gather you, and from there will He fetch you" (Deut. 30:4). This is the promise made by God. Every Jew will be saved; every Jew will be returned to the fold; not a single Jew will be lost. But *nefutzoteinu me'arba tekabetz* refers to building up *Eretz Yisrael* as the home of the Jewish people, not just the home of individual Jews. If *Klal Yisrael* could actually be ingathered from all parts of the world in *Eretz Yisrael,* we believe there would be a public "*hashra'at hashekhina,*" a public revelation of divine glory. The restoration of *Eretz Yisrael,* and the ingathering of the exiles for whose arrival and return to *Eretz Yisrael* we petition God day in day out, would not depend upon a few *nidaḥim.*

Teka beshofar is related to the community and is not a *berakha* for individuals. As such, the emphasis should not be on the *nidaḥim.* True, when we conclude with words of praise to God, we say that He is not only interested in *nefutzot Yisrael,* in the great multitudes of Jews, but He is also concerned for every lonely soul—"*mekabetz afilu nidḥei Yisrael.*" In *Havineinu,* however, Shmuel emphasized the focal point of the *berakha.*

THE RIGHTEOUS

"*Veyismeḥu tzaddikim bevinyan irekha uvetikkun heikhalekha uvetzemiḥat keren le'David avdekha uva'arikhat ner le'ven Yishai meshiḥekha,* May the righteous rejoice in the rebuilding of Your city, the restoration of Your Temple, the flowering of Your servant David's glory, and the radiant light of the son of Jesse, Your anointed." This combines in one sentence the three *berakhot* of *Al HaTzaddikim, Binyan Yerushalayim* and *Tzemaḥ David*. In one sentence, Shmuel took the standard *berakha* for the *tzaddikim,* the righteous, and elevated it from the daily monotony of work and gray everyday needs of human beings to dizzying heights.

We don't have to pray for the health and contentment of the scholar, of the righteous and the elders of our people. True, we hope that they lead a quiet, prosperous life, but for that the Aramaic prayer *Yekum Purkan* recited on Shabbat would have been enough. There is no need to repeat such a prayer three times a day. The *berakha* of the *Shemoneh Esreh* aims at a higher goal, a much nobler objective. Not one of physical health or welfare or prosperity or quietude or peace of mind, important objectives as they might be. The author of *Havineinu* sublimated this petition and turned it into an exalted prayer for the community, not one for individual well-being and happiness. For the *tzaddik* is not interested in his own welfare. What the righteous and elders of the people dream of is the triumph of the Master of the Universe over wickedness, of divine goodness defeating satanic malice and hatefulness, of the fulfillment of our prophetic aspirations for the restoration of Jerusalem, the *Beit HaMikdash,* the Messianic kingdom and the exclusive rule of God over all.

What prompted Shmuel to combine these blessings was one letter, the *vav haḥibbur,* the conjunction. Shmuel combined the blessings of "Restore our judges" and "For the slanderers let there be no hope" because they are connected by a *vav*—it is a combination of judgment and punishment. So too the *vav* of *VeLiYerushalayim* indicates that the hopes of the righteous will be fulfilled when God returns to Jerusalem and resides in the *Beit HaMikdash*.

SHOME'A TEFILLA, WHO ANSWERS OUR PRAYER

The last sentence of *Havineinu* is "*Terem nikra ata ta'aneh,* Before we call, You will answer." This corresponds to the *Aneinu* prayer, not to *Shema koleinu* of the *Amida*. In the regular *berakha* of *Shema koleinu,* we ask God to hearken to our prayer and to accept our supplications when we plead with Him and beg Him for mercy. In *Havineinu* and *Aneinu,* however, we express the hope that God will anticipate our prayer and offer His salvation even before we have a chance to offer our petition to Him.

Prayer is indispensable if man wants redemption, if he wants to be helped, if he wants to be sustained by God and supported by Him. God accepts prayer, but without prayer no assistance will be forced on him from God. This is the theme of *Shema koleinu*. Prayer is the greatest privilege that God has granted man. It is a pure act of grace, of *ḥesed*. Logically, man has no right to approach God. A little man living on a little planet in a little solar system, in a galaxy which is insignificant to the cosmos knocks on the door of the Eternal, of the *Melekh malkhei hamelakhim* whose word guides billions of stars and determines the course of the flying nebulae on the outskirts of the universe. It is an act of *ḥesed* that God granted man that he is capable of and entitled to knock on His door whenever he wants. He allows him to pray not only for necessaries, for the indispensable, for the inevitable, for the sustenance of his life; he has the right to pray even for frivolities, for luxuries, for things which are unnecessary. Whether God will accept his prayer or not is a different story. Indeed, it would be calamitous if God had accepted all our prayers! Prayer must be well formulated. The diction should be clear, the presentation should be immaculate, one should be standing upright. Prayer is a presentation before the King of Kings! In order to pray, one must have not only a contrite heart, but a very disciplined mind as well. Prayer is not only an emotional act but an intellectual one as well.

However, at times, one is incapable of prayer because he is not in control of his mind, and even his heart is in rebellion. Either he himself is not aware of his own plight and misery, or his mind has crumbled under the strain of a combat for which Providence did not qualify him. No prayer can rise out of the dismay of a tortured existence which was shattered into pieces. Such an existence is an existence of *tzara,* of personal catastrophe. Crisis and tragedy rob man of his cherished talents of communing with God. The *onen,* the individual who suffers the death of a close relative, is free from the duty of prayer. In fact, many say he is *enjoined* from praying, for a mind which conjures up images of horror and despair is not fit to pray. A haunted individual can only cry, sulk and moan out of his unbearable pain, but he cannot pray. These vocal manifestations of pain may consist of a few words or disjointed sentences—and many a time a speechless, wordless, and unintelligible shriek and cry in the night. In such situations, in the dark night of loneliness, there is no *tefilla*, there is *ze'aka*. Interestingly, when Maimonides (*Hilkhot Taaniyot* 1:1) speaks about prayer on a fast day, he doesn't call it *tefilla*, but rather *ze'aka*. Of course, on a *taanit* prayer was proclaimed because of a sudden crisis. *Ze'aka* is a shriek when tragedy strikes and destroys human hopes and expectations and one is overpowered by breathtaking grief, fear, and desolation. He loses the ability to speak, to commune, to express himself. The impact of the distress is too destructive to allow man to engage in regular prayer. There is only one outlet for all his spiritual distress: *ze'aka*. So too is the sound of the *shofar* that is interwoven into our Rosh HaShana prayers. It is a *ze'aka*, a speechless *tefilla*, a wordless prayer said when we cast off our pretenses and claims to wisdom, to intelligence, to telling God what we need, to dictate to the Almighty a plan of action. We come before Him naked, in all our agony and misery. And God accepts our cry. He hears not only the prayer of intelligent man, proud man, unique man, creative man; he also accepts the *tefilla* of downtrodden man, lonely man, the man who has lost the ability of speech, the capability of expressing himself. He answers our prayers *terem nikra*, even before they have been formulated. Shmuel introduced this into *Havineinu* because *Havineinu* is recited when man is troubled, when he finds himself in distress, when he has no peace of mind to express himself, to elaborate his requests, his needs. Shmuel tried to formulate a synopsis of the *Shemoneh Esreh*. But when he comes to the end, he says, Master of the Universe, all I can do is cry. I am in despair and cannot express my needs anymore.

THE OBLIGATION TO PRAY

The Torah tells us: "When war shall come upon you in your land against an aggressor who attacks you, you shall sound short blasts on the *ḥatzotzerot*, the trumpets... On your days of joy, holidays, and *rashei ḥodashim*, you shall sound the *ḥatzotzerot* over your burnt offerings" (Num. 10:9–10). Sometimes, the *ḥatzotzerot* will announce joy and happiness and victory, but more often they will announce distress and disaster. It is interesting to see how Maimonides treats these verses. In the list of mitzvot for *Hilkhot Taaniyot,* he says that the section contains one mitzva, "*vehi litzok,* to cry out before God in times of disaster" (Maimonides, *Hilkhot Taaniyot, hakdama*). Then, in the text (*Hilkhot Taaniyot* 1:1), he repeats the mitzva, but replaces *litzok* with *lizok,* changing the *tzadi* into a *zayin*. Such a slight variation, sometimes unnoticeable, always intrigued me, and still does.

However, there is another difficulty with this text which must first be resolved. Maimonides considers the first verse regarding *ḥatzotzerot* to be a separate, autonomous mitzva entity, but does not include the second. To understand this, let us consider his definition of the *ḥatzotzerot* which were blown by the priests in the *Beit HaMikdash* on "your days of joy, holidays, and *rashei ḥodashim.*" "On all of the holidays and on *rashei ḥodashim,* the priests would blow the *ḥatzotzerot* at the time of the sacrifice and the Levites would recite *shira*" (Maimonides, *Hilkhot Kelei HaMikdash* 3:5).

In other words, *tekiat ḥatzotzerot,* according to Maimonides, was not a separate mitzva, but rather is one of the aspects of *shira*. The Torah required that the priests blow the *ḥatzotzerot,* while the *Levi'im* sang. Playing the *ḥatzotzerot* is another kind of *shira* but it is not a separate mitzva. *Mitzvat shira* was divided, so to say, between the *Kohanim* and *Levi'im*. During *nisukh hayayin,* the wine libation, the *Levi'im* sang and simultaneously the *Kohanim* blew the *ḥatzotzerot*. Since Maimonides requires simultaneity for the *ḥatzotzerot* and the recital of *shira* by the *Levi'im,* the conclusion is plain and obvious: *tekiat ḥatzotzerot* was not counted as a separate autonomous entity, because it is not a separate mitzva, but a component of the general mitzva of *shira*. However, when there is a threat of war or when the community is confronted with disaster, the commandment to blow *ḥatzotzerot* is a distinct mitzva and is counted as such.

We noted earlier that Maimonides uses the term *litzok* with regard to *minyan hamitzvot,* while in the halakhot themselves, he changed the *tzadi* to a *zayin* and substituted *lizok* for *litzok*. What is the distinction between *lizok* and *litzok*?

Overall, in Tanakh *litzok* means to complain, and whether it is in a whisper or a loud voice is secondary. For example, God will respond if the orphan or widow will "*yitzak* to Me" (Ex. 22:26). It doesn't mean that the orphan or widow will yell or raise his or her voice; but rather the oppressed person will complain to God who sits in judgment over people. *Yitzak* means "he will protest." "A certain woman, the wife of one of the sons of the prophets, *tza'aka* to Elisha" (II Kings 4:1). She did not yell at Elisha but complained to him.

"*Lizok*" has an additional connotation, namely, that of mobilizing, assembling, congregating. There are many passages in the Bible where the term is meant in the sense of prayer as well as a summons addressed to others to do likewise and to join in prayer. The best example is "*va-yizak ze'aka gedola umara,* he cried with alarm, with a bitter cry" (Esther 4:1). Mordecai didn't do that because he became hysterical; rather he summoned the community to join in to prayer. Another example: "*Va-yizak [Shmuel] el Hashem kol halayla,* he cried out to God all the night" (I Sam. 15:11). Samuel summoned the people to join him in prayer for Saul. Had the people done so, the wrath of the Holy One would have been mitigated, and Saul wouldn't have lost his kingdom.

(Incidentally, we note parenthetically a similar story regarding Moses. When he was told that he would not enter *Eretz Yisrael,* Moses pleaded for forgiveness. Had the people joined him in prayer, the Holy One would have been forced to respond. But they did not join. Thus we read in *Parashat Va'etḥanan* that with tears in his eyes Moses tells them, "*Va'etḥanan,*" I prayed alone (Deut. 3:23). It was not *vanitḥanen,* we prayed. I was a lonely, solitary prayerful person; I prayed, no one else joined in with me. But God became angry and did not listen to me "*lemaankhem,* because of you." Moses did not enter *Eretz Yisrael* because instead of addressing the rock, he hit it. It was not the fault of *Am Yisrael* that Moses made a mistake. But had the people possessed the sensitivity and love for Moses similar to that love that Moses felt for them, they would have torn the decree into shreds. It was their fault. "*Lema'ankhem.*")

The Torah had stated that in a time of distress "*vaharei'otem baḥatzotzerot.*" Maimonides added a word, "*lizok uleharia beḥatzotzerot.*" The purpose of *ḥatzotzerot* is "to summon the people" (Num. 10:2). Maimonides united *ze'aka* with *ḥatzotzerot* because they form one mitzva—to pray, but not only for myself in isolation. The mitzva is to draw as many people as possible into prayer, to create a prayerful community of individuals who display love for those who suffer. The *kiyyum hamitzva,* the fulfillment of the *ḥatzotzerot,* is not just prayer, but prayer which unites, prayer which takes individuals with love for each other and turns them into one community, into a mystical, metaphysical entity. *Ze'aka* is based upon an act of sympathy and compassion. The individual is supposed to arouse the community, and protect it from distress. Love for the people is indispensable for *ze'aka*. Maimonides says,

> But if [the people] fail to call out [to God] and to sound [the *ḥatzotzerot*], and instead say "what has happened to us is merely a natural phenomenon and this difficulty is merely a chance occurrence," this is a cruel conception of things (*Hilkhot Taaniyot* 1:3).

It is cruel because *ze'aka* expresses the love of the individual for the community, and the dedication of the community to the individual.

A solitary person prays in isolation, silently, in complete privacy. *Tefilla* is the monologue of the individual who stands before the Almighty, who is the One God—an individual in the absolute sense of the word. *Ze'aka,* on the other hand, means that I exist only within the community, within the many. My existence is justified because I feel love for the community. I get involved with the *tzibbur* and I summon the *tzibbur* to pray with me—not *lehitpallel* before God, but *lizok* before Him.

There are structured, architectural designs to *tefilla*. It consists of *berakhot,* of benedictions. It starts with *Avot,* with the dawn of our history, and climbs up to the apex, when in *Sim Shalom* it speaks of eschatological fulfillment. It starts with Abraham, the father to whom the Holy One made the great promise, and concludes with *Sim Shalom,* the period when all promises will be fulfilled. The benedictions are divided into private and communal requests. The omission of a *berakha* results in the duty to repeat the prayer. In a word, *tefilla* has structural integrity. This is the *mitzva bekhol yom,* every day; this has nothing to do with *tzara*. However, when man is in distress, he cannot create anything structurally beautiful. He can just cry and pronounce a few words. *Tze'aka* has no structure at all. It is an outcry of a person who is hopelessly entangled. Unlike *tefilla, tze'aka* is a special mitzva which is limited to *sha'at tzara*.

Why did the Torah combine the two verses pertaining to *ḥatzotzerot*? One speaks of a day of crisis and the mitzva of *terua*; the other of a day of rejoicing and the mitzva of *tekia*. The *tekia baḥatzotzerot* is an expression of joy and triumph and gratitude and happiness, and the *terua baḥatzotzerot* expresses desolation, *ḥurban,* and fear of total destruction. Prima facie, they are mutually exclusive. Yet I believe that a common element is to be found in one thing, which is that man is finite and his capabilities are limited. Man cannot resolve the total mystery of the universe, nor can he achieve perfection or achieve anything in totality. The Holy One put at the disposal of man only small segments of creation. Man was endowed with speech; however, the latter too was not given to him in totality. He is capable of communicating and communing with others, but the communication is again limited and is restricted to peripheral problems.

Man wants to express himself, but he has no words for it. So what does man do if he lacks words? He sings. The melody expresses more than the non-melodious words of celebration or the non-melodious cries of battle. However, song does not satisfy him either. So he grabs the instrument and he plays! Man is a limited being, and the symbol of man's limitedness, finitude, and frustration as far as communication is concerned is the *ḥatzotzerot,* the musical instruments which man built and constructed. If his tongue cannot do it, he expects his nimble fingers to make up for his lack of words. This is what combines our two verses of the *ḥatzotzerot.*

The Creator endowed us with an intellect that enables us to appreciate our distress and He answers our prayers even when in our distress we can only cry out without formulating our prayers. Indeed, *"Terem nikra ata ta'aneh,* Before we call You will answer."

Chapter 6

Praying for the Defeat of Evil

PSALMS 1–2: VANQUISHING EVIL

The Talmud (Berakhot 9b) says that the verse "May the words of my mouth be acceptable..." (Ps. 19:15) would be appropriate either before or after the Amida. Why, then, was it set at the end?

> R. Judah the son of R. Simeon b. Pazzi said, "Since David said it only after eighteen psalms, the Rabbis too enacted that it should be said after eighteen blessings" (Berakhot 9b).

The Talmud explains that the first two chapters of Psalms constitute one psalm.

The Talmud continues:

> For R. Judah the son of R. Simeon b. Pazzi said, "David composed one hundred and three psalms, and he did not say '*Halleluya*' until he saw the downfall of the wicked, as it says, 'Let sinners cease from the earth, and let the wicked be no more. Let my soul bless the Lord, *Halleluya*'" (Ps. 104:35).

The Talmud again explains that chapter 104 is in truth only the one hundred and third Psalm because the first two chapters are one unit.

In fact, I have never come across a Psalter in which the two chapters appear together. Our Bibles separate them, and they deal with two distinct subjects. Why, then, does the Talmud fuse them into one? First comes a textual reason:

> R. Samuel b. Naḥmani said in the name of R. Yoḥanan, "Every chapter that was particularly dear to David he commenced with *Ashrei* [fortunate] and concluded with *Ashrei*. He began [chapter 1] with *Ashrei* as it is written (Ps. 1:1), '*Ashrei Ha'Ish,* fortunate is the man,' and he concluded it with *Ashrei,* as it is written (Ps. 2:12), '*Ashrei kol ḥosei bo,* fortunate are all who take refuge in Him'" (Berakhot 9b-10a).

What is the logic that prompted the Rabbis to join the two chapters? Textual evidence is not enough; there should be one idea, a common denominator that underlies the textual unity. Chapter 2 deals with rebellion against God. It describes an era when the world (or part of the world) is determined to dethrone the Almighty: "The princes conspire against God and against His anointed" (verse 2). But, as the Psalm continues: "He who is enthroned in heaven laughs; the Lord scoffs at them" (verse 4). Who is "His anointed"? Anointed means elected, and refers to *Knesset Yisrael,* the community God has chosen. The powers ready to break the heavenly yoke and rebel against the Almighty are defined as the enemies of the Jewish people, of *Knesset Yisrael.* Why? Because we are the people who gave the world the Bible and we have proclaimed God's kingdom on earth as an ideal. We are the people who said that man cannot rule himself because the beast in man is never far from the surface. Of course we believe that wickedness will be defeated: "So now, O kings, be prudent; accept discipline, you rulers of the earth!" (verse 10)—we appeal to humanity not to cast off the moral, divine yoke. According to *Ḥazal,* this Psalm depicts the eschatological destruction of wickedness, the defeat of evil and the triumph of justice. It is typical that the Rabbis asserted the involvement of Israel in the triumph of justice. The triumph of evil would mean the end of the people Israel; the defeat of evil is the redemption of Israel. This is how *Ḥazal* read Psalm 2.

What of the first chapter with its vision of the person who is "like a tree deeply rooted alongside brooks of water" (verse 3) and its conclusion that "the wicked shall not be vindicated in judgment" (verse 5)? *Ḥazal* interpreted that verse too in eschatological terms. There will be a Day of Judgment, a *Yom HaDin,* when God renders His ultimate judgment on the history of humanity. Though at present the righteous may be persecuted or suffer or may not be recognized, they will eventually be like a tree deeply rooted upon brooks of water.

The two chapters refer to two levels in which the destruction of evil and the triumph of righteousness occur. One is the public, political or the communal level; the other is the individual level. Chapter 2 speaks of universal wickedness—the cruelty and insensitivity at the political level that immoral power engenders. There may be a society of individuals, each of them kind, good, hospitable and sensitive in his private life, willing to extend a helping hand and so forth, who as a state, as a group, as a community, are collectively wicked, cruel and insensitive. The individual in isolation doesn't commit any crimes, but the society, the state, the empire, is endlessly guilty. Think of the collective cruelty of slavery in the United States, the home of a remarkably generous people. Think of the ruthless cruelty of children when a group turns on a fellow pupil in the classroom. Then again, there are people who are generous as a collective but composed of individuals who are insensitive.

A state commits crimes that an individual will not. I don't know exactly what happened at My Lai, but clearly something did happen. American soldiers are usually kindhearted and compassionate; we know how they acted when they came upon the extermination camps in Germany. Yet American soldiers could assemble women and children and shoot them down. This is collective cruelty. In a war, the individual loses his ego, his uniqueness. He is a member of a group and has no will of his own, no conscience of his own. His individuality disappears; he is dissolved completely. He becomes integrated into the collective, and the collective—exhausted, angry, and frustrated—is sometimes ruthless and cruel. There are many reasons for it. When the individual has completely lost his individuality, his uniqueness, and his spiritual personality, he is like a member of a class, a member of the species, and the will of the collective dominates him.

Until recently the Jewish people acted like individuals. They had no collective instruments with which to implement decisions; they had no statehood. As individuals, Jews were kind and compassionate, incapable of murder or bloodshed. The crime rate was low in Jewish communities; hospitality was on the highest level. I pray that as a state we act the same way, that we not defile our name in the framework of the state, the group, the collective. I wish that the pages of our history as a state would be as clean as the annals of the Jewish people for the past nineteen hundred years, when we were a stateless nation.

The first chapter of Psalms deals with kindness and righteousness versus wickedness, cruelty, and insensitivity on the individual level; the second chapter deals with the same problems on the political level. That is why *Ḥazal* say that they form one chapter. No matter how many defeats that kindness, righteousness, and morality suffer, no matter how many times they are defeated on the field of battle and ruthlessness emerges victorious, the final battle will be won by the righteous over the wicked.

HE SAW THE DOWNFALL OF THE WICKED

The Talmud said that David did not say "*Halleluya*" until he witnessed the defeat of the wicked at the end of Psalm 104. Indeed this is the first time that David uses the phrase "*Halleluya*" but it is not the first time that the Book of Psalms mentions the absolute defeat of the wicked. What is new in the last verse of Psalm 104?

If we read the Talmudic discussion carefully, we notice that it does not refer to the downfall of the wicked, but rather to David *witnessing* the downfall of the wicked. When the Egyptians were drowned in the Red Sea, "The angels wanted to sing a hymn to God. God said to them, 'My creatures are drowning in the sea, and you will sing a hymn to Me?'" (Sanhedrin 39b). God does not rejoice in the death of the wicked. The Egyptians too are human beings, and every human being is unique and endowed with a divine spark.

Halleluya is the highest form of praise. It is the song of sublime ecstasy. Only when David witnessed "sinners will cease from the earth" was he able to say, "Let my soul praise You, *Halleluya*!"

This Judaic concept is further illustrated in the story the Gemara proceeds to tell. There were gangsters who lived in the neighborhood of Rabbi Meir and caused him a lot of trouble. Rabbi Meir used to pray to God for their death, that God do away with them. His wife Beruriah told him: Does *yittamu ḥattaim* mean that wicked people must be destroyed? It does not! It says *ḥataim* (sins). Beruriah read *ḥataim* as a plural of *ḥet* (sin) without a *dagesh forte,* not as sinners (with the *dagesh*). The sin must be erased, not the sinner. When sin disappears, then there will no longer be wicked people. Pray that they rediscover their own humanity, and then you will not have to encounter the wicked. So Rabbi Meir prayed for them, and those criminals, those sinners, became ethical personalities.

The Torah ascribes the first sin to the seduction of the serpent, who convinced Eve that sin is sweet and the fruits of sin are delicious. The Torah does not say that Eve acted on her own, because we understand sin as an extraneous factor to which the human being succumbs. "The inclination of man's heart is evil from his youth" (Gen. 8:21) means that he lacks the power of resistance. It is sometimes difficult to defy the environment, but that does not mean that sin is inborn. If sin as such were purged from the world, reality would be repaired. Wickedness would disappear; the social and economic order, cultural concepts, and external circumstances would no longer cause man to sin. Isaiah (1:18) portrays repentance as the cleansing of a stained garment to which detergent has been applied. Water is the symbol of forgiveness and absolution because when water washes away dirt, this reflects the fact that the layer of dirt is not part of the garment. Sin, likewise, is not an integral part of man. It is a layer of dirt, and when sin is gone from the earth, the sinner can rehabilitate himself.

That is exactly what R. Judah the son of R. Simeon b. Pazzi meant when he said that David did not recite *Halleluya* until he saw the downfall of the wicked. The Psalms prior to chapter 104 refer to the destruction of sinners, not the elimination of sins; the disappearance not of wickedness, but of wicked people. And until that point there was no *shira,* no *Halleluya.* At the end of *Borkhi nafshi* (ch. 104) a new idea emerges. For the first time, David discovers that instead of hoping for the destruction or extermination of the wicked people, we should pray for the rehabilitation of the *rasha* (evildoer), to reform and rehabilitate him into a humane personality. We may pray for, and behold a vision of, a world purged of evil. And the world purged of evil will surely be free of evildoers.

What enabled David to see the problem of evil differently? In Psalm 104 he speaks of the beauty of God's work and His revelation in nature. One can discover God in every beam of light, in the rushing tides, in the flight of the bird, in the roar of the sea, and in every mount and forest. God's residence is in the universe. Though He transcends the universe He dwells in it as well, in every phenomenon of the cosmos. If God dwells in the universe surely He does reside in man as well. And if God is present in man, then there is no need to condemn man absolutely, even the most wicked one.

"God's glory is forever, God rejoices in his creatures" (Ps. 104:31). If this is the case, "I will sing a hymn to God while I live; I will sing praises to my God while I endure" (Ps. 104:33). It is not necessary to ask for retribution as in the previous chapters. It is not necessary to speak about the multitude of enemies, the evil that they inflicted. Instead, "I will rejoice in God" (Ps. 104:34) because the world reveals a different possibility. Now, one can pray to God that the good in man prevail over the bad, that the divine image gain the upper hand over the devil in man. That is the new discovery in this Psalm. David did not want to say *Halleluya* until he saw the defeat of the wicked, meaning the disappearance of evildoers because sin is no more. For this reason the Talmud immediately tells the story about Beruriah. Without the story the statement about the birth of *Halleluya* remains enigmatic.

PRAYING AGAINST EVIL IN THE LITURGY

When the *mesadrei hatefilla,* those who arranged the liturgy, composed our prayers, they introduced the motif of triumph of righteousness and the complete defeat of wickedness and cruelty. Yet they did not speak about the *reshaim*. For example, consider the second paragraph of *Aleinu, Al ken nekaveh lekha*. We pray for the elimination of idols from the land and for the restoration of the world to the kingdom of God. We then continue to pray that "all fleshly beings, *vekhol bnei basar,* will call Your name." What does the reference to "flesh" mean? It signifies man as one who has succumbed to the flesh and surrendered his ideals and principles. We then pray that "all the wicked of the earth, *kol rishei aretz,* turn to You." Here we are not speaking of the weak person who has given in to his shallow desires but about the most wicked, the tyrants of the earth who oppressed humanity.

We do not pray that they disappear or be crushed. Rather we hope that they will turn to God.

The only place where there is prayer against the wicked people themselves is the passage in the *Amida*: *VeLaMalshinim*. *Malshin* means informer. During a time of religious persecution, when Jews practiced Judaism clandestinely, the Roman government made use of informants to report on them. The penalty was death. So we can't blame the Jews of the second century for ordaining this petition.

The Gemara in Megilla 17b tells a very strange story about the composition of this passage. Shimon HaPakuli was the one who composed the *Amida* prayer at Rabban Gamliel's request. Apparently Shimon HaPakuli left out *VeLaMalshinim*. Then Rabban Gamliel asked: Who can write the prayer against the *minim*, the informers? It was Shmuel HaKatan who composed the prayer. Why Shmuel HaKatan? *Pirkei Avot* (chapter 4) lists the mottos of the sages. Shmuel HaKatan's favorite saying was a verse from Proverbs (24:17): "When your enemy falls do not rejoice; when he trips, your heart should not gladden." This explains why Shmuel HaKatan was chosen to compose this benediction. Shmuel was a man without enmity. The sages did not want the passage written by a person with hate in his heart.

We have touched on two principles: first that God dwells with human beings; secondly that every person is capable of repenting, of rehabilitating himself. When we ask that the dominion of evil be wiped off the earth, or that wickedness should disappear like smoke, we recognize that sin does not flow inherently from the human being. Man is not a sinner by nature, because if that were true he would have no hope at all.

Chapter 7

Berakhot in Judaism

THE PURPOSE OF BERAKHOT

> Rav Yehuda says: one who desires to be virtuous should fulfill the rules of [Tractate] *Nezikin* (the laws of damages). Ravina says: [He should fulfill] the rules of [Tractate] Avot. Some say: [He should fulfill] the rules of [Tractate] Berakhot. (Bava Kama 30a)

This last dictum regarding "the rules of Berakhot" embraces the two preceding dicta. The Torah's worldview with respect to interpersonal matters ("the rules of *Nezikin*") and matters between man and God ("the rules of Avot") coalesces and finds its full expression in the rules of Berakhot. This is the topic of our discussion.

What is the content of a *berakha*? What is the meaning of the word "*barukh*"? Does Judaism require man to recite *berakhot* so as to praise the Almighty, or to thank Him?

The conventional translation of the word "*berakha*" is "blessing" or "benediction," but this merely begs the question: what exactly are blessings and benedictions? The accepted but superficial explanation is that the act of reciting a *berakha* is one of praising God, and the formula "*Barukh Ata Hashem*" means "Praised be God's name." However, this explanation is incorrect. Every kabbalist, from the Ari HaKadosh to the Vilna Gaon and the author of *Tanya*, rejects this explanation, and when we consider how the Torah uses the expression "*barukh,*" it will become clear that the sages of the Kabbala were entirely correct in their assessment.

The Torah attributes great significance to *berakhot*. At the dawn of time, the Creator blessed His newly-created world: "God blessed them and God said to them: 'Be fertile and increase; fill the earth and master it'" (Gen. 1:28). He likewise blessed the Sabbath day: "And God blessed the seventh day and sanctified it" (*ibid.* 2:3). After the Deluge, the Creator granted His blessing to Noah: "God blessed Noah and his sons, and said to them: 'Be fertile and increase, fill the earth. The fear and dread of you shall be upon all the beasts of the earth and upon all the birds of the sky…'" (*ibid.* 9:1–2). God also promised Abraham: "And you shall be a blessing. I will bless those who bless you, and those who curse you, I will curse" (*ibid.* 12:2–3).

It is obvious from these verses that a *berakha* should not be identified with praise. The Almighty did not praise creation or laud the seventh day; His *berakhot* to Abraham and Isaac included no words of acclaim. Similarly, in the blessings of our patriarchs to their sons and of our teacher Moses to Israel, they did not intend to praise and extol their descendants and the people of Israel.

The question therefore emerges: What is the meaning of the *berakha* that the Holy One gave to the world, that the patriarchs gave to their sons, and that Moses gave to all of Israel? If we can understand the content and substance of these blessings, we will understand what it means to bless the Almighty.

The Torah linked the secret of the *berakha* with an even greater mystery: the profound secret of male and female. It is stated in Genesis: "God created man in His image; in the image of God He created him; male and female He created them. God blessed them and God said to them: 'Be fertile and increase; fill the earth and master it'" (Gen. 1:27–28). This is a foundational verse in Judaism, which asserts that the Creator imbued human nature with the desire to procreate and produce ever more offspring, and that the biological expression of human fertility is through the joining of male and female.

The Creator gave the biological, organic world in general, and the human being specifically, the power to procreate and multiply. Upon creating plant life, the Holy One commanded: "And God said: 'Let the earth sprout vegetation, seed-bearing plants, fruit trees of every kind on earth that bear fruit with the seed in it" (*ibid.* 11). That is, the botanical world must increase and spread out. When He created the beasts and the birds, the Holy One said: "Be fertile and increase, fill the waters in the seas, and let the birds increase on the earth" (*ibid.* 22). He likewise gave man the potential to procreate and multiply.

The blessing to "be fertile and increase" is thus the embodiment of this potential in the natural world. The *berakha* is a law of nature, inscribed by the Creator upon organic matter in accordance with His primal will, which drives plants, animals, and human beings to increase and multiply without limit.

When buzzing bees hop from flower to flower, they blindly, mechanically, cross-pollinate the plants. When a spring wind scatters spores across the land, which is in turn covered by a colorful coat of plant life, it is a manifestation of the Creator's will in saying: "Let the earth sprout vegetation, seed-bearing plants."

The powerful sex drive is nothing more than a heavenly echo of the Creator's commanding *berakha* from the dawn of creation, saying: "Be fertile and increase, fill the waters in the seas, and let the birds increase on the earth." When human beings are troubled by sex desires, overcome by the curse of loneliness, yearning for a helpmate, they will be assuaged only when heeding the commanding blessing of their Creator: "Be fertile and increase; fill the earth and master it." In short, the *berakha* evinces the natural drive to procreate, to multiply, to reproduce.

The Torah addresses the *berakha* to "them," to a couple. The blessing is not addressed to the solitary individual. Human reproduction is not asexual, but the product of the merging of male and female. The blessing is thus first found in the framework of "male and female He created them"; that is, only when male and female are joined are they blessed with God's *berakha*: "God blessed them and God said to them: 'Be fertile and increase.'" The entire *berakha* is stated in the plural.

Moreover, Judaism developed the original and magnificent idea that the blessing of "be fertile and increase" was not limited to the natural world, but resonates in the spiritual, metaphysical world as well. This seems paradoxical, but it is indeed the case that the Creator modeled the spiritual world as well in keeping with the pattern of "male and female He created them." There, too, there are those who influence, and those who are influenced; those who give, and those who receive; those with an active creative potential, and those with the passive capacity to be formed and shaped. This is the meaning of the sages' statement: "When the Holy One created Adam, the first human, He created him with two faces" (*Bereishit Rabba* 8:1). That is, every human being has two facets, male and female. Every person both influences and is influenced. He or she both gives and receives, possessing both the power to create and containing the primal matter that is made subject to creative forms. For example, a teacher who imparts words of Torah and wisdom to his students is the giver of form, the *dukhra*, the masculine facet; his attentive students, whose thoughts and feelings are stimulated and made fertile by the teacher's ideas as expressed in his words, represent the *nukva*, the feminine facet. His effect on them is as the Torah describes: "May my discourse come down as the rain, my speech distill as the dew, like showers on young growth, like droplets on grass" (Deut. 32:2).

Then, suddenly, a clever and seasoned student is aroused and asks his teacher a question, which stirs the thoughts of the teacher until a new approach begins to form. The teacher's face shines with a new light. The student planted the tiniest seed, but sometimes it develops into a beautiful flower. In such cases, there is a reversal of roles: the student, the wide-eyed youngster with the expression of curiosity, becomes the influencer, the *dukhra*, while the teacher suddenly becomes the passive *nukva*, and receives influence.

No person, no matter how uneducated, is ever only a student and never a teacher, and no person, no matter how wise and knowledgeable, is ever only a teacher and never a student. "Male and female He created them."

The Holy One blessed not only the physical human being when enjoining him to "Be fertile and increase; fill the earth and master it," but also man's spiritual persona, as though instructing him, "Rise! Ascend the rungs of spiritual development! Reach the towering summits of thought and spirit!" Even though every personality is imbued with both of these elements, the *dukhra* and the *nukva*, it must, perforce, connect with other personalities in order to express itself fully. The masculine element of each personality must connect with the feminine element of one's fellow, and its feminine element must connect with the masculine element of one's fellow.

The *dukhra* and *nukva* aspects of the two friends' personalities become interdependent, as trees require the wind to cross-pollinate and cross-fertilize. A person who is isolated, without companionship, will remain sterile. "God blessed them, saying: 'Be fertile and increase.'" There must be a "them." Blessing requires companionship. The greatest *berakha* with which human beings are blessed is expressed in the ability and capacity for self-actualization, that is, for expressing both his masculine and feminine aspects. God blessed Abraham as he departed for the Promised Land, "And you shall be a blessing": you will have the power to draw deeply from the wellsprings of wisdom that shall be revealed to you, thus fully developing your *nukva* potential, and you will then have the power to transmit those very achievements, and future achievements as well, to the people of Israel, preparing it to accept the path of the Torah, the prophets, and the sages of our tradition and also to impart blessing to other nations.

THE MASCULINE AND FEMININE ASPECTS OF MAN

The realization of the idea of male and female is the greatest and most sublime blessing. Human beings must become blessed with the *berakha* of the feminine, that is, one must develop the capacity to receive the blessings of bountiful influence, rising ever higher as they absorb beauty and spiritual riches into one's person. Not all plants grow in fertile soil, from which they can draw water and nutrients, and not every plant enjoys the precious light and warmth necessary for it to grow and flourish. First and foremost, man must be endowed at birth with the aptitude and capacity to absorb wisdom, understanding, and virtue; second, he must be placed in the right environment, with nurturing light and warmth; third, no one can receive bounty and reach spiritual heights unless he is concurrently influencing others by giving them from his spiritual treasures and possessions. Benevolent influence enriches not only the recipient, but above all the influencer himself, as R. Ḥanina said: "I learned much from my teachers, from my peers more than from my teachers, and from my students most of all" (Ta'anit 7a).

Not all Jewish leaders were equally privileged to fully realize the *berakha* of "male and female He created them," of "be fertile and increase." Our sages recount:

> Once they were reclining in the upper chamber of Gurya's house in Jericho, and a heavenly echo descended upon them and announced, "There is someone here who is worthy of having the Divine Presence alight upon him, but his generation is unworthy of it." The sages looked at Hillel the Elder. (Sota 48b)

Hillel had all of the qualities and virtues that, had they all been fully utilized, would have lifted his character to the level of our teacher Moses, to the level of a prophet. However, it was not to be. The *berakha* of "male and female He created them" and "be fertile and increase" could not reach its perfect fulfillment in the persona of Hillel the Elder. The generation, the environment, was not ready for the realization of the *berakha*, and so Hillel could not attain the level of a prophet, even though he had the necessary abilities and qualities.

Even in my own limited experience, I have seen immensely talented individuals who did not have the fortune of fully developing their talents and qualities and therefore did not achieve the greatness of which they were worthy. The blessing of "male and female He created them" and "be fertile and increase" was not fully realized through them. On the other hand, I have seen people of middling talent achieve great things by fully maximizing the blessing of "male and female," of influencing and being influenced, of giving and taking, of learning and teaching. The blessing of "be fertile and increase" was fulfilled in all its bounty through them. The *berakha* of "be fertile and increase" means the manifestation of man, not only in the biological sense, but also through the full development and expression of his unique personality, and through the expansion and integration of his powers.

"And God blessed the seventh day and sanctified it" (Gen. 2:3). R. Avraham ibn Ezra (*ad loc.*) explains: "The meaning of '*berakha*' is an increase of goodness. On this day, the body's reproductive strength is renewed, as is the soul's power to discern." Nahmanides agrees with this interpretation, calling it true and accurate.

Thus, when we begin our blessings to the Holy One with the traditional word "*barukh*," we mean the same thing that God meant in His *berakha* to Adam and Eve. Our Torah is always consistent; if the Creator's blessing to His world means an increase of goodness, influence, bounty, renewal, and fertility, then when the Torah commands us to bless God—"You shall eat and be satiated, and you shall bless the Lord your God for the good land that He has given you" (Deut. 8:10)—it means that we, as it were, bless God in the same vein: increase of goodness, renewal, expansion. This begs for an explanation!

Let us delve a bit deeper into the subject. This sense of the word "*berakha*" seems paradoxical, almost absurd! How can man, flesh and blood, a filthy speck, a wilting flower, a dissipating fog, bless the omnipotent Creator of the world!? The absurdity is heightened when we recall that the blessing is inextricably linked with the idea of "male and female He created them." Yet the Torah commands us to bless God!

The *baalei kabbala* imagined and explained the relationship between creation and its Creator by way of the merging of male and female. The *sefirot* of *Tiferet* (Splendor) and *Yesod* (Foundation) are *dukhra,* whereas *Malkhut* (Kingship) is *nukva.* "God created man in His image; in the image of God He created him; male and female He created them." According to the sages of the Kabbala, from *Zohar* to *Tanya* and *Nefesh HaḤayyim,* the meaning of this verse is that God's manifestation in this world is through the lens of "male and female": *Malka Kadisha,* the Holy King—*Tiferet* and *Yesod*—is male, and the *Matronita,* Matron; *Ḥakal Tapuḥin,* the Field of Apples; *Re'aya Mehemna,* the Faithful Shepherd; *Kalla,* Bride, is female.

One who has studied a bit of Kabbala is familiar with the notion of the "secret of the merging" ("*sod hazivug*"), and consequently knows the meaning of the liturgical poem with which we greet the Sabbath queen, *Lekha Dodi.* "Go forth, beloved, toward the Bride; we will greet the Sabbath."

"And God blessed the seventh day and sanctified it." This blessing is the special song in honor of the Sabbath day, the source of all blessings, which symbolizes the *sod hazivug.*

A Jew sits at his festively laden table on the Sabbath eve and sings, in awe and love: "I sing with praise to enter the gates of the Field of Apples that are holy." He continues, with longing: "Right and left, and between them the Bride, adorned… Her husband embraces her and her *Yesod,* which brings her joy…" While he sings, he feels deeply that these lines, written by the holy Ari, contain the entire secret of Judaism. Our simple Jew ascends, impassioned, as he continues singing: "Draw near, O groomsmen, make preparations… to form new souls and spirits." Come, O bride and groom and attendants, and greet the *Malka Kadisha*, the *Shekhina* (Divine Presence).

I am not a kabbalist, and this is not the place to delve into the esoteric Torah. Nevertheless, I think it was the author of *Tanya* who once said that just as there are esoteric matters within the exoteric Torah,[1] so too, there are exoteric matters in the esoteric Torah. Every kabbalistic idea can be explained in a way that every Jew can apprehend and understand. I will avail myself of this view and will attempt to explain, in a straightforward, exoteric manner, what the Kabbala means by "*dukhra*" and "*nukva*." Once we understand this enigmatic issue, we can grasp the idea of *berakhot*.

The Creator is the Holy King, the all-powerful Maker of all, the foundation and purpose of all creation, who created the world through His utterances. We believe that the creation of the world was not a one-time act, but a continuous process of renewal and life-giving, as we say in *Shaḥarit*: "Who, in His goodness, renews the work of creation every day" and "You give life to all." If the Master of the world were to withdraw from our world even for a moment, all would return to formlessness and emptiness. It is only because of His providence over us that we can exist in His world. And inasmuch as we exist, before Him it is as though we are mere ether, nothingness.

In this relationship between the Creator and the world, He is in the role of male, omnipotent, *dukhra*. He influences, and we are the receivers of His influence. He gives, and we receive. He is manifest as *dukhra*, and we as *nukva*. "When I behold Your heavens, the work of Your fingers, the moon and stars that You set in place, what is man that You have been mindful of him, mortal man that You have taken note of him?" (Ps. 8:4–5). In the infinite space of the universe, from the most distant cosmic nebulae to the concrete existence of this world, the "voice of the Lord is power; the voice of the Lord is majesty" (*ibid.* 29:4) that echoes and resonates. Man is negligible, worthless. Powerless, mortal,

---

1. When the holy Ari began studying *Beitza*, he would read, with great excitement, "*bei TZa"H*"—"within is the Rock of Ages (*TZur Ha-olamim*)." In the verse "And these are the kings who ruled in the land of Edom" (Gen. 36:31), all of the aspects of the "shattering of the vessels" are alluded to, according to the *Tikkunei Zohar*.

wracked with pain and disease—man is but dust. Greatness and might belong to the Everlasting.

However, if man's relationship with his Creator, the "Holy King," were limited to this aspect alone, there would have been no room for the giving of the Torah and for His revelation to Israel at Mount Sinai, amid thunder and lightning, to establish a covenant of truth with us. Ultimately, all covenants are bilateral; each party gives and takes. Each party is both *dukhra* and *nukva*.

It must be, then, that the Master of the world needs us, as it were. It is in this sense that we refer to Him with names like *Shekhina*, *Matronita*, and *Kalla*—in short, as *nukva*. The *Shekhina*, the Divine Presence in this world, is the recipient of influence, as it were; and we are the givers, the influencers. This means that the Holy One, as it were, conferred some of His grandeur and sovereignty on mortal man, the withering flower and broken vessel, revealing Himself to him with the manifestation of the *Shekhina*.

The omnipotent *Malka Kadisha*, the Creator and Sustainer of all worlds, as it is written, "You give life to all" (Neh. 9:6), is concealed and hidden. "The Most High dwells in secret" (Ps. 91:1). Who can see Him? The *Malka Kadisha* is even called *Shekhina* because He dwells among us—"who dwells among them amidst their impurity" (Lev. 16:16). Yet we, who are always connected to Him, nevertheless never see Him. Scripture states: "The Lord came down in a cloud; He stood with him there" (Ex. 34:5), meaning that even when the Holy One is close to man, within man's four cubits, to the extent that man feels His presence and senses Him before him, He is still cloaked in the thick cloud that no eye can penetrate.

To the eyes of the physicist, the cloud is a mathematical formula; to the biologist, it is a biochemical reaction. To the physiologist, it is a feeling; to the psychologist, an impulse. The Master of the world Himself does not want to, and, as it were, is unable to dispel the cloud. It is the task of man to dissipate it. It is man who must seek and find: "If you have sought and found, you are credible" (Megilla 6b).

The *Shekhina*, as it were, cannot reveal Herself; She is the *nukva* aspect, the "King held captive in His tresses" (Song 7:6). Man must free the *Malka Kadisha* from His chains, bring Him out of hiding, scatter the dense cloud, so that He may illuminate the world with His radiance.

The Master of the world is all-powerful, except when it comes to His own revelation. With respect to His revelation, we human beings are the active influencers while the *Shekhina,* as it were, is the recipient of influence. This is likewise expressed in the sages' dictum about the principle of free choice: "All is in the hands of Heaven, except for reverence of Heaven" (Berakhot 33b). Reverence of Heaven, *yirat Shamayim,* is none other than the perception of Heaven, *re'iyat Shamayim*—"seeing" ("*re'iyah*") and "revering" ("*yir'ah*") share the same Hebrew root.

When is man in awe of God's glory? When he senses His presence and discovers Him, when man himself is the discoverer. The manifestation of the *Shekhina* depends on man himself. Man can, if he wants, seek and find God in any phenomenon, at any time, in any place—in the sunrise and the sunset, in the sea and in the flowering plants, in the stars and the sand, in the world around him and within himself. When a Jew discovers the Master of the world—the *Shekhina, Malkhut, Kalla*—he assumes the aspect of *dukhra,* while She is *nukva.* By virtue of this discovery, his disclosure of God's presence, he cleaves to the *Shekhina* and increases holiness in this world.

Likewise, when a Jew partakes in a meal, once he recites the formula "Blessed are You," the *Shekhina* is present, found in every slice of fruit, every blossom, every sip of water, every gesture of the hand. He discovers the Creator in each of these; every phenomenon is an occasion for a direct encounter with "You." Consequently, the *berakha* of "be fertile and increase" is realized, the *Shekhina* expands, goodness and holiness are increased further, and the Master of the world merges with His world.

STUDIES IN THE FORMULA OF BERAKHOT

The meaning of the formula "*Barukh Ata*"—"Blessed are You"—that a Jew recites before eating is similar to that of Moses' petition, "May the power of the Lord be increased" (Num. 14:17). In other words: Lord of all worlds, please reveal the glory of Your dominion to the eyes of all, as it is stated: "And all flesh, as one, will see that the mouth of the Lord has spoken" (Is. 40:5). By virtue of my discovery of You, my God, in this apple that I am eating, in this cup from which I sip wine, You and I merge with one another. The Master of the world is present when the *berakha* is recited, because its meaning is the disclosure of the *Shekhina.*

This is how the psalm "*Barkhi Nafshi*" is explained: "Bless the Lord, O my soul; O Lord, my God, You are very great; You are clothed in glory and majesty. Wrapped in a robe of light, You spread the heavens like a tent cloth" (Ps. 104:1–2). By blessing You, God, I discover You, and Your light extends gloriously and majestically throughout all of creation.

If you ask me what Judaism is, I will respond: Judaism is contained in the words "*Barukh Ata*." The recognition that the Almighty, as it were, needs our *berakhot*, means that He, as it were, needs to be discovered by us and needs our constant aspiration to seek and find Him.

Transgression causes the concealment of God's face from the sinner, as it is written: "But your iniquities have been a barrier between you and your God, your sins have made Him turn His face away and refuse to hear you" (Is. 59:2).

A Jew who is mired in iniquity thickens the cloud that cloaks the Creator, ensuring that it will not soon be dissipated. Severe transgressions, like hard-heartedness, insensitivity, and coarseness, create barriers between us and God but do not distance Him from us, for He "dwells among them amidst their impurity." What, then, must the sinner do? He must rediscover the Holy One. He must become the heroic *dukhra* and help the Almighty, as it were, be revealed to him again. When the sinner once again discerns and identifies his purpose, he becomes a penitent, a *baal teshuva*. The power of a *baal teshuva* is greater than that of a wholly righteous individual because he managed, through his own efforts, to rediscover his Creator, who had hidden from him in a thick fog.

When I was a young child, I studied Torah with a Hasidic teacher. Once, on the day before Tisha B'Av, we studied *midrashim* about the destruction of the Temple. We reached the 24th introductory passage in *Eikha Rabbati*:

> ...Enemies entered the Sanctuary and burnt it. Once it was burnt, the Holy One said, "I no longer have an abode on earth; I shall remove My *Shekhina* from there and go up to My former habitation." At that time the Holy One wept and said, "Woe is Me! What have I done? I caused My *Shekhina* to dwell below for the sake of Israel; but now that they have sinned, I have returned to My former habitation. Heaven forfend that I become a laughter to the nations and a byword to human beings!" Then Metatron

> came, fell upon his face, and said before Him: "Master of the world! Let me weep, but You do not weep." He replied to him, "If you do not let Me weep now, I will withdraw to where you have no permission to enter, and I will weep there," as it is written: "For if you do not give heed, I shall weep in secret" (Jer. 13:17).

When I heard this description, I asked my teacher, in my innocence, a simple question: Why does the Holy One need to cry and mourn the destruction of the Temple? He can rebuild it in an instant! The teacher then answered: "If you, my dear pupil, would be fluent in the teachings of Chabad, you would understand that for many things there must first be an arousal from below, an *it'aruta deletata*."

At that time I certainly did not fully understand my teacher, but the question and its answer became clear to me after many years: The Sovereign of the world is omnipotent, but when His great name is desecrated, Israel must kindle its zeal and fight on behalf of God's name. The sanctification of God's name always comes from below, never from above.

This is what Metatron discussed with the Holy One. Metatron is the angel who represents nature and the universe as a whole. When Metatron saw the Holy One agitated and weeping, as it were, he fell down before Him and said: "Master of the world! Let me weep, but You do not weep!" In other words, he asked: Why are You weeping? Are You not all-powerful? Was it not by Your utterance that the heavens were created, and by the breath of Your mouth all of its hosts? With one utterance, You can restore the crown to its former glory and make everything as it was!

And so the Master of the world responded: Metatron, you do not properly understand the matter. I must weep because I have no control over My heart. The Temple was destroyed and can no longer serve its purpose of revealing My *Shekhina* because the soul of Israel has been contaminated by sin; without Israel to sanctify Me from below, My power to save Myself is weakened, as it were, and so My *Shekhina* must withdraw, acting as the *nukva*, weeping in the hidden recesses.

INVOKING GOD'S NAME IN BERAKHOT

We have thus far explained that the opening of *berakhot* with "*Barukh Ata*" is the Jewish prayer for the Creator to reveal Himself to us, as when

Moses prayed, "May the power of the Lord be increased." In addition to "*Barukh Ata*," halakha requires that God's name and God's kingship (*malkhut*) be invoked. The sages said: "Any *berakha* that does not include [God's] name and [God's] kingship is not a *berakha*" (*Berakhot* 40b). That is, a *berakha* must include God's explicit four-lettered name (YKVK), the Tetragrammaton, though the appellation "*A-donai*" ("Lord") is pronounced in its stead. It also must invoke God's kingship: "*Melekh ha'olam*" ("King of the world"). Why did they establish this as the fixed language of *berakhot*? Why isn't it sufficient to recite simply: "Blessed are You, who creates the fruit of the vine, ... who brings forth bread from the earth"?

The invocation of God's name and kingship teaches us two major principles of Judaism, which we will discuss below. Let us first address the mention of God as "*A-donai*." The Talmud informs us:

> R. Yoḥanan said in the name of R. Shimon bar Yoḥai: From the day that the Holy One created the world, no person called the Holy One "Lord" ("*Adon*") until Abraham arrived and called Him "Lord," at it is written: "And he said: O Lord (*A-donai*) God, how shall I know that I am to possess it?" (Gen. 15:8). Rav said: Even Daniel was not answered but for the sake of Abraham, as it says: "O our God, hear now the prayer of Your servant and his plea, and show Your favor to Your desolate sanctuary, for the sake of the Lord (*A-donai*)" (Dan. 9:17). It should have said, "for Your sake"; rather, [it means] "for the sake of Abraham, who called You "*Adon*."

In this statement, R. Shimon bar Yoḥai expresses a highly original viewpoint. Abraham's greatest discovery was in calling the Almighty by the name "*Adon*." Moreover, Daniel's best argument in petitioning the Creator to rebuild the Temple is "for the sake of *A-donai*." That is, the rebuilt Temple will spread the name "*A-donai*" throughout the world, and therefore You must rebuild it and shine Your countenance on its ruins.

Now the name "*A-donai*," which is incorporated in the texts of our *berakhot*, is only one of the seven sacred names that may not be erased. The Tetragrammaton is holier than the name "*A-donai*," because YKVK is considered God's "explicit" or "special" name, and it was permitted to pronounce it only in the Temple, nowhere else. The name "*A-donai*," on the other hand, could be pronounced in all places. Our sages recount that the Tetragrammaton was transmitted only to a worthy person, and only once every seven years (Kiddushin 71a).

According to the Kabbala as well, YKVK is higher than the name "*A-donai*." There are opinions that the Tetragrammaton signifies all of the *sefirot*, from *Ḥokhma* to *Malkhut*, and generally emphasizes *Tiferet*. "*A-donai*," on the other hand, signifies only the *sefira* of *Yesod*.

The Men of the Great Assembly fixed the formula of *berakhot* for Israel, so that they bless the Creator with the name *A-donai* and R. Shimon b. Yohai says that the use of this name signifies the great contribution of Abraham. Why is this so?

With the Tetragrammaton alone, Abraham would not have been able to teach the world about the divinity of the Holy One. With faith alone, without any concrete, practical morality, one cannot teach people anything. It was only by revealing the name "*A-donai*" in the world that Abraham could teach them not only to recognize the Master of the world, but also to follow in the way of God. Thus, Abraham was the teacher of everyone in the world.

THE NAME OF LORDSHIP IN BERAKHOT

What is the meaning of "*A-donai*"? Lordship: ownership in the simplest sense of the word. The Almighty is the Creator of the world and is therefore its Owner, as it is written: "The earth is the Lord's and all that it holds, the world and its inhabitants." Why? "For He founded it upon the ocean, set it on the nether-streams" (Ps. 24:1–2). He owns the world because He created it, and one who creates something thereby becomes its owner. The name "*A-donai*" thus stems from the name YKVK, which refers to God's creation and sustaining of the world.

Let us explain this in halakhic terminology taken from monetary law. There is a dispute among *Amoraim* (Bava Kama 98b) about whether or not a craftsman acquires the improvements to a vessel. For instance, if someone gives expensive raw material to a craftsman for him to forge a utensil from it, for pay, and the craftsman indeed improves and completes the utensil, who owns the added value of the finished product? One view maintains that the craftsman does not acquire the improvements to the completed utensil; rather, the utensil in its entirety, both its substance and its betterments, belong to the original owner, who owes nothing to the craftsman except for his wages. The other view maintains that any improvement to the utensil that the craftsman produced through his toil and effort belongs to the craftsman. The original owner does not pay wages, but pays the price of the added value, just as any buyer pays the seller the price of the object.

Maimonides rules: "If one gave [a carpenter] wood to make a chest, cabinet, or closet, and it broke after they were completed, [the carpenter] must repay him the value of the chest, cabinet, or closet, for the craftsman does not acquire via the improvements to the utensil" (*Hilkhot Sekhirut* 10:4). R. Tam (cited in *Piskei HaRosh*, Kiddushin 2:11), however, states that a craftsman does acquire ownership status through the improvements to the object.

Whatever ruling is adopted vis-à-vis a human craftsman, all agree that with respect to the Creator of the world, the Craftsman acquired ownership rights. I must emphasize that this is the halakhic truth in that the Master of the world acquired the world He created and formed. It is not a biased judgment in favor of the Creator. The Talmudic dispute applies to a craftsman, who improves on raw materials but does not create those materials *ex nihilo*. A craftsman who contracted with a customer to refashion his raw materials in exchange for payment is obligated to return the materials plus their improvements to the customer, having completed the work and been duly compensated. Once the payment is made, the finished product belongs to the customer, and the craftsman has no right to withhold it. The *Amoraim* disagree only about the interim period, after the object is finished but before the craftsman receives payment: is the customer, who owns the raw material itself, entitled to claim that the enhancement already belongs to him, or is the craftsman entitled to say that the enhancement is his? However, if the craftsman found ownerless material, took it without explicitly claiming ownership, and turned it into a utensil, all agree that the craftsman has acquired the utensil and its improvements, even though the raw material was ownerless. His craftsmanship and labor grant him rights to the object.

The Yerushalmi (Ma'asrot 1:5) states: "One who sows an ownerless field is obligated in the tithes (*ma'asrot*)." Even though the sower did not intend to claim the field itself (had he done so, it would not be a case of one sowing an ownerless field, but of one sowing his own field), the produce belongs to the sower who cultivated the field, and he is obligated to tithe it. The land has no owner, so no one can claim, "My land has been improved." However, if one enters another's field without permission and sows it, the produce belongs to the field owner, for he can claim, "My land has been improved."

The Holy One created the world *ex nihilo*. No one else can claim ownership of the world and say of it, "My land was improved," for the earth is God's. The Master of the world is the One who created both the hylic matter and the form of the world. There was no obligation to any other with respect to the world's creation. It was an act of pure grace; "the world is built in kindness" (Ps. 89:3). In such a case, Maimonides would agree that the Craftsman acquires the improvements to the utensil.

There is another Talmudic passage (Berakhot 31b):

> "And she swore an oath and said, Lord of Hosts (*A-donai Tzeva'ot*)…" (I Sam. 1:11). Rabbi Elazar said: From the day that the Holy One created His world, there was no person who called the Holy One "*Tzeva'ot*" until Hannah came and called Him "*Tzeva'ot*."

When we say that the world is the Almighty's handiwork, we do not limit our statement to the known universe, to natural processes, to the infinite expanse, to the Milky Way; we mean that the Creator is Lord over the tiniest particles. This is the meaning of "Lord of Hosts"; the expression *Tzeva'ot* includes all of the smallest and most negligible specks. All belongs to the Creator, as it is written: "The earth is the Lord's and all it holds, the world and its inhabitants" (Ps. 24:1).

It is interesting, even astonishing, that halakha defines *hekdesh* (the public trust for consecrated objects) as a form of legal ownership. Objects consecrated for the upkeep of the Temple are considered to be the property of *hekdesh*. *Hekdesh* acquires objects from those who sanctify them, and the acquisition is effected through speech or through any of the common ways of effecting a transaction. The Talmud speaks of "God's treasury" (Ḥullin 139a), meaning that wherever the consecrated object is, it is in God's domain. Therefore, if one vowed to bring an offering but did not bring it, the treasurer of *hekdesh* may collect it from him against his will, because the vow to bring an offering constitutes a form of debt. The idea that "*hekdesh* is God's money (*mamon gavo'a*)" is common in halakha.

Why does the Torah ascribe monetary ownership to the Almighty? It is not because the Holy One requires money; rather, the primary meaning is that consecrated monies are not owned by any other. The goal is for man not to see himself as master. To the rich man, the Almighty says: "Silver is Mine and gold is Mine" (Hag. 2:8); your money is not yours. To the world's kings and rulers, who govern vast territories, He whispers: "the land is Mine; you are but strangers resident with Me" (Lev. 25:23). The expression "Mine" is primarily an implication of its negative: "not yours." No man truly acquires property.

A Jew who is scholarly and erudite, a scientist and thinker, a gifted homilist and preacher, may delude himself into thinking that his wisdom and talent are really his own, since he toiled many sleepless nights to acquire those virtues and qualities. But then the liturgical poet comes and says to him: "*Hadei'a vehadibbur lehai olamim.*" "Knowledge and speech—are the Eternal's." The prophet admonishes him: "Let not the wise man glory in his wisdom" (Jer. 9:22). The Men of the Great Assembly formulated the prayer: "You grace man with knowledge and teach understanding to humanity."

A person may be renowned. He may be in full possession of all of his mental and physical faculties at an advanced age, and with a clean bill of health from his physician. He is loved and adored by all, and he concludes that his accolades and his health are his own. A painter, a sculptor, a composer, or any artist who breathes new life into sound, color, or stone may think that what they have created is theirs. To them, King David says: "Yours, Lord, are greatness, might, splendor, triumph, and majesty—yes, all that is in heaven and on earth; to You, Lord, belong kingship and preeminence above all. Riches and honor are Yours to dispense; You have dominion over all; with You are strength and might, and it is in Your power to make anyone great and strong" (I Chron. 29:11–12).

Birkhot hanehenin, the blessings recited upon deriving benefit and pleasure from the physical world, are based entirely on the notion of God's lordship. The recitation of a *berakha* is the obtainment of permission from the Master of the world to enjoy something from His world, so as not to commit sacrilege. We learn (Berakhot 35a):

> The sages taught: One is forbidden to derive benefit from this world without a *berakha,* and anyone who derives benefit from

> this world without a *berakha* has committed sacrilege [*me'ila*, which is a form of theft—*me'ila* and theft are synonymous concepts]...Rabbi Levi raised a contradiction: It is written: "The earth is the Lord's and all it holds," and it is written elsewhere, "The heavens are the Lord's, and the earth He has given over to mankind" (Ps. 115:16). This is not difficult: [The first verse] is before the *berakha*, and [the second verse] is after a *berakha*.

Even after a *berakha*, it makes little sense to explain that God has "given" us the earth in the simple sense of a regular, full grant. Had this been the case, we would not need to recite another *berakha* after eating, yet it is well known that *Birkat HaMazon*, the *berakhot* after a meal, is explicitly ordained by the Torah.

Hence, the verb "give" ("*natan*") is used in the sense of giving permission, not of granting a gift. This is the sense in which the word appears in the verse: "I knew that you did this with a blameless heart, and so I kept you from sinning against Me. That was why I did not allow you (*netatikha*) to touch her" (Gen. 20:6).

Even after permission is granted, based on the verse "and the earth He has given over to mankind," man must still know that, "The earth is the Lord's and all it holds," that benefit without a *berakha* is theft, denial of God, and heresy. So says R. Hanina b. Papa: "Anyone who derives benefit from this world without a *berakha*, it is as if he stole from God and the community of Israel" (Berakhot 35b). That is, it is as if he denies the Jewish conception of God's lordship over the world, which Abraham discovered and which Daniel established as the basis for the redemption of the Jewish people. A *berakha* that does not invoke God's lordship is not a *berakha*.

THE IDEA OF DIVINE LORDSHIP IN OTHER REALMS

The principle of *adnut*, of God's lordship, finds expression in other realms as well. For example, the idea of *tzedaka* is usually translated as "charity," an act of kindness for another. At first glance, this explanation appears correct, for we owe no debt to any poor person. Therefore, anything that we give him is a favor; for he has no legal claim on it.

However, Maimonides demonstrated in the *Guide of the Perplexed* (3:53) that this is a mistaken conception. Had the Torah conceived of *tzedaka* in this way, it would have called it "*ḥesed*"—kindness—a benevolent act that is not owed. Since the Torah calls it "*tzedaka*," though—a term related to "*tzedek*" ("justice")—we have a clear indication that it is an act of justice, not merely a matter of kindness. Doing justice is an obligation. In truth, this insight is contained within the halakha as well.

Human imagination has not yet invented, in any legal system, the strange idea that charity can be collected by force. Is not the essence of charity that it is freely given? Yet the halakha states specifically about *tzedaka*: "We seize collateral for [debts to] *tzedaka*, even just before Shabbat" (Bava Batra 8b). If a person of means refuses to give *tzedaka* according to his ability, it is permissible to seize collateral and carry items from his home, even if Shabbat is about to begin. Most of the *Rishonim* agree with this rule and explain that the duty to give *tzedaka* generates a lien on one's property, much as a loan would.

Tzedaka and *tzedek* are thus the same thing. When one understands of his own accord that justice demands a particular course of action—for example: to pay off a loan, to refrain from stealing, not to oppress the poor—this accepted and widespread honesty is called "*tzedek*." However, when man, with his weak and superficial mind, does not understand certain acts as *tzedek* but thinks they are acts of kindness, he does not understand the meaning of the letter *heh* in *tzedaka*. In the sages' worldview, the letter *heh* expresses weakness: "It shall be a sign to you upon your arm (*yadkhah*—with an extra *heh* at the end)" (Ex. 13:15) teaches that *tefillin* are placed on the left, weaker arm ("*yad kehah*"). Just as the left arm is still an arm, albeit the weaker one, so *tzedaka* is identical with *tzedek*, though it is a weaker form of *tzedek*.

Why did the Torah mandate *tzedaka* as a debt, pledging our bodies and assets to its fulfillment as for any routine indebtedness? Because it is the will of the Master of the world, unto whom is all gold and silver, that we pledge ourselves to *tzedaka*. Everything that He has given us is conditioned on our acts of *tzedaka*. This is expressed in the words of Rabbi Elazar of Bartota: "Render unto Him what is His, for you and whatever is yours—are His" (Avot 3:7). Likewise, King David said: "all is from You, and it is Your gift that we have given to You" (I Chron. 29:14).

Our patriarch Abraham was the first to discover God's attribute of *tzedaka* in the world, as it says: "that he may instruct his children and his posterity to keep the way of the Lord by doing what is just (*tzedaka*) and right (*mishpat*)" (Gen. 18:19). Note that this verse refers to *tzedaka,* not *tzedek;* others understood *tzedek,* but no one before Abraham understood *tzedaka.*

Not only *tzedaka,* but many other mitzvot of the Torah can only be comprehended once we understand God's mastery over the world: the sabbatical and jubilee years and *teruma, maaser, ḥalla,* and *bikkurim* are all based on the premise that "The earth is the Lord's and all it holds, the world and its inhabitants."

Judaism abhors haughtiness in all of its forms. The Torah says of the king of Israel: "Thus he will not act haughtily toward his fellows" (Deut. 17:20). Likewise, it is avowedly opposed to slavery, as R. Yoḥanan ben Zakkai said: "The ear that heard My voice on Mount Sinai when I said, 'For the children of Israel are slaves unto Me' (Lev. 25:55), and not slaves unto slaves, now goes and acquires a master for itself? Let that ear be pierced" (Kiddushin 22b). The Torah severely admonishes against injury and affronts to the dignity of others, especially among the most vulnerable segments of society: "You shall not mistreat any widow or orphan" (Ex. 22:21). "One who publicly embarrasses another has no share in the world to come" (Avot 3:15). All of these, and indeed, all of human morality, stem inexorably from God's lordship over the world, as it is written: "Let not the wise man glory in his wisdom; let not the strong man glory in his strength; let not the rich man glory in his riches. But only in this should one glory: that he understands and knows Me..." (Jer. 9:22–23).

INVOKING GOD'S KINGSHIP (MALKHUT) IN BERAKHOT

We now arrive at the final element of the formula for *berakhot*: God's kingship. "Any *berakha* that does not invoke God's name and kingship is not a *berakha*" (Berakhot 40b; *Mishneh Torah, Hilkhot Berakhot* 1:5).

What is the meaning of *malkhut*? Why is a blessing that does not invoke the descriptor "King of the world" ("*Melekh ha'olam*") not considered a *berakha*? Does the Almighty need for us to call Him "Your Majesty"?

The entire world is His; "The earth is the Lord's and all that it holds." His ownership over the world goes beyond simple ownership, rising to the level of consecration. We have already emphasized that consecrated property is divine property, and so anyone who derives benefit from this world without a *berakha* has committed a form of sacrilege.

Sacrilege (*me'ila*) is more severe than theft, as it consists of both theft and a transgression against God. A thief does not bring an offering to atone for his theft, but one who commits sacrilege must bring a guilt-offering (*asham me'ilot*). The reason is quite simple: returning a stolen object to its original owner is strictly a matter of civil law, whereas one who misappropriates the property of the King of the world desecrates the name of Heaven and prevents His glory from filling the whole world.

Even with respect to a mortal king, we learn (Sanhedrin 22a): "One may not ride his horse, sit upon his throne, or wield his scepter." That is, one who sits on the royal throne is deemed to have betrayed the king and arrogated his power, and so the king may not permit another to perform such acts. He may only permit another to use things that are in the legal realm of personal, private property. However, with respect to the king's honor, the sages said: "If a king relinquishes his honor, his honor is not relinquished" (Kiddushin 32b).

Thus, when Jews invoke the "King of the world" while reciting a *berakha*, they ask for permission to enjoy this world without it constituting sacrilege. This, however, must be explained further.

The entire world is consecrated to its King, so we may still ask: how can we derive benefit from the world, even after obtaining permission by means of reciting a *berakha*? The Torah teaches that one can derive benefit from consecrated property only after redeeming it. Anything which possesses sanctity for its value ("*kedushat mamon*") and not for the sacred use of the object itself ("*kedushat haguf*") is redeemable, as it is written: "and if he who consecrated the land wishes to redeem it, he must add one-fifth to the sum at which it was assessed, and it shall pass to him" (Lev. 27:19).

What is "redemption"? The Torah permits deriving benefit from consecrated property after it has been redeemed and desacralized at a price that is generally the same as the value of the benefit that a person wants to derive. Only after redeeming the consecrated property may one use the property of the King of the world.

And so we are again faced with a profound mystery: The entire world belongs to the Almighty. Every fiber of one's being—body and soul, thoughts and feelings, desires and abilities—are His, as we say in the *Seliḥot*: "The soul is Yours and the body is Your work… The soul is Yours and the body is Yours." In a sense, everything is consecrated to Heaven, and so deriving benefit from them is an act of sacrilege and treason. The only way to permit the derivation of benefit from divine property is by redeeming it—that is, by "compensating" the Almighty, as it were, with something equivalent to the object I wish to enjoy. But what can I give the Holy One for my soul, my body, my entire human existence, my "I"? How can I compensate Him for all He has given me!? To enjoy the world, man must pay ransom for his soul. He must redeem his body and spirit.

"Nowadays, we do not consecrate," says the Talmud (Yoma 66b). Since the destruction of the Temple, there has been no Temple maintenance to fund, so we do not, *ab initio*, consecrate property for the upkeep of the Temple. But what recourse does one have if he indeed consecrated something? The Talmudic sage Shmuel says: "Consecrated property worth one *maneh* that was desacralized with the value of a *peruta* is redeemed" (Arakhin 29a). In other words, one may, *ab initio*, redeem an object consecrated for its value upon with something of minimal value—a *peruta*—and it thereby is desacralized, and may be enjoyed, not subject to sacrilege. Maimonides rules accordingly: "It is permissible nowadays to redeem consecrated property for even a *peruta*, which is cast into the Dead Sea" (*Mishneh Torah, Hilkhot Arakhin* 8:10). The ransom need not have the same value as the consecrated object being redeemed.

God is giving us a great bargain in allowing us to redeem property consecrated to Him, even properties worth thousands of gold *denarii*, for a *peruta*, a penny, the coin of the lowest denomination. The *peruta* is the offering; the ransom is our redemption.

Consider: the Torah admonishes us not to charge exorbitant prices (Lev. 25:14), so how can we be so brazen as to swindle the Almighty, as it were, by redeeming ourselves, our families, and the entire world for the equivalent of a *peruta*?! A Mishna provides the answer: "[The law of] overcharging does not apply to consecrated property" (Bava Metzia 56a). The Master of the world permits us to "swindle" Him, as it were. For one penny, a minimal ransom, He permits us to enjoy "the earth and all that it holds, the world and its inhabitants." The Lord, King of the world, demands a ransom of man in the amount of no more than a *peruta*, yet if one does not pay it, he has committed sacrilege.

THE JEWISH PEOPLE ACQUIRES ITS WORLD FOR A RANSOM OF THREE PERUTOT

Judaism demands that we redeem the world—and a single *peruta* suffices. The ransom that the Almighty demands from man is a microcosm of the sacrifice that He, as it were, brings of Himself. God does not demand anything of man that He does not demand of Himself. A major principle of the Torah is to "walk in His ways" (Deut. 8:6), *imitatio Dei*.

THE FIRST PERUTA: A HEDGE OF LILIES AND THE MYSTERY OF TZIMTZUM

The first *peruta* that God demands of Israel is to live within the "hedge of lilies" (Song 7:3) safeguarding the observance of mitzvot and proper actions, which is akin to the idea of *tzimtzum* (withdrawal or contraction). Kabbalists, most prominently the Ari HaKadosh in *Etz Ḥayyim* and the first Lubavitcher Rebbe, expressed the idea that the creation of the world was created by an act of withdrawal or contraction. When the Infinite created the world through His utterances, He contracted Himself, as it were, in order to give creation a place to exist. Had He not chosen the mode of withdrawal and instead chosen the mode of expansiveness, the world could not exist. Of the Infinite, without contraction, it is written: "For His name, alone, is sublime" (Ps. 148:13). The Almighty relinquished several of His attributes, so to speak, in order to give our world its existence.

This is true not only of the metaphysical possibility of the world's existence, but also of the continued existence of the Jewish people as a singular unit within the world. If the Holy One desired for there to be an eternal people in the world because He wanted to give the world the Torah, He could have chosen the entire human race and given the Torah to the whole world at once. Yet the King of the whole world, whose kingship we declare on Rosh HaShana when we recite the verses of *Malkhuyot*, elected a tiny, impoverished nation to be His kingdom of priests, His holy nation. The Almighty emphasizes that He could have selected as His chosen "people" all of humanity: "Now then, if you will obey Me faithfully and keep My covenant, you shall be My treasured possession among all the peoples, for all the earth is Mine" (Ex. 19:5). "It is not because you are the most numerous of peoples that the Lord set His heart on you and chose you—indeed, you are the smallest of peoples" (Deut. 7:7). Of all walks of life, says God, I have chosen you to be My treasured people. This is an act of *tzimtzum*.

What is *tzimtzum*? A Midrash (*Yalkut Shimoni*, Ex. 365) tells us:

> When the Holy One said to Moses, "Let them make Me a sanctuary that I may dwell among them" (Ex. 25:8), Moses was alarmed and taken aback. He said, "The heavens to their uttermost reaches cannot contain You" (I Kings 8:27), yet You say to me, "Let them make Me a sanctuary that I may dwell among them"?
>
> The Holy One said to him: Moses, it is not as you think. Rather, twenty beams to the north, twenty to the south, and eight to the west, and I will descend and contract My Presence below. Sometimes the heavens to their uttermost reaches cannot contain Me, and sometimes I descend and contract My Presence into the space of one square cubit, as it is written: "There I will meet with you, and I will impart to you—from above the cover, from between the two cherubim that are on top of the Ark" (Ex. 25:22).

Every Jew must likewise espouse this attribute of restriction by limiting his action in many ways. Halakha itself is, in practice, a doctrine of *tzimtzum*. This is the currency by which a Jew can redeem the entire world from the realm of the sacred, for the benefit of humanity.

In the halakhic system, one form of redemption is by means of a method that I call the "hedge of lilies" ("they do not even breach a hedge made of lilies"—Sanhedrin 37a). Unthreatened by police action or penal codes, without compulsion to conform or face imprisonment, the Jew nevertheless observes and fulfills the Torah and mitzvot. It is not easy for the Jew to uphold every rule of the *Shulḥan Arukh*. Sometimes, and this is especially true in modern society, observance entails major hardships. The laws do not constitute a barrier of iron between him and that which is prohibited, but a "hedge of lilies." A hedge of lilies is easily trampled, yet nevertheless the Jew who desires the mitzvot pays the *peruta* of ransom, in exchange for which God permits His creatures to enjoy and live in His world.

Adherence to the *Shulḥan Arukh* requires this *peruta* constantly. The more private a relationship, the more hidden our conduct, the fewer the witnesses to our behavior—the softer the lilies that form the hedge.

When a Jewish man betroths a Jewish woman, a *berakha* is recited: "Blessed are You ... who has sanctified us with His commandments and commanded us concerning forbidden relations; He has forbidden to us those betrothed to us and permitted to us those married to us by means of a canopy (*ḥuppa*) and betrothal (*kiddushin*)." In exchange for this "and permitted to us," the man pays two *perutot*. The first is the tangible one gives to the woman he is marrying. The second is the figurative *peruta* we have been discussing—this *peruta* one pays to the Almighty. The sages state the following (*Midrash Ḥazit* 7:3 and *Pesikta Rabbati*, as expounded by Rashi on Song of Songs 7:3):

> "Hedged about with lilies"—fenced and safeguarded by a fence of lilies. A light fence is sufficient so that none of them breaches it to enter. The groom enters the wedding canopy, his heart yearning for the canopy and for marital love. He comes to consummate with her, and she says to him, "I have seen a drop of blood the size of a mustard seed." He turns his face away, though no snake has bitten him, no scorpion has stung him.

The bride and groom, concealed by darkness of night, are tempted to sin. They are alone together, and they passionately desire one another. No one is there to see them. No one will reproach them. But the Master of the world is present, so they hold back from transgression. This is the *peruta* with which they redeem themselves before God, enabling them to live in His world.

Rashi continues: "One was walking on the road"—under the heat of the burning sun, and he is famished and thirsty. "And he sees the first ripening figs at the tops of the trees"—ripe figs, bending downward, calling out to him, Come, take us and you will profit! "He reached his hand up to take, and is told that they belong to a Jew"—these figs are not yours, they have an owner, and it is forbidden for you to benefit from them. "He withdraws his hand because of theft. This is the meaning of 'hedged about with lilies.'"

Who said these words to the passerby? The King of the world, before whom he recites a *berakha*. The figs are sacred; they belong to the Almighty, who gave them to another, not to you. You may not steal them. But you are hungry and thirsty—and He knows this! This is the coin that the Creator demands from you: you may enjoy the figs once you reach your own vineyard.

The same phenomenon repeats itself every day, with respect to matters of Shabbat, *kashrut*, education, etc. The Master of the world expects us to ransom ourselves, to redeem ourselves. True, He does not demand much—no more than a penny, for what is this payment in comparison to the great privilege the Jew merits through observing the Torah and mitzvot?

THE SECOND PERUTA: HUMILITY AND ANONYMITY

The Master of the world brings an even greater sacrifice than the one mentioned above: His own disappearance. The Torah says, "This is My name forever" (Ex. 3:15), but "*le'olam*, forever," is spelled "*le'alem*, to be obscured" (Kiddushin 71a). The Holy One owns everything. He is Omnipresent; "the whole world is filled with His glory" (Is. 6:3). No place is devoid of Him. He renews the work of creation each day. He sustains all worlds, overtly and covertly. The entire natural order is subservient to Him, fulfilling His will.

Nevertheless, He conceals Himself and remains hidden. There is none like Him, yet He does not manifest Himself before all as the Lord of the world. When He appears, He is concealed in a thick cloud: "The Lord came down in a cloud." He is unseen; it is up to us to discover Him. Sometimes our brazenness toward God is superseded only by our foolishness, to the extent that we imagine that there is no Lord over us. Yet the Almighty is the most humble. "The Most High dwells in secret; in shadow dwells Shad-dai." This name, Shad-dai, implies that "His divinity is sufficient for Him" (see Rashi to Gen. 17:1). Indeed, His hiddenness stems from His *tzimtzum*, and His obscurity is another sacrifice He makes.

Man spends his "*peruta*" in his interactions with friends and others. Every human being longs for respect and admiration, recognition and fame. These aspirations are expressed especially in his desire to be remembered after his death, to gain a measure of eternity. He wants to be remembered by history. He wants schoolchildren to learn about him and memorize specific formative dates from his life, in keeping with the verse: "Their grave is their eternal home, the dwelling-place for all generations of those once famous on earth" (Ps. 49:12).

Along comes Judaism and demands anonymity from man. A Jew must always restrain himself. He must do his job and then vanish; he must not stand out. This is the penny ransom that a Jew must pay to the Creator, with which he redeems something worth far more than a penny, for with it he builds a great altar of self-negation: "For I am dust and ashes" (Gen. 18:27).

Consider: what do we know about the personal lives of the sages of the Jewish tradition? We had a sacred and authoritative institution whose members were called the Men of the Great Assembly ("*Anshei Knesset HaGedola*"). It was they who ensured that the Oral Torah would endure for all generations. Our sages said of the *Anshei Knesset HaGedola* that they "restored the crown to its glory." Rabbinic laws like *muktzeh* and *shevut*, which govern our observance of Shabbat, were conceived and enacted by the *Anshei Knesset HaGedola*. The *Anshei Knesset HaGedola* formulated our liturgy, the *berakhot*, and the recitations of *Kiddush* and *Havdala* over wine to mark the beginning and end of Shabbat.

But who were they? What were their personal stories? We know next to nothing about them. Only a few names have come down to us—Ezra the Scribe, Nehemiah, Shimon the Just—from a membership of 120. They did not seek to perpetuate their own names. They strove diligently to bring the Jewish people together and to crystalize the Oral Torah, and when they finished their tasks, they disappeared. When one of their number—Nehemiah—said "O God, remember it to my credit" (Neh. 13:31), the sages were displeased, for it is forbidden for a Jew to seek congratulations (Sanhedrin 93b).

What do we know about Rabban Yoḥanan ben Zakkai, Rabbi Akiva, Abaye, and Rava? What do we know about R. Yitzḥak Alfasi (Rif), R. Moshe ben Naḥman (Nahmanides), and their respective eras? What do we even know about the Vilna Gaon and R. Ḥayyim Volozhiner? Or about R. Ḥayyim Brisker and his son, my father? We have very few biographical details and almost no comprehensive biographies, whereas the nations of the world have many monumental works about their leading lights.

R. Ḥayyim Berlin tells that when a biography of Rabbi Akiva Eiger was published in 1862, R. Ḥayyim's father, the Netziv, did not even want to look at it. In R. Ḥayyim's words, which I cite here verbatim:

> He said that this is included in that which is said with respect to mourners: "We do not erect monuments to the righteous, for their words are their memory." What do I care when his birthday was, when he died, what he looked like, or whether he was like this or like that? The main thing is to pay attention to his words of Torah.

This paradoxical view is characteristically Jewish and flows from the depths of our moral consciousness.

The Mishna (Eduyot 1:4) speaks directly to this issue: "Why do we mention the rejected words of Shammai and Hillel? To teach future generations that they should not insist on their views, for our greatest patriarchs did not insist on their views." Why does the Mishna mention the views of the House of Shammai, which halakha does not follow, alongside the words of the House of Hillel, which it does? Why does it mention the words of an individual when he is opposed by a majority, which we follow? More generally, why are the sages of the Oral Torah even mentioned by name? Isn't mentioning names opposed to Judaism, which demands privacy, as it is written: "It is the glory of God to conceal a matter" (Prov. 25:2)? The main thing is the idea, the words of Torah themselves, not the names of those who utter them!

Rather, the reason that the House of Hillel, the House of Shammai, and other sages are mentioned in the Talmud is to model humility for us. When the majority of sages in the study hall decided against them, these individuals submitted and stopped fighting for their opinions. They did not keep struggling just to prove that they were right. If not for this reason, we would not know about the House of Shammai and the House of Hillel. The Mishna would state simply: one says that the *berakha* over wine is recited prior to the *berakha* on the day, and the other says that we first recite a *berakha* on the day, then on the wine, etc. The Talmud mentions the names of individuals only when necessary. In general, the final authority in a passage is cited anonymously.

"*Aḥerim omerim.*" "Others say." Do we know who these "others" that the Talmud cites are? On occasion, the Talmud asks, "Who are the 'others'?" But do we know who the *tanna kama*, the first, anonymously-cited sage of a Tannaitic statement, is? Or the *tanna batra*? Who were the *ḥasidim rishonim*? Who were the *tovlei shaḥarit*? They were all anonymous soldiers of the Jewish people who did not see fit to tell us anything about themselves. They came, they did their duty, and they vanished.

THE THIRD PERUTA: SILENCE AND THE ACCEPTANCE OF SUFFERING WITH LOVE

The third coin with which a Jew pays ransom to the Almighty in order to benefit from His world likewise is a form of *imitatio Dei*. The Talmud (Gittin 56b) states: "The academy of R. Yishmael taught: 'Who is like You among the mighty ones (*ba'elim*)?' (Ex. 15:11) means 'Who is like You among the mute (*ba'ilmim*)?'" Though God's might and power fill the world, He sees and hears the offenses of transgressors and responds with silence and infinite patience.

Likewise, the ransom that Israel pays to the Holy One is in the form of silence and patience. How so? We do not demand immediate answers to our questions about how He runs the world, even if the questions are acute and serious, pertaining to circumstances that seem completely absurd to us. If God were to demand an immediate answer to the question, "Why did you sin against Me?" the sinner would face immediate punishment. Yet the Holy One is slow to anger; He waits for the transgressor to repent.

We ask questions and seek answers, but one of the hermeneutical rules by which the Oral Torah is explicated is forbearance: "two verses that contradict one another until the third verse comes and decides between them." We Jews, who so excel in the art of questioning and refuting in the realm of halakha, nevertheless know that sometimes, in our private lives and in public life, we must refrain from posing questions.

We bless the Almighty and say "*Barukh Ata…*" not only for good and pleasurable things like a goblet of wine or a cluster of grapes, a wedding or circumcision, but also for the bad, over pain and suffering. We have cultivated the ability to serve God from within suffering, to discover Him even when a barrier of physical and psychological pain stands in the way. We have learned not to ask questions but to bless God for everything, with the exact same *berakha*. This is a distinctly Jewish trait. This is the *peruta* of ransom that we pay for our enjoyment and delight in God's world. What is harder and more painful than rending one's garments over the loss of a loved one? Yet we recite a blessing to God at that moment, "*Barukh Dayan ha'emet.*" "Blessed is the true Judge." A Jew scatters clumps of earth on a fresh grave, in which is buried that which was most precious, good, and beautiful to him in this world. And this bereft Jew declares: "*Yitgadal veyitkadash shmeh rabba.*" "May His great name be magnified and sanctified." In the throes of tragedy, the Jew seeks the Master of the world, just as he discovers Him when he experiences miraculous salvation.

Furthermore, Judaism demands a level of emotional discipline and psychological fortitude to an extent which can transcend human capabilities. One loses a parent, sibling, or spouse, God forbid, on the day before Pesaḥ, and the burial takes place that day. The grieving Jew returns home in the late afternoon, removes his shoes, and begins sitting *shiva*. His home is gloomy and desolate, attesting to the fresh loss of a loved one. The entire household wails with heartbreak.

Then the sun sets and the festival of Pesaḥ begins. Halakha suddenly commands the end of the mourning period: A festival cancels mourning. Light candles in honor of the holiday! Recite the *berakha* of *Sheheḥeyanu,* blessing God "who has given us life, sustained us, and brought us to this time"! Go to the synagogue, and upon your return, recline at the Seder like princes. Rejoice because God delivered our ancestors and delivers us. "This is the day that the Lord has made—let us exult and rejoice on it" (Ps. 118:24).

How can halakha demand such behavior? I accept many obligations that halakha imposes: Shabbat, *kashrut,* family purity, *tefillin,* and honesty in business. But how can halakha demand that I deny my grief? How can halakha expect me to recite *Hallel* while my soul is cloaked in heavy mourning? But this is what halakha demands. This is how we must behave. The Master of the world is "long-suffering," and we too must, to the degree possible, espouse this trait.

This can be illustrated with an actual event. It was the first night of Shavuot in Volozhin. The entire yeshiva was filled with light. Hundreds of students were sitting and learning Torah. Suddenly, the fatherly figure of the Netziv, Rabbi Naftali Tzvi Yehuda Berlin, appeared, and he called out: "*Rabbotai,* let us go dance in honor of the giving of the Torah."

The entire yeshiva, with the Netziv at the head, went out to dance in a sacred circle, with fiery passion. While they were dancing, an agent from the telegraph office ran over and handed the Netziv an open telegraph. He gave it a quick glance and then placed it in his pocket, saying, as an afterthought, "It's nothing; let's keep dancing." Thus, the entire holiday of Shavuot passed in Volozhin amid dancing, rejoicing, and celebration through Torah study. At the end of the festival, the Netziv made *Havdala*, concluding with the *berakha*, "Blessed are You … who separates the sacred from the profane." Suddenly, as the sanctity of the holiday vanished in that moment, the Netziv fainted. The telegraph that arrived on the first night of Shavuot had informed him of the death of his little sister.

This is a story of patience and forbearance. This is the greatest ransom that a Jew must pay to the Almighty; it is worth more than a *peruta*.

R. Avira expounded (Berakhot 20b):

> The ministering angels said before the Holy One: Master of the world, in Your Torah it is written "who shows favor to no one and takes no bribe" (Deut. 10:17), yet You show favor to Israel, as it is written "The Lord shall show favor to you" (Num. 6:26)? He replied to them: Should I not show favor to Israel? I wrote for them in the Torah: "You shall eat and be satiated, and you shall bless the Lord your God" (Deut. 8:10) [meaning that there is no obligation to bless the Lord until one is satiated]; yet they are meticulous even if they have eaten an olive-bulk or an egg-bulk.

"Showing favor," "*nesi'at panim*," literally means "lifting [one's] face toward." Showing favor means peering at and through another's face into his very soul. When Israel sins, the Holy One shows them favor; He does not examine their externalities, which have become profaned through impurity. Rather, His infinite gaze penetrates deep into the soul and character of Israel, and in the depths of its humanity He discovers that the innermost soul of Israel remains pure, unsullied by sin. The Holy One seeks, as it were, the sacred aspects of the Jew, and He finds them buried in the ashes of the profane.

Why, and on what merit, does He do so? Because this is how the Jewish people "showed favor" throughout its history. Even in the difficult times, when the Divine Presence was hidden, when everyone treated

Israel with fearsome cruelty, completely inundating them in grief and pain, they never demanded immediate answers to the piercing questions: Why? What for?

Even when a Jew is suffering, confined to his home, impoverished and despairing, when all his satiation consists of an egg-bulk or an olive-bulk of food, and sometimes without even these minimal amounts, he nevertheless recites passionately: "Blessed are You, Lord our God, King of the world, who nourishes the entire world with His beneficence, with grace, with kindness, and with compassion." This poor Jew places the Almighty before him always, and even shows Him favor.

Chapter 8

Communal Prayer and the Structure of the Synagogue

THE TEIVA IN WHICH THERE IS A TORAH SCROLL

Maimonides writes: "In the morning, the people are all seated and the *sheliaḥ tzibbur* goes before the ark (*teiva*) and stands in the midst of the people. He begins with the Kaddish and the people answer 'Amen, may the great name…'" (*Hilkhot Tefilla* 9:1). We need to understand Maimonides' reason for having the *sheliaḥ tzibbur* stand in the midst the people.

It appears that this rule can be understood on the basis of Maimonides' further comments:

> And they build within it [the synagogue] an ark (*heikhal*) in which they place a Torah scroll, and that ark is built to be in the direction they face while praying in that city, such that their faces will be opposite the ark when they rise in prayer… And when they set up the *teiva* in which there is a Torah scroll, they set it up in the middle, with the rear of the *teiva* toward the ark and its front toward the people. How do the people sit in the synagogue? The elders sit facing the people with their backs toward the *heikhal*, and all the people sit… such that the faces of all the people are toward the sanctuary (*kodesh*) and toward the elders and toward

> the *teiva*. And when the *sheliaḥ tzibbur* rises in prayer, he stands on the ground before the *teiva* with his face toward the sanctuary, just like the rest of the people (*Hilkhot Tefilla* 11:2–4).

Kesef Mishneh (*ad loc.*) comments that the *teiva* mentioned by Maimonides is not the holy ark but "a small wooden platform on which the Torah scroll is placed at the time for reading it." But that view is very problematic, and there is no doubt that the *teiva* is the holy ark, as Maimonides says: "the *teiva* in which there is a Torah scroll." Further proof can be adduced from a passage in Megilla (26b): "Rava said: A *teivuta* [Aramaic for *teiva*] that has decayed may be made into a small *teiva* [using the parts that remain sound] but may not be made into a *kursayya*" –which Rashi explains there (and earlier in the passage) is "a wooden platform" on which one generally "places a cloth and then places the Torah scroll on it."

From the fact that it is prohibited to turn a *teiva* into a reader's desk, it is clear that the *teiva*'s degree of sanctity exceeds that of the reader's desk. While each of them serves as a place for the Torah scroll, they differ in the nature and duration of the scroll's occupancy at that place: it resides regularly in the *teiva* but is located on the desk only while being read. Accordingly, when Maimonides refers to the *teiva* in connection with the rule that the level of sanctity to which resources are applied may be increased but not decreased (*Hilkhot Tefilla* 11:14), it must without doubt be the *teiva* in which the scroll is regularly placed, and that must be the case here as well.

Indeed, Maimonides' statement quoted above lends itself by its very terms to this interpretation. If there is no Torah scroll in the *teiva*, why should the *sheliaḥ tzibbur* stand near it while praying, for it is merely a wooden chest! And note *Hilkhot Taaniyyot* (4:1), where Maimonides reproduces the statement in the Mishna (at Taanit 15a) that the *teiva* is brought out to the city square and cinders are placed atop it (in times of severe drought). Where the Mishna reads "and they place cinders atop the *teiva*," Maimonides substitutes "and they place cinders atop the *teiva* and atop the Torah scroll." It is clear that he is speaking of a *teiva* in which there is a scroll.

Moreover, in *Hilkhot Lulav* (7:23) Maimonides writes with reference to circling the synagogue with the lulav: "And all Israel, wherever situated, have already adopted the custom of placing the *teiva* in the center of the synagogue and circling it each day [of Sukkot] as they circled the altar, in remembrance of the Holy Temple." Here, too, it seems obvious that the reference is to the *teiva* containing a Torah scroll, for an empty *teiva* cannot at all symbolize the altar and there would be no reason to circle it. In short, it is clear that when Maimonides uses the term "*teiva*," he means an ark in which the Torah scroll regularly resides.

This understanding implies that Maimonides took the view that there are two "arks" (*aronot*) in the synagogue. One, which he calls "*heikhal*" (sanctuary) or "*kodesh*" (holy), is the one "in the direction toward which they pray in that city"—that is, toward Jerusalem. That ark apparently never leaves its place and is never taken outside. The other, in which a Torah scroll also is placed, is situated in the middle of the synagogue. The *sheliaḥ tzibbur* stands before it, and it sometimes is brought out to the city square on fast days.

Further clarifying the matter, it appears that the ark fulfills two concepts. First, it completes the sanctity of the synagogue. In the Tabernacle and the Holy Temple, the Ark of the Covenant within the Holy of Holies made the holiness of the sanctuary complete. Here, correspondingly, the ark realizes an aspect of the form and sanctity of the synagogue. In writing about that realization, Maimonides chooses his words with precision: "and they build within it a sanctuary (*heikhal*) in which they place a Torah scroll, and that sanctuary is built in the direction toward which they face in that city while praying." In other words, building the sanctuary and the ark are an essential part of fashioning a synagogue. And see *Hilkhot Beit HaBeḥira* 1:5, where Maimonides writes: "And these are the essential matters in building the Temple: they make within it a Holy [chamber] and a Holy of Holies, and before the Holy there should be an area called the hall (*ulam*) and the three together are referred to as the Sanctuary (*heikhal*). Thus, the ark that Maimonides refers to as *heikhal* or *kodesh* corresponds to the Holy of Holies, the Holy [area], and the *ulam* in the Temple.

Second, there is a distinct law that the Israelites' camp should surround the Tabernacle; its source is the statement, in the account of the Israelites' travels through the desert, that "they encamp around the Tabernacle" (Num. 1:50). That was the law for later generations in

Jerusalem, for the city corresponds to the Israelites' camp and surrounds the Temple on all sides, and the rule applies as well to the synagogue, its structure, and its seating arrangements. In other words, the Israelites' camp was sanctified by their encampment around the Tabernacle, which, in turn, surrounded the Ark of the Covenant. In the synagogue too, therefore, the Torah scroll should be in the middle, for the Ark of the Covenant was at the center of the Israelites' encampment.

AN ASSEMBLY OF TEN

But it is remains necessary to understand why, in Maimonides' opinion, the *sheliaḥ tzibbur* was to stand in the middle, opposite the *teiva* situated there, and not before the *heikhal*, as is our practice. Moreover, what is the connection between the Torah scroll and prayer or *devarim shebikedusha*, and why should the *sheliaḥ tzibbur* stand before a Torah scroll in the first place, whether in accordance with our custom or Maimonides'?

To answer these questions, we should note Maimonides' words in *Hilkhot Tefilla* (8:5):

> They do not recite Kaddish except in a group of ten... for every group of ten Jews is called an "assembly" as Scripture says (Num. 14:27), "How long will this wicked assembly," and they numbered ten... and every sacred utterance must be amidst an assembly of Israel, as Scripture says (Lev. 22:32), "I will be sanctified amidst the Children of Israel."

Maimonides draws a parallel between a verse speaking of "amidst" and another speaking of "assembly." In his view, it seems, there is a substantive and logical parallel between "amidst" and "assembly," a view reflected in his precise wording: "every sacred utterance must be amidst an assembly of Israel." Still, we must consider the nature of that connection.

The explanation turns out to be quite simple. Scripture's decree that "I will be sanctified amidst the Children of Israel" conveys a particular halakha—that the sanctification of His great name, whether according to the simple meaning of the verse, in the sense of giving one's life for the sake of observing His commandments in a time of duress

(God save us from it), or in the sense of reciting a *davar shebikedusha,* requires the presence of all Israel. "Amidst the Children of Israel" means in a gathering of all Israel; His name is not sanctified unless the whole nation, Israel in its entirety, sanctifies it, and only when all of them are present can sanctification of His name, may it be blessed, occur. And so, Maimonides writes, "every *davar shebikedusha* must be amidst an assembly of Israel, as Scripture says, 'I will be sanctified amidst the Children of Israel'"—that is, amidst the nation in its entirety, along the lines of the verse "And the entire assembly of the Children of Israel will be forgiven" (Num. 15:26).

As a practical matter, however, that would be impossible in the generations following that of the wilderness, so a different halakha was set: the rubric of "assembly" applies to every grouping of ten Jews. And that is what Maimonides meant when he wrote, precisely, that "every group of ten Jews is called an 'assembly.'" But the group of ten is not the specific unit that, in itself, affords authorization for the recitation of *devarim shebikedusha*; rather, it is the agent and representative of all Israel. Anyone who recites Kaddish and *Kedusha* in a group of ten is considered to have sanctified His great name in the presence of the entire nation, for every grouping of ten is considered a miniature assembly symbolizing the presence of the entire congregation of Israel. And wherever a gathering of ten assembles, the entire congregation of Israel is considered to be present, and the *davar shebikedusha* is associated with all Israel.

THE FUNDAMENTAL NATURE OF PRAYER

If this seems to be correct with regard to *devarim shebikedusha,* it is indisputable with respect to prayer; however, we must first consider the fundamental nature of prayer and what its fulfillment entails. We begin with the passage in Berakhot 21a, in which R. Yoḥanan declares the rule of voluntary (as distinct from obligatory) prayer: "would that a man prayed the whole day long." The *Rishonim* offered differing understandings of this statement. Rabad wrote:

> I am of a different opinion on all this, for when R. Yoḥanan said "would that a man prayed the whole day long," he was referring only to the *Shemoneh Esreh* [eighteen-blessing weekday *Amida*],

> comprising pleas… But R. Yoḥanan was not there referring to the [seven-blessing] *Amida* for Sabbaths and festivals, which comprises only praises." (Comment on Maimonides, *Hilkhot Tefilla* 1:9)

In his view, then, voluntary prayer is grounded in the concept of prayer as pleading—along the lines of the Gemara's comment with respect to making up a statutory prayer whose time has passed: "since prayer is supplication for mercy, a man may go on praying as long as he likes" (Berakhot 26a). But Maimonides (*ad loc.*), following Rif (Berakhot ch. 3, Rif 13a), offered a different explanation: "If a man wishes to pray all day, he is permitted to do so, and all the prayers he adds are as if he brought voluntary animal offerings." In his view, voluntary prayer parallels the bringing of voluntary sacrifices and is grounded in the possibility of bringing such sacrifices.

It appears that "both are the word of the living God," for prayer entails two separate essential qualities, both contained within the term "service of the heart." The first is a plea for mercy, which flows from man's experience of exhaustion and weariness, his sense that he is a poor, downtrodden creature, powerless to save himself, to solve his problems, or satisfy his needs, be they spiritual or physical. Man knows that even if he dwells in royal palaces, his life hangs by a thread. In this way, King David turns to God with "the prayer of a sufferer when he is faint and pours out his plea before the Lord" (Ps. 102:1). This notion of absolute reliance on the Holy One Blessed be He, rooted in the recognition that if, God forbid, He fails to come to man's aid, man will be eternally lost, constitutes one element of prayer, expressed in full force in one of the *Shir HaMaalot* psalms: "Unto You I lift up my eyes, who dwells in heaven; behold, like the eyes of servants toward their masters, like the eyes of a maidservant toward her mistress, so are our eyes toward the Lord our God, until He favors us" (Ps. 123:1–2).

The second element is sacrifice. Prayer encompasses a realization of sacrifice, and the worshipper stands in the place of the person bringing the sacrifice. When R. Joshua b. Levi said that "they instituted [the *Amida*] prayers to correspond to the daily sacrifices" (Berakhot 26b), he meant not merely to note that prayers were a substitute for sacrifices but to determine that they themselves were like actual sacrifices. This is shown by the law that on certain occasions—such as when one is drunk or needs to relieve himself—a man's prayer is *"to'eiva,* an abomination" (see Berakhot 22b; Eruvin 64a). The term *"to'eiva"* is not used in the context of other commandments, where a failed effort to perform is characterized as "invalid" (*pasul*) or the individual is referred to as "not having discharged his obligation." Only in the context of sacrifices is the term used, quintessentially in the phrase "the sacrifice of the wicked is an abomination," and if we encounter it as well in relation to prayer, it is because prayer, too, is a form of sacrifice. Similarly, the priests' obligation to bless the community is tied, in the Temple, to the sacrificial service and, outside the Temple, to prayer (see Y. Taanit 4:1; Maimonides, *Hilkhot Tefilla U'Nesiat Kappayim* 14:14).

Were you to ask me what the worshipper sacrifices, I would answer "himself." "Service of the heart" means not only service through and within the heart but also sacrifice of the heart. The heart sacrifices itself, in the manner of "May my prayer be as incense before You, my lifted palms as an evening sacrifice" (Ps. 141:2). Man's body, spirit, soul—everything he possesses—belong to the Holy One Blessed be He, and man, through prayer, returns God's property to Him.

Maimonides explains these two elements early in his treatment of the laws of prayer. He writes:

> And when Ezra and his court recognized this [that the Jews in Babylonian exile had lost the ability to compose their prayers properly], they arose and established for them eighteen ordered blessings, the first three... and the middle ones contain pleas for all things and encompass overall categories of individual and communal needs. And they also determined that there would be as many prayers as there were sacrifices (*Hilkhot Tefilla* 1:4–5).

This duality of prayers as pleading and prayers as the bringing of a sacrifice is apparent in the very wording of the prayers. In the *Shemoneh Esreh,* we recite two successive blessings that, at first glance, appear redundant: *Shema koleinu* ("Hear our voice") and *Retzeh* ("Be pleased, O Lord our God, with Your people Israel and their prayers"). Why is this plea repeated? Because *Shema koleinu* concludes the sequence of the middle, petitionary blessings, while *Retzeh* transforms the prayer into a sacrifice, for the concept of causing God to be pleased relates to sacrifices. Each aspect requires its own plea for acceptance of the prayer.

It follows that, according to Rif and Maimonides—who are of the view that voluntary prayer is rooted in the possibility of free-will sacrifices—the conclusion to be drawn is that when one prays a voluntary prayer, it is like bringing a free-will sacrifice, and when one prays one of the obligatory prayers, it is like bringing a mandatory communal sacrifice, that is, the regular daily offering. This was instituted by the Men of the Great Assembly, as Maimonides writes (*ibid.*): "The two daily prayers correspond to the two daily offerings ... and they likewise instituted one prayer at night, for the organs of the animal sacrificed as the daily offering were burned throughout the night ..."

Still, one might ask, how can an individual perform a mandatory communal sacrifice, which could only be brought from communal funds in the name of all Israel? Moreover, how can a congregation pray even an obligatory prayer, given that ten Jews could not bring the regular daily offering, which was owned and could be brought only by all Israel? Given these constraints, how can prayer be regarded as paralleling sacrifice?

The answer is clear. We have already explained, in connection with *devarim shebikedusha,* that the determinative factor is not the group of ten physically present in one place; rather, it is the invocation of all Israel as represented by that group. A *davar shebikedusha* recited in a particular place by a congregation of ten individuals is regarded as having been pronounced by all Israel in unison. That is the rule of "I will be sanctified amidst the Children of Israel": wherever any congregation of Israel is present, the congregation of all Israel is present.

Our explanation is adequate with respect to *devarim shebikedusha,* which lend themselves to being attributed, wherever and whenever recited, not merely to congregation X in place Y, but to all Israel. And even if one thousand *devarim shebikedusha* are recited by one thousand congregations in one thousand places, each of them can be credited to all Israel. But seeing prayer in that light leads to a strange and radical conclusion—that each and every time a congregation in a particular place prays, its prayer is regarded as the prayer of all Israel and as a regular daily sacrifice, in accord with the verse, "May my prayer be as incense before You, my lifted palms as an evening sacrifice." If so, it follows that all Israel each day brings thousands of regular daily offerings—something clearly unimaginable.

With respect to prayer, accordingly, we must willy-nilly modify the formulation: all the prayers of the congregations of Israel, in all their dwelling-places, become commingled into a single communal prayer, in which all Israel is enmeshed, and that one united prayer is accepted as a single and unique regular daily offering, morning and evening. With respect to *devarim shebikedusha*, we could say that each and every *Kedusha* constitutes a unique entity attributed to all Israel. That possibility is unavailable with respect to prayer in general, however, where we must take the position that all the many communal prayers are blended into a single prayer. "I will be sanctified amidst the Children of Israel" is then carried out by each congregation of worshippers not as an independent unit but as participants in the universal prayer. In contrast to *devarim shebikedusha*, the attribution of "all Israel" to each group of ten does not lead to multiplicity of prayers. Only a single prayer, parallel to the single regular daily offering, rises up from Israel as a whole.

It further appears that, in the context of prayer, even an individual's prayer is accepted as that of the congregation, for the individual's prayer could not otherwise become mandatory prayer in the sense of a mandatory community sacrifice. An individual may not bring a regular daily sacrifice, so we must infer that the individual's prayer also is caught up with the congregational prayers, and all of them together are transformed into a single prayer of all Israel. In that respect, there is a fundamental distinction between voluntary prayer and obligatory prayer. Voluntary prayer is individual from beginning to end. It corresponds to the individual sacrifice, brought as a voluntary gift, and counts and is accepted as an individual's prayer. Statutory prayer, in contrast, even when recited by an individual, is accepted as the prayer of the community, for it was instituted to correspond to the regular daily sacrifice. Taking the place of the sacrifice, it, too, is unique. In the blessing *Shema koleinu*—pertaining, as noted above, to petitionary prayer—we say that God "hears prayers and pleadings," in the plural, but also that He "hears the prayer of Your people Israel with mercy," referring, in the singular, to the prayer of Israel as a whole. In the blessing *Retzeh*, however, in which the rubric of sacrifice is applied to prayer, we refer, in the singular, to one prayer alone: "Be pleased, O Lord our God, with Your people Israel and its prayer... and the burnt offerings of Israel and its prayer be pleased to accept with love." Communal prayer is distinct in that not only is it accepted as the prayer of all Israel but in it the very act of praying also becomes a collective act. By dint of the scriptural decree "I will be sanctified amidst the Children of Israel," which makes each grouping of ten or more into a representative of all Israel, the act of a group of ten that pray is conjoined with the entire nation, and those who pray congregationally throughout the world are amalgamated into a community and take part in the self-same prayer.

The essence of prayer as an entity is public prayer, that is, the prayer of all Israel. Individual prayer is something that the community does not participate in and that does not constitute an act of communal worship. Israel as a whole is implicated in the prayer of a group of ten, for, by law, they represent the entire congregation of Israel; but there is no such intertwining in solitary prayer, which remains the action of an individual. Still, that distinction does not affect the pleased acceptance of the prayer before God. Even an individual's prayer is combined with that of the many, and, like a sacrifice, it ascends with all the prayers of Israel and the Holy One Blessed be He accepts it as part of all Israel's great prayer. The individual's prayer is combined with that of the whole not on the level of action and deed, but on the level of acceptance; on that level, the individual's prayer is intertwined with all the other prayers of Israel, and the Holy One Blessed be He, who hears the prayer of His people Israel with love, accepts it as well, for "He did not despise or abhor the lowliness of the poor" (Ps. 22:25) and "He turned to the prayer of the destitute and did not despise their prayer" (Ps. 102:18).

ONE SHOULD JOIN HIMSELF WITH THE COMMUNITY

Let us now turn to a passage at the end of the Talmudic chapter *Tefillat HaShaḥar*: "Abayye said, 'One should always join his soul with that of the community'" (Berakhot 29b). The Gemara there cites this statement in connection with the wording of the traveler's prayer, which is to be recited in the plural. Maimonides observes that "Communal prayer is always heard, and even if there are sinners among them, the Holy One Blessed be He does not despise the prayer of the multitude; accordingly, one should join himself with the community" (*Hilkhot Tefilla* 8:1). But the context of Maimonides' comment makes it apparent that, unlike the

Gemara, he is not dealing with the wording of the prayer, and we must ascertain what he means when he speaks of "joining." In light of what we have said, that becomes clear: the worshipper must intend that his prayer become amalgamated with that of the congregation, for without that amalgamation, his prayer cannot be accepted as a sacrifice. Note also the related observation earlier in the Gemara:

> R. Isaac said to R. Naḥman, "For what reason did my master not come to the synagogue to pray?" He said to him, "I was unable to." He said to him, "My master should have gathered ten [to his home] and prayed [with them]." He said to him, "Doing that would be difficult." "My master could tell the *sheliaḥ tzibbur* to notify my master when the congregation prays." He said to him, "What would be the purpose of that?" He said to him, "As R. Yoḥanan said in the name of R. Simeon bar Yoḥai, what is the significance of the verse 'As for me, may my prayer to You, Lord, be at an acceptable time' (Ps. 69:14)? What is an acceptable time? The time when the community is praying."

This, too, demonstrates the linkage between the acceptance of individual prayer and the acceptance of communal prayer.

This notion provides a basis for resolving a seeming anomaly in the viewpoint of Rif and Maimonides, noted above. They write that one may not pray a voluntary *Musaf* service because the community could not volunteer a *musaf* sacrifice; yet, as many have pointed out, the community cannot volunteer a regular daily sacrifice, but that does not stand in the way of allowing a person to pray a voluntary *Shaḥarit* or *Minḥa* service, which corresponds to a voluntary *olah* sacrifice. Why should *Musaf* differ? There, too, we might say that he may pray a voluntary prayer as if he were bringing an individual's voluntary *olah*, even though the *Amida* was instituted to correspond to the communal sacrifice.

In light of our analysis, the answer is clear. Voluntary prayer differs from mandatory prayer in that it is not commingled with the community's worship. It is in its entirety an individual's prayer, rendered as such and accepted as such; it is feasible because the Holy One Blessed be He does not only hear prayer, He hears prayers. In no way is it a realization of the regular daily sacrifice; rather, it is a realization of an individual's *olah* sacrifice.

All of this is possible only in the *Shaḥarit* and *Minḥa* prayers, whose texts themselves make no reference to the sacrifices to which the prayers correspond. Accordingly, the prayer can be transformed into something corresponding to an individual's sacrifice. In the *Amida*'s *Retzeh* blessing, to be sure, we ask that our prayers be considered and accepted as a sacrifice and as worship, but we do not specify the nature and character of the sacrifice referred to. The *Retzeh* blessing usually transforms the prayer, through commingling, into an obligatory communal sacrifice; but it sometimes transforms it into an individual's sacrifice. In the *Musaf* prayer, in contrast, we mention the nature of the sacrifice to which the prayer corresponds; and *Tosafot* note in this regard that a missed *Musaf* prayer may not be made up later (as a missed *Shaḥarit* or *Minḥa* may) because "the seven blessings of *Musaf* were instituted only for the sake of (Hos. 14:3) 'we render for bullocks the offering of our lips'" (*Tosafot*, Berakhot 26a, s.v. *Iba'aya*), i.e., the *Musaf* prayer was instituted only to fulfill the obligation of the *musaf* sacrifice. Accordingly, the *Retzeh* blessing transforms the prayer into a communal *musaf* sacrifice; the *Musaf* prayer simply cannot be transformed into a voluntary individual sacrifice, for its entire content is at odds with that. And that is why Maimonides and Rif ruled that this prayer cannot be offered voluntarily.

But despite the connection between them, individual prayer must still be distinguished from communal prayer. The merging of communal prayer into a single act of worship akin to the regular daily offering, on the one hand, and, on the other hand, the integration of an individual's prayer with that of the community are tied to two distinct factors. The individual's prayer, though not set forth amidst the congregation and though the worshippers do not represent a congregation, is nevertheless accepted with grace and love together with the other prayers because of a specific halakha, the primary subject of King Solomon's prayer: "That Your eyes be open to this house [the *Beit HaMikdash*] night and day, to the place of which You said My name will always be present there, to hear the prayer that Your servant will direct toward this place; and You will hear the plea of Your servant and Your people Israel, which they will direct to this place" (I Kings 8:29). The import of the passage, which underlies the halakhic conclusion, is that the Temple is the place where prayers are received, as the passage goes on to explain: "They will pray to You via their land, which You gave to their ancestors; the city that You chose; and the house that You built for Your name" (I Kings 8:48). It follows that every man must direct his face—or, at least, his heart—toward the city and the Temple, as explained in the *baraita* at Berakhot 30a and in Maimonides, *Hilkhot Tefilla* 5:3.

Note also Maimonides' comment that "All should pray toward the Temple, wherever they might be" (*Hilkhot Tefilla* 1:3). His remarks imply—and the point is something of a novel one—that the obligation to face toward Jerusalem and the Temple predated the legislation on prayer of the Men of the Great Assembly, described later in halakhot 4–7, and appears to constitute a Torah-law (*deoraita*) obligation with respect to prayer. The nature of this law at first appears problematic, but it makes perfect sense, given the foregoing. The Temple is the place where prayer and sacrifice are pleasingly received, and all prayers are accepted only via the city of Jerusalem and the Temple. Given that, the joining and amalgamation of prayers can be carried out only by directing them to a single place, the Temple, where God's presence is to be found.

While Maimonides rules that directing one's face toward Jerusalem is not a *sine qua non* of discharging the obligation to pray, we may say that directing one's heart is a *sine qua non*. It is part of the worshipper's obligation to regard himself as if he is standing before God's presence, as may be inferred from Maimonides' comment that "a blind person, and one unable to know which direction is which, and one traveling on shipboard, should direct his heart toward God's presence" (*Hilkhot Tefilla* 4:3). The Mishna states that in such cases, "He should direct his heart to the Holy of Holies" (Berakhot 28b), but Maimonides seems to have chosen his words carefully so as to explain that this halakha is within the rubric of the obligation to direct one's heart toward God's presence. Such direction is a *sine qua non*, as Maimonides explains in defining the necessary intention: "What is [proper] intention [in prayer]? That he clear his heart of all thoughts and regard himself as if he is standing before God's presence" (*Hilkhot Tefilla* 4:16); and if that is the case, it may be the rule with respect to directing one's heart toward Jerusalem and the Temple.

This factor is what bonds individuals' prayers to those of the community and permits their acceptance as a sacrifice. For communal prayer, however, where the act of praying itself is associated with all

Israel, directing one's face and heart toward Jerusalem does not suffice. For the act of prayer itself to subsume and integrate all Israel into it, a special amalgamating force is needed—namely, a Torah scroll.

Consider this passage in the seventh chapter of Berakhot: "R. Huna said: 'Nine [men] and the ark join [to form a *minyan*].' R. Naḥman said to him: 'Is the ark a person?' Rather, R. Huna said: 'Nine who appear as ten join...'" (Berakhot 47b). It seems obvious that R. Huna never meant to say that the ark is included among the ten. What he meant was that the ark, containing the Torah scroll, joins the nine who are present with all Israel, for the Torah scroll unites the dispersed of Israel. And it is interesting—as *Tosafot* (48a, s.v. *veleit*) point out—that what R. Naḥman firmly rejected was, in fact, accepted as halakha with respect to declaring a leap year:

> [A court of] three may declare a leap year. R. Eliezer says [it must be] ten, as Scripture says, "God stands in the congregation of God" [Ps. 82:1], but if there are fewer, they bring a Torah scroll and spread it out before them. They arrange themselves in a semi-circle, sitting in order of seniority... (*Pirkei DeRabbi Eliezer*, chapter 8).

We rule according to our passage in Berakhot that the Torah scroll cannot merge the group of nine with all Israel, but it appears that the principle implicit in R. Huna's remarks applies to a group of ten as well. Because they comprise a congregation, and the rule of "I will be sanctified amidst the Children of Israel" applies to them, they are joined with all Israel so that the prayers of all will constitute a single prayer and a single communal sacrifice. That amalgamation is accomplished through the means of a Torah scroll, which has the capacity to combine all the wandering and dispersed of Israel into a single entity that presents the sound of pure, unsullied prayer.

(We are speaking, of course, of the ideal situation; the presence of a Torah scroll is certainly not a necessary condition. It may be added that the practice of the *sheliaḥ tzibbur* holding a Torah scroll while announcing and blessing the new month on the preceding Sabbath reflects the fact that declaring the new moon is dependent on all Israel, and the local congregation in which the announcement is made is acting not on its own but as part of all Israel. Accordingly, the Torah scroll is the appropriate amalgamating factor.)

In light of what we have said, the practice of the *sheliaḥ tzibbur* praying before the ark containing a Torah scroll can be understood perfectly, as can Maimonides' view that he stands before the *teiva* rather than before the *heikhal*. Praying in the presence of the Torah scroll is necessary because it is the scroll that joins this congregation and its act of prayer to all Israel. By way of that connection, and in view of Maimonides' understanding that "I will be sanctified amidst the Children of Israel" teaches that every group of ten represents all Israel, this congregational prayer is linked with that of every congregation praying anywhere in the world, and they are amalgamated into a single prayer—not only with respect to the acceptance of the prayer before God but also with respect to the very act and entity of prayer. It likewise can be understood why, in Maimonides' view, the *sheliaḥ tzibbur* stands before the *teiva* rather than before the *heikhal* even though each contains a Torah scroll. As explained in *Pirkei DeRabbi Eliezer*, when they are amalgamated by means of the Torah scroll, they form a sort of semi-circle—the Torah scroll in the middle, and all the assembled surrounding it. Since the Torah scroll serves as the amalgamating factor in the congregation, it stands to reason that the people gather around it, with the scroll in the middle. And that is the practice as well in the synagogue during congregational prayer, as Maimonides writes: "The order of congregational prayer is as follows: In the morning, all the people are seated, and the *sheliaḥ tzibbur* goes down before the *teiva* and stands in the midst of the people."

Chapter 9

The Synagogue as an Institution and as an Idea

1.

The synagogue nowadays is not the most popular institution in the Jewish community. When I say Jewish community, I have in mind not the secular but the religious community, the community which is concerned with man not only as a biological but as a transcendental being as well. However, even the religious or searching community, whose members logically should have flocked in droves to the synagogue, is not too much in love with it. The activities and interests of this community do not revolve about the synagogue. The members of this community stay away from the synagogue.

There are a variety of reasons responsible for this paradoxical phenomenon and I wish to enumerate some of them.

First, the unpopularity of the synagogue is the result of the anti-establishment mood of our times. This rebellious frame of mind has precipitated, sometimes in a frightening way, an upsurge of shallow, amorphous emotionalism, which rejects religious institutionalism and objectivism.

Second, the commitment to the State of Israel, which the Diaspora Jew has accepted willingly, overshadows all our commitments to local institutions. The impact of that commitment upon the Western

Jew, the completely alienated Jew, but who is still committed to Judaism, leads him, as far as charity is concerned, to assign the major part of his charity money to the State of Israel and its institutions while the synagogue comes second.

Third, we rabbis are not without blame either. The American Jew of twenty or thirty years ago, at the time I arrived on these shores, was ceremony- and protocol-minded as far as the synagogue was concerned. He was almost a prisoner of rigid decorum and inflexible social mores. The personality of the American Jew of that period was two-dimensional, flat. He was straight, without twists, without bends and turns. I am referring lo the average American Jew. He was basically naive, like the American in general. He was simple and open-minded, and he was a sturdy personality. He liked the decorum of the synagogue, the solemnity, the formality, and the dramatic character of the service.

The young man of today is a complex personality. There is no simplicity to him. With his critical, sophisticated approach, he feels alienated from a scrupulously well-organized synagogue. The young man of today is volatile, very excitable; his emotionalism is not deep-rooted. He would like to attend a service which is more fervent and less fixed. He would also like to see the synagogue become a house of study rather than just a house of prayer. The young Jew is curious and sensitive. Somehow, I believe that we rabbis have a share in the process of alienation of the young religious Jew from the synagogue by not reacting to his needs.

The unpopularity of the synagogue in the American Jewish community, the young community, expresses itself in a variety of ways. First, young couples do not care to join the neighborhood congregation. Like nomads, they wander from synagogue to synagogue, displaying impatience with all and liking none.

Second, the religious, observant Jew, the young Jew in America, is not overly concerned nowadays with *tefilla betzibbur*. Even fully committed Jews do not care to attend services daily; even those who can afford, in terms of time, to come to *shul* will avail themselves of any pretext in order to explain their absence from the morning services; how much more difficult it is to get a *minyan* for *Minḥa* and *Maariv*, especially in the wintertime.

Years ago one who lived in a Jewish neighborhood was surrounded by many synagogues, and each synagogue used to have three *minyanim* in the morning, *minyanim* in the afternoon, and there was no problem. The Jews of that day were not consistent. They were not very observant, and still they used to come to shul. Now even in an area where there is a strong, well-organized religious, Jewish community, young Jews, professionals, intellectuals, who come to *shiurim*, do not come to *Minḥa*. Furthermore, the most difficult problem which the educators in the day schools face is to train the children to attend morning services. The majority of the children are not present at the morning services.

The children *daven* at home, but they do not come to *minyan*. Of course, there are many extenuating circumstances. In the winter it is difficult to get up so early and arrive in time for the *minyan*. The main reason that the child does not come is that he does not see his father do so. The American Jew, even the religious Jew, does not consider *tefilla betzibbur* important.

This unpopularity expresses itself in yet another way. The approach to the synagogue as an institution on the part of many young, religious Jews is a cynical one. Quite often one hears them mock the synagogue as well as its rabbi. Of course, the young generation of today is very intolerant and sits in judgment over middle-aged and old mortals. They never take into consideration the difficulties which the rabbi encounters in his quite often heroic efforts to protect the traditional character of the synagogue.

2.

Is there a cure? Is there a way to resolve this problem? I do not know; I have no solution to offer. However, I believe that a deeper understanding of the synagogue as an idea, not only as an institution, is required. To understand the synagogue as an institution is easy. However, institutions are nurtured by ideas. Behind every stable, fixed, standardized, institution, there is a beautiful idea, a great vision, and a great experience. No one has ever tried simply to explain the synagogue to people as an idea, as a vision rather than as an institution. Such an explanation might be helpful. We have seen how rabbis and *baalei batim*, while overemphasizing the institutional character of the synagogue, have completely neglected to bring out the idea, or *weltanschauung*, which lies at the very root of the institution. We simply did not explain to the young people what *tefilla* is and what *Beit HaKnesset*, the house dedicated to prayer, means, and how deeply rooted these ideas are in our philosophy of man and his destiny.

Basically, *tefilla* reflects the Judaic philosophy of man, the paradoxality, the exciting vision of man and also the tragedy of man. The greatness and the smallness of man are both reflected in *tefilla*, in the idea of the *Beit HaKnesset*. And in my lecture tonight, I shall attempt to explain two ideas which underlie prayer in general and the institution of the *Beit HaKnesset* in particular.

3.

Let me start immediately with two postulates. First, man is in exile. Man is a homeless being. Second, exiled man, or homeless man, must pray; he has a strong need to pray; through prayer he redeems himself from his loneliness.

I wish to explain these two premises. When we use the word exile, we immediately, by mere association, think of the Jew. Exile, as a historical experience, is known only to the Jew. No other nation has ever led an exilic existence. I do not mean to say that there have been no population shifts in general history, and that no other people has ever been displaced from its native soil. The opposite is true. History is full of accounts of mass population movements or *völkerwanderungen*. Yet no movement of populations from one country to another resulted in an exile experience in the manner in which we Jews have felt it.

It is self-evident with regard to any immigration that the first generation of immigrants, or exiles, suffers from a sense of alienation and loneliness. The immigrants, particularly in a case in which the immigration was not voluntary but coercive, feel homeless and displaced for a while. However, with the passage of time the nostalgia of the immigrants subsides. Everyone who has come here from across the ocean can confirm this experience. The sense of dislocation and estrangement disappears gradually. The commitment to the old country weakens. Images and memories are extinguished piecemeal and with their slow extinction, the experience of exile disappears. As a rule, for there are exceptions, the second and third generations know nothing of the old country, of the bond between their parents or grandparents and the native soil they left behind. The new country is home. The old one sinks into oblivion and becomes the forgotten land.

The Jews behaved differently. It is very hard to guess how they managed to do it, but somehow they did manage to preserve their historical identity as a people and to maintain a very strong sentimental relationship to a land from which they were exiled nineteen hundred years ago. That we have maintained such a relationship, or rather commitment, is best proven by the State of Israel. Without that strange commitment, a nineteen-hundred-year-old commitment, to a land from which we were exiled, the State of Israel would have never come into existence.

The Jew has beheld, and still beholds, a messianic vision. He has awaited, and he is still awaiting, the arrival of the Redeemer and the triumphant return to a Promised Land. The Jew has never forgotten the promise. The Jew in the Middle Ages, in the dark and narrow ghettos, the Jew of the Renaissance period, the Jew of the Reformation era and that of the Age of Reason, the Jew of the capitalist society, of modern times, and the contemporary Jew of communist society, whose parents were agnostics and atheists, whose grandparents fought together with Lenin and Trotsky and Bukharin, for socialism and the Marxist millennium—the Jew in all those periods could not forget the promise of return. While praying, he has turned, and he still turns, his face toward that mysterious country, a land he never visited, never saw, whose climate is alien to him, and whose rocks radiate an oppressive heat which the Nordic Jew cannot tolerate. Yet in spite of everything, he managed to maintain the commitment. He never forgot the strange land; he longed and craved for it. It is odd, but the Jew, who is a realist, clever and pragmatically minded, turned into a dreamer whenever the name of that promised, mysterious, unknown land was mentioned. He adored her and surrounded her with a transcendental halo. That is the reason why the experience of exile would last for hundreds and thousands of years.

As an exile, the Jew prayed; his homelessness cried out of his very being. If you analyze the *Shemoneh Esreh*, six of the eighteen or nineteen benedictions are concerned with one burning passion, with one strong desire, the termination of the exile.

4.

Judaism says that not only the Jew is in exile, but that man as such, man in general, leads an exilic existence. As we said above, when we speak of exile in historical terms, the Jewish experience is unique. However, if we approach the idea of exile, of *galut*, from an existential, metaphysical viewpoint, then the *galut* experience is a universal one, shared by all men. Our exile, or exile experience, is a reflection of the universal metaphysical exile awareness with which man—not only the Jew—is burdened. Man was cursed by the Almighty and expelled from Paradise and became a homeless being.

Contemporary philosophy is concerned with the fate and destiny of man in general and his loneliness experience in particular. Before the First World War, philosophy was asking about the nature of the universe: space, time, quantity, quality, causality were the categories with which philosophy operated. But in the 1920s, philosophy decided that instead of asking what the world is, one should rather ask the old Socratic question: who am I? In fact, existentialism is nothing but an attempt on the part of man to understand himself and his fellow man, and inject a little bit of rationality into his existential awareness, because this awareness is quite often fraught with tragic absurdities.

5.

This question, which modern philosophy asks, has been answered by Judaism a long time ago. The Psalmist already declared: "*ger anokhi imakh, toshav kekhol avotai,* I am a stranger with You, a sojourner, as all my fathers were" (Ps. 39:13). I am a stranger, I am a homeless being. I am in exile, even though "*toshav kekhol avotai,*" I have lived for so many years on this globe.

Man is homeless because he was expelled from his Paradisiacal home, and he, like the historical Jew with regard to the Promised Land, has never forgotten that once upon a time, so many millennia ago, he lived in Paradise. Of course, he lost it; however, he has not forgotten it. Man's home has been, and still is, the Paradise upon which God showers so much beauty and grace. Outside of Paradise, man finds himself lost in the vast spaces and boundless distances of an unknown, strange, and frightening world, which is at best indifferent and at worst hostile toward man.

Judaism looked upon man from a dialectical viewpoint. Hence, his homelessness should also be understood in a dialectical manner. On one hand, man is a great being and he is homeless in his greatness. Human homelessness and human greatness merge into one existential awareness. On the other hand, man is a small, helpless being, a fallen being, and he is homeless in his smallness. Human homelessness and human smallness merge into one existential awareness.

The question, now, is: What is the homelessness which man experiences when he thinks of himself as a great being, as a proud being, as a genius, as a demi-god; how does he then experience his homelessness? Likewise, we are curious to know, how does man experience his homelessness when he thinks of himself as a little being, as a small being, when he is dejected and despondent? How does he then experience his solitude? Let us explain.

Man experiences his homelessness as a small being, in the human reality called vulnerability; man is, as just stated, exposed to all the vicissitudes of an environment that, at best, is unconcerned and indifferent. This feeling of being vulnerable, of being exposed, is the feeling of homelessness.

Man is an exposed being. He is exposed to disease and he is exposed to death. Of course, the beast is also exposed. The beast of the field is also vulnerable. However, the beast is not homeless. Even a stray dog is not a homeless dog because a beast knows nothing and does not anticipate anything. Man is aware of himself and his environment and anticipates events; since he has an awareness of time and he looks forward to the future, he is conscious of his vulnerability. We speak quite often of our desire to achieve security, but total security is unattainable, since the very awareness of man is fraught with a feeling of insecurity.

How, then, can we speak of a home for man if the home fails to provide him with security? The Song of Songs (3:7–8) depicts the hall with the litter, or bed, of Solomon, guarded by "threescore mighty men, of the mighty men of Israel, all handle the sword and are expert in war," yet every man has his sword upon his thigh, because of the dread in the night, "*mipaḥad baleilot*."

I remember how, as a little boy, I was studying with my *rebbe Shir HaShirim*, and when we came across this passage I asked him, "What is the dread in the night, *mipaḥad baleilot*?" He did not answer me.

But the question nevertheless kept bothering my mind. I came home and I asked my mother, "What is *mipaḥad baleilot*? What is the dread in the night?" My mother didn't answer me. She told me, "Read *Shema,* and go to bed." When she tucked me in, I forgot the dread in the night.

But what is indeed "the dread in the night"? Who is afraid? Who takes so many security measures in order to protect himself against the mysterious dread in the night? King Solomon is afraid. King Solomon is afraid of the dread of night? King Solomon has no mother to tuck him in. If he is afraid, he cannot overcome his fear. He experiences distress.

Who is King Solomon? King Solomon is modern man, wise and powerful man, ingenious, an expert in all fields of science and technological research, who sends off a manned vehicle to the moon; his computations are almost flawless. He, modern man, Solomon, is afraid *mipaḥad baleilot,* of "the dread in the night." King Solomon is powerful; why, then, is he afraid? His men are indeed mighty men, expert in war. Nevertheless he is afraid. All the mighty men do not make King Solomon secure and safe. He is as insecure, despite his mighty warriors, as the poor shepherd in the Galilean hills. And this fear, the dread of the night, has not yet been alleviated. Man can send a vehicle to the moon, but what does the wise, mighty, sophisticated, technology-minded King Solomon do if he comes face to face with the fear of the night—a degenerative disease?

Our evening and morning prayers reflect our fright in the night and our joy in the morning. In the evening, we recite the blessing "*Barukh Hashem le'olam amen ve'amen,*" whose central phrase is "*be-yadkha afkid ruḥi,* I entrust my spirit to Thee." Man surrenders his total existence to God. Man is ready to bring the supreme sacrifice. The fear in the night manifests itself in the recital. The Jew accepts God's inscrutable will. He does not know whether God's grace will be bestowed upon him and that he indeed will rise from his slumber. When he does rise in the morning, he recites with a happy mind the prayer *Elokai neshama shenatata bi.* Man is a happy and surprised person. There is an element of excitement and wonder in that blessing. God bestowed a precious gift upon him—a new life. He praises the Almighty for every heartbeat and every activity he can engage in. The dread in the night, *mipaḥad baleilot*, turns into a great ecstasy, *Ahava Rabba*.

This is the homelessness of man as a small being, as a little being. It comes to expression in the experience of the dread of the night, in a feeling of insecurity and fright. As we said before, human beings are frightened. In the young, the fright is not pronounced; it is covered up by one's trust in his parents, even in himself. But as man advances in age and gets older, he becomes a frightened person. I have never seen an old man who is not frightened. Some people know how to manage their fright; some people know how to sublimate their fright into creativity. Others do not. On the whole, the American Jew does not know how to handle old age. He cannot sublimate old age to wisdom, to dignity, or to creative efforts. While modern old man lives in luxury and travels around the globe many times a year, he does not know how to redeem himself from the awesome fright of *mipaḥad baleilot*. And *mipaḥad baleilot* makes man homeless.

Let us now examine the antithesis: how does man merge his greatness with his homelessness? How does he experience both at the same time? Let us open the Book of *Kohelet* and see how the old king of Jerusalem experienced his existential exile. King Solomon, or King Kohelet, who has risen above his fellow man, experiences his homelessness in a certain restlessness, in frustrating boredom, in questing for the boundless and for the unachievable. Great man is homeless because he is never satisfied with his own creative gesture. He is always driven by a satanic, insatiable urge to conquer and to control beyond and above the bounds which God has assigned to him. No matter what the ultimate end may be, the human being is not happy with his modest home, with the status quo. He journeys into parts unknown and, of course, he is always disenchanted. The human creative fantasy knows no bounds. The whole phenomenon we call civilization is an expression of human homelessness and human restlessness. Why is man restless? What is he looking for? He searches for a home in the Paradise. Where is the Paradise? The Paradise is in God. Man's restlessness is man's questing for God, sometimes knowingly, consciously, intentionally, and other times unconsciously and unintentionally. Man searches for God even when he, driven by pride and impudence, tries to move away from God.

6.

Homeless man was commanded to pray. "*Batzar lekha,* In thy distress..." (Deut. 4:30). What sort of distress? Homelessness. "When all those things are come upon thee, thou wilt return to the Lord, thy God." Little homeless man has a need for prayer because he is frightened by his vulnerability and his exposure to an unfriendly nature. Great homeless man prays for fulfillment and total realization. Both are questing for God, even though from time to time the quest is misunderstood by man. He may erroneously think that what he is searching for is another field, another million dollars, another luxury. In fact, he is searching for the *Ribbono shel Olam*. And how can you find the *Ribbono shel Olam*? The road to Him winds through prayer. Thus homeless man, in his quest for a home, is questing for God, whom he can reach only through prayer.

In prayer both great man and small man find their home. Through prayer great man finds home, peace, and serenity, and through prayer small man liberates himself from his fright, the dread in the night. Unfortunately, the modern Jew does not know how to pray. The experience of returning home the very moment one starts to read his prayers is unknown to the modern Jew.

I remember that as a small child I was raised in a Chabad town where there was a synagogue called the *Alter Chassidishe Shul*. There was a tradition that the founder of Chabad, the *Baal HaTanya* Rav Shneur Zalman, once prayed in that *shul*. There was indeed one seat completely enclosed so that no one could sit in it. This was the seat he supposedly sat in when he passed through the town. He had come to that town with the Russian army, which was being pursued by Napoleon. The population of that town consisted almost exclusively of poor people: workers, tradesmen, particularly peddlers, who used to travel to and visit the villages within a fifteen-mile radius of the town. You cannot imagine the primitive conditions in which the Russian peasants lived fifty or fifty-five years ago [the early twentieth century]. Yet after spending a full week in those primitive shanties the people used to come home every Friday afternoon. As a child I used to watch the people coming into the *shul* one by one, with water glistening from their payot and beards because they had immersed in the *mikva*. I still remember the tune with which they started to recite, immediately upon entering the *shul*, the 107th Psalm. *Hodu lashem ki tov*. They sang a hymn of gratitude to

God. For what? For delivery from captivity, for freeing people from a prison, for freedom; they would cling to God; they came home in spite of the fact, which they knew very well, that the next day, after sunset, they would return to the primitive villages surrounding the town. The experience of deliverance and redemption represents exactly the idea of prayer. To pray means to allay the fright, the dread in the night; to pray means to return home.

As a matter of fact, why not pray in the fields, in the woods, in the streets? God is ubiquitous. Why does the halakha require a house consecrated to prayer? It must be understood that even a *yaḥid*, an individual, should try to say his prayers in the synagogue. Why is that necessary? It is not the physical structure which is important. It is not so much the roof and not so much the big galleries and the high windows. These are not important. You know we have never cared about the architecture of the synagogue. People speak a lot about it nowadays, but the halakha was not concerned. What is important according to the halakha is something else. *Bayit* in Hebrew has a double connotation. *Bayit* means a house, the physical structure, four walls, a roof, and a floor, and *bayit* means a home. We err when we translate *Beit HaKnesset* as "the house of prayer." This rendition is not true. There is no need for a house of prayer, because I can pray to God and I can kneel to Him and have a rendezvous with Him anywhere on the globe, even on the outskirts of the universe. I am confronted with God everywhere. *Beit HaKnesset* is not a house but a *home* of prayer. The structure is symbolic. *Beit HaKnesset,* if understood as a house of prayer, is an institution; however, if translated as a home of prayer, it turns into an exalted idea, namely, the home of man, of homeless man, which is at the same time the home of God. "*Me'ona Elokei kedem*" (Deut. 33:27), God's dwelling place. Solomon, when he dedicated the Temple, asked a pertinent question: "But will God in very truth dwell on the earth? Behold the heaven and the heaven of heavens cannot contain Thee; how much less the house that I have built" (I Kings 8:27).

And what is the answer to this question? The *Beit HaMikdash* is not the home of God but the home of man where he keeps an appointment with God. God does not need a home for Himself. God feigned homelessness in order to induce man to build a home for man. And whatever name is assigned to this home is to be understood in terms of human, not divine, homelessness. It is the home of God, because it is the home of man. God comes to that house in order to keep His appointment with man.

7.

Solomon, while answering the principal question pertaining to the construction of the Temple, also enumerated those people who need to pray the most because they are the most homeless people. "If a man trespass against his neighbor" (I Kings 8:31). Two people quarrel. Two friends part from each other, and turn into enemies. The friends, I mean the two people who lost their friendship, the most precious gift in the world, started to fight. They were friends. They confided in each other, but due to certain circumstances, sometimes completely unreasonable, they fought. The friendship was terminated and they became enemies. Now they are both homeless. If you lose a friend, you become a homeless being. We expect that this homeless being, "and the oath come before Your altar in this house" (I Kings 8:31), will travel to Jerusalem, to the home of prayer; he has lost a home and now he must find another which will replace the one he lost. Homelessness applies not only to individuals but to a community as well. Not only a person but an entire nation can find itself homeless and lonely. "When Your people Israel are smitten down before the enemy, because they have sinned against You, and shall turn again to You, and confess Your name, and pray, and make supplication to You in this house" (I Kings 8:33). When Your people are smitten down before the enemy, and they are exiled, homeless people, "*veshavu elekha*,"—they will come back, they will find their home. Where? In the home of prayer. In a word, man—be he an individual, be he a community—is homeless because he is vulnerable. He is terrorized by the dread in the night. He needs a home that will give him security, at least a sense of security, and shelter. "Who shall know every man the plague of his own heart, and spread forth his hands toward this house, then hear You in heaven Your dwelling-place, and forgive, and do, and render unto every man according to all his ways, whose heart You know—for You alone know the hearts of all the children of men" (I Kings 8:38–39). That is exactly the idea of *Beit HaKnesset*. As we said above, *Beit HaKnesset* is the home of God because it is the home of man.

8.

Beit HaKnesset conveys a second meaning as well. There is a strange passage in Tractate Shabbat, at the end of the second chapter (32a): "R. Ishmael, the son of Eleazar, said, there are two reasons why ignorant people do not live long, their life-span is shortened: because they call the *aron hakodesh,* the holy ark, *arna,* an ark, and also because they call a *Beit HaKnesset, beit am.*"

The nature of the first violation, of omitting the word *hakodesh* from the phrase *aron hakodesh* concerning the ark, is understandable. By referring to the sacred ark, which contains the law, as *arna,* one equates the sacred ark with an ordinary closet or box. This is secularizing the Torah which is kept in the ark. That is why it is sacrilegious, and hence punishable.

However, the nature of the second sin, of substituting the word *beit am* for *Beit HaKnesset,* is *prima facie* not obvious. What does *Beit HaKnesset* mean in simple language? "House of assembly." Similarly, what does *beit am* mean? "House of the people," or "house of the multitude." What is the semantic difference between *Beit HaKnesset* and *beit am?* The Talmud considered the substitution of *am* for *knesset* a very serious offense.

9.

The answer to this problem lies in a halakhic concept, namely, the idea of *sheliḥut.* At first glance, we are inclined to look upon the institution of *sheliḥut* from an exclusively legalistic, formal viewpoint which does not contain anything transcending the civil, juridic, pragmatic boundaries of that particular institution. As a matter of fact, *sheliḥut,* as a formal legalistic, civil institution, is known not only to Jewry but to the whole civilized world. Roman law and English common law were both familiar with the institution of proxy. What does the institution say? In plain legal terms, it says that I can transfer authority to or bestow authority upon another individual to act on my behalf as my deputy or agent. The more complex communication between people became, the more the distances separating people from each other extended, the more pressing became the need for action by proxy or deputy. However, when we study the laws of *sheliḥut* carefully, analytically, we arrive at a different conclusion: that *sheliḥut* according to the halakha is not just a formal, utilitarian institution. It is not just formal transfer of authority to my agent to sign an agreement or to finalize a transaction on my behalf.

In Judaism *sheliḥut* represents something more. Judaism has formulated *sheliḥut* in a very unique way. The idea belongs not only to the juridic, formalistic realm, but it also has a personalistic note, which sometimes extends into the metaphysical. Unlike the agent in common law, the *shaliaḥ* in Judaic law acts not for the *meshale'aḥ*, i.e., instead of him, but together with him. The alter ego, the *shaliaḥ*, actually undergoes a miraculous metamorphosis and turns into the *meshale'aḥ*. He enacts the part of the latter. He impersonates the latter, like an artist on a theatrical stage, but with one distinction. While the artist, the actor, impersonates a certain character in the drama in an artistic, fictional manner, the *shaliaḥ*, according to *Yahadut*, impersonates the *meshale'aḥ* in an existential, personalistic way. The very phrase *sheluḥo shel adam kemoto* says that the *shaliaḥ* assumes the identity of the *meshale'aḥ*. There is a personal union of *shaliaḥ* and *meshale'aḥ*.

When a *shaliaḥ* is appointed he is not just told *yesh lekha reshut*, you have the authority to act on my behalf, but also, at least initially he is told *yadekha ke'yadi*, my hand is like thy hand, thy hand is like my hand; *pikha ke'pi*, your mouth is like mine; *devarkha ki'devari*, your words are to be considered like my words. Something great and exciting happens. The barriers fencing in an egocentric man's existence are torn down, and the lonely captive, who until now had no friends, a narcissist addicted to vainglory and self-love, breaks out into the free, open spaces of an existence in good fellowship, of being together. *Sheliḥut* forges friendship.

The *shaliaḥ*, in order to "play" the part of the *meshale'aḥ*, must get acquainted with the *meshale'aḥ*, with the latter's cares and anxieties. He must share in his distress and rejoice with him in times of triumph. Even an actor on the stage cannot play the part of a certain character if he does not understand the character. Otherwise his acting would be stiff, mechanical, lifeless. How can the *shaliaḥ* impersonate the *meshale'aḥ*, play the part, at an existential, personalistic level, if the bond of sympathy, of kindness, of concern, and of curiosity does not prevail? The egotist, the self-loving person, who does not acknowledge the presence of others in this world, can hardly assume the identity of his next-door neighbor. How could he? The neighbor does not exist for him.

Basically, *sheliḥut* is an ethical performance in *Yahadut,* and that explains a certain halakha. *Ma atem bnei brit af sheluḥakhem bnei brit,* just as you are members of the covenant, so must your agents be members of the covenant (Kiddushin 41b). The *shaliaḥ* must be like the *meshale'aḥ,* a *ben brit,* a member of the covenant, a Jew, because the abyss separating members of the covenantal society from those who profess another faith must not separate the *shaliaḥ* from the *meshale'aḥ.* If existential destinies differ, if historical memories are not the same, if misunderstanding prevails, if full sympathy and mutual concern are not present, the *sheliḥut* cannot be achieved. The halakha requires the compassionate understanding that results from sharing in a destiny, that draws upon similar historical memories. In a word, *sheliḥut* is nurtured by *ḥesed,* a merger of personal experience and mutual sharing in distress and in joy.

This emphasis explains why *sheliḥut* is valid not only in civil transactions, but also in certain personal relationships between man and God. In fact, the prototype of *sheliḥut* is *sheliḥut* in *korbanot.* There is a rule that *ein korbano shel adam karev ela im ken omed al gabav,* no sacrifice must be offered in the absence of the *baal hakorban,* the person who has pledged the sacrifice. However, the same rule says there is no need for the *baal hakorban,* the owner of the sacrifice, to be present *in corpore* at the sacrificial offering. The presence of a *shaliaḥ* appointed by the *baal hakorban* suffices.

The *shaliaḥ* represents the *baal hakorban,* or owner, at the sacrificial ceremony in the Sanctuary, in the *Azara.* He is not just a formal agent. The latter suffices to sign an agreement, or to sell shares and stock, but to represent the *meshale'aḥ lifnei Hashem,* in the house of God, while the sacrifice of the *meshale'aḥ* is being offered, then formal agency or formal proxy is not enough. The *shaliaḥ* apparently takes on the identity of the *baal hakorban* and acts the latter's part existentially.

10.

The prophet of the Bible is the messenger of God. God is the *meshale'aḥ,* and the prophet is the *shaliaḥ.* Prophets are called *malakhim in* the Bible. "*Vayishlaḥ malakh vayotzieinu miMitzrayim*" (Num. 20:16)—the *malakh* the Bible refers to was Moses. However, God does not just send off the prophet with a message. He does not leave the prophet alone. He moves along with the prophet and acts and speaks through him. We all know the famous expression: *Shekhina medaberet mitokh gerono shel Moshe,* God spoke out of the mouth, or throat, of Moses.

In conjunction with the above it is interesting to recall yet another passage in the Bible. When Moses complained (Ex. 3:11) "Who am I that I should go unto Pharaoh and that I should bring forth the children of Israel out of Egypt?" God answered him in three cryptical words: "*Ki ehyeh imakh,* because I will be with thee": In other words, God told Moses, "Listen, Moses. The *sheliḥut* which I have entrusted to thee is unique. You are not a proxy. You are not an agent. You are not a deputy." The *meshale'aḥ* will not absent himself from the *shaliaḥ*. He will walk along with the *shaliaḥ* silently and whisper into the ear of the *shaliaḥ* and guide him as to what he is supposed to do and how to act.

11.

The whole institution *of tefilla betzibbur,* and the synagogue, which is dedicated to *tefilla betzibbur,* rests upon the idea of *sheliḥut.* Let me explain. What is a *tzibbur*? Of course, in the vernacular we identify *tzibbur* with the *minyan.* We do not say *tzibbur. Tzibbur* is the scholarly phrase for which *minyan* is the colloquial expression. What, then, is a *minyan*? Ten Jews together. The number ten.

Is this equation of *tzibbur* with *minyan* correct? Technically, it is correct. However, philosophically, it is wrong. Perhaps it is wrong not only philosophically, but halakhically as well. In order to understand the word *tzibbur,* we have to simply give our attention to the term *korban tzibbur.* What is the connotation of *tzibbur* as regards *korbanot*? After all, we know that *tefillot* resulted from *korbanot.* Prayer, or the three institutional prayers, morning, afternoon, and evening, are just the correlates of the sacrifices offered by the *tzibbur* in antiquity. What is the halakhic semantics of the term *tzibbur* concerning *temidim* and *musafim,* concerning *korban tzibbur*? Of course, *tzibbur* with regard to *korban* is to be equated with *eida,* with *Adat Yisrael,* and not with a *minyan.* In other words, *tzibbur vis-a-vis korban* signifies the entire Jewish covenantal community. If ten people should get together and jointly bring a sacrifice, the latter would not be considered as a *korban tzibbur,* but as a *korban hashutfim,* since the term *tzibbur* halakhically is related to the entirety of the Jewish community.

Hence, the term *tzibbur,* or *tefilat hatzibbur,* refers not to ten people, but to the *Klal Yisrael,* or rather, *Knesset Yisrael.* God hearkens to prayer of the community as a whole, to prayer offered by the *Adat Yisrael* in its entirety. No one must be excluded: "*Venikdashti betokh Bnei Yisrael,* I will be hallowed among the Children of Israel" (Lev. 22:32). Only within all the people, in the midst of the community, will I be sanctified. And the halakha derives from these words the famous conclusion: *Kol davar shebikedusha lo yehei paḥot me'asara,* one is not allowed to recite words of sanctification if fewer than ten people are present (*Megilla* 23b).

The question is obvious. On the one hand, the Bible states "*betokh Bnei Yisrael,*" only in the midst of all the people shall I be sanctified and glorified, and not in the presence of just a part of the people. On the other hand, however, the halakha sanctions the recital *of Kedusha* in the presence of ten old men. How can we reconcile the words in the Bible, *venikdashti betokh Bnei Yisrael,* which imply that *Kedusha* must be recited in the presence of the entire community to the exclusion of no one, with our daily practice, where we are satisfied with ten people?

The answer lies in the self-evident fact that the halakha, in permitting ten people to recite *Kedusha,* to say "*Amen, yehei shemei rabba,*" to answer "*Barukh Hashem hamevorakh le'olam va'ed,*" operated with the idea of *sheliḥut* which, as I said before, is not to be equated with proxy. The ten are the representatives of the *Klal Yisrael.* They are the *sheluḥim of* the people as a whole. And in keeping with our interpretation *of sheliḥut,* they are not only representatives, they are not only ambassadors of the *Klal Yisrael,* they *are* the *Klal Yisrael.* In a strange mystical way, they impersonate, not fictionally, not artistically, but existentially, and become *Klal Yisrael.* In other words, when ten people in the synagogue offer their prayers, the entire *Knesset Yisrael* prays with them. They are the *Knesset Yisrael.* That is why *Kedusha* has been permitted in the presence of ten.

Let me add another thought. When we pronounce the term *Knesset Yisrael,* we refer not only to a multitude consisting of thirteen million people, our contemporaries, *ken yirbu,* but to a mystical entity or individuality. *Knesset Yisrael,* the way Nahmanides and other mystics, the classical *baalei hakabbala,* understood the term, is not just a conglomeration of people, it is not just a crowd. It is more than that. It is a separate entity, a living individuality provided with an "I" awareness. The kabbalists spoke about the invisible *Knesset Yisrael.* There is a visible *Knesset Yisrael,* which consists of contemporaries, of thirteen million people now. And there is an invisible *Knesset Yisrael,* which embraces not only contemporaries, but every Jew who has ever lived. It includes all those whose names have been immortalized and made unforgettable as well as all those Jews who lived in anonymity, who died silently and were buried in unmarked graves, without leaving a single memory, without leaving a single footprint on the shifting sands of human destiny. All of them, great or small, big or little, are part and parcel of that invisible *Knesset Yisrael* which is represented, and to be more exact, impersonated, by the *minyan* of ten old, frail, sickly people.

Furthermore, the *Knesset Yisrael* holds in her embrace every Jew who will ever live on the face of the globe. Generations yet unborn, who will at some point in the dark, awesome future serve our people in a variety of ways—all of them belong to the invisible *Knesset Yisrael,* represented by the ten people who on a rainy afternoon go to *shul* and say, *Ashrei yoshvei veteikha od yehallelukha sela.* The entire *Knesset Yisrael.*

Fundamentally, there is only one prayer. Fundamentally, there is only one *tzibbur*: the invisible *Knesset Yisrael,* embracing the past, the present, and the future, prays with every *minyan.* The *tzibbur* in the synagogue is the micro-*Knesset Yisrael* of ten which represents, personifies, the macro-community of the invisible *Knesset Yisrael,* the eternal community. The idea of *sheliḥut* even in the context of prayer reaches, as is the case with prophecy, into the mystical and transcendental. The invisible, eternal *Knesset Yisrael,* cutting through all ages *me'olam ve'ad olam,* is present in every micro-community of ten. The macro-community, the invisible, infinite *Knesset Yisrael,* contracts itself. The all-embracing macro-community practices *tzimtzum* in order to find room in a small, finite community of ten.

We asked above why the halakha is so meticulous regarding the name *Beit HaKnesset.* What is wrong with *beit am*? Why did our sages say that it is a serious offense to substitute *beit am* for *Beit HaKnesset*? The answer now is simple. The *Beit HaKnesset* is the home of the great, invisible *Knesset Yisrael* which cuts through all ages and millennia. A *beit am* is just a house for contemporaries. However, to pray with contemporaries is not enough. One must pray with the entire covenantal community which is present in the *Beit HaKnesset*, and the sanctity of the *Beit HaKnesset* is due to that *mysterium tremendum*. The latter suspends all three time dimensions: the past is not gone yet, the future has already arrived, and we, the ten people, the *minyan* who live in the present, unite both, past and future. A *Beit HaKnesset* is the home of prayer, as was pointed out above, because it is the home of the great *Knesset Yisrael*, and *ipso facto*, the home where the Almighty has a rendezvous with the *Knesset Yisrael*.

Chapter 10

Old Prayers and "New" Jews

PRAYER AND CEREMONIALISM

How does the halakha conceive of prayer?

Jewish prayer is not some ceremonial form of divine worship, as it is in the Catholic Church and in certain Protestant denominations.

Every ceremony has at least three characteristic features:

1. The ceremonial emphasizes the superficial. What is important are not one's feelings, but rather his declarations and gestures. What is meaningful are not one's intentions, but rather his prose. What is valuable are not one's inner thoughts, but rather his external actions. In short, ceremony is founded upon the great falsehood of hypocrisy, saying one thing while having another in one's heart.

2. The ceremonial seeks in every instance to tear a person away from reality and lead him into a world of illusion. Ceremonies do not exist in real life; real life is simple, gray, and monotonous. He who wishes to enjoy the beauty of a ceremony must slip into a different realm, a realm of pseudo-reality.

3. A ceremony must always have a master of ceremonies schooled in performing the ritual in an impactful manner. The layperson can only be a spectator, not an active participant.

The essence of Jewish prayer leaves no room for any of these three characteristics of the ceremony.

What is the essence of prayer according to the halakha? The religious act of prayer is, from a halakhic standpoint, exquisitely unique and fundamentally different from many of the Torah's other commandments. The distinctiveness of prayer consists of the fact that its essence and substance lie not in the outward, physical behavior of the person praying—in the recitation of a particular text or the adoption of certain postures and gestures, like standing or bowing—but rather in the subjective sphere, in a state of mind/disposition, in a feeling, in a religious experience. Prayer requires intention. However, the intention associated with prayer is not simply an accompanying religious exercise, as it is in the case of other commandments, but rather constitutes the central motif and substance of prayer itself. It expresses not only the petitioner's resolution to fulfill a commandment, but also his entire spiritual disposition. In short, prayer is, in halakhic terms, an *avoda shebalev*, an act of worshipping the Master of the Universe with one's heart (Taanit 2a).

It is true that the halakha has never really put much stock in subjective, formless, free-flowing states of mind and inner experiences. Indeed, it has always demanded that the powerful currents of feeling and thought be channeled into objective molds and forged into specific, concrete actions: the feeling of loving-kindness into the act of giving charity, the feeling of sanctity into ethical behavior, and so on. Subjectivity and inwardness alone are like a disembodied soul: intangible, insubstantial, indistinct, and ephemeral. Feeling flares up magnificently, like a beautiful sunrise on a clear summer morning, but also evanesces very quickly in the fog of uncertainty. The physical act endows the subjective disposition with stability and durability. Therefore, the halakha dictated that the worship of the heart—prayer—not remain locked up in the heart, but rather express itself outwardly and take on concrete form in an established rite, thrice-daily prayer, and other objective practices.

However, all of these demands touch only upon the technique of prayer (in halakhic terms, the *ma'aseh hamitzva* [performance of the commandment]), the means by which the *avoda shebalev* is manifest, but not upon the core of prayer itself, which remains hidden in the recesses of the heart, in the mysterious tremble of the God-thirsty soul. To use halakhic terminology, I would say that the *kiyyum hamitzva* [fulfillment of the commandment] is realized *balev* [in the heart]: "Make not your prayer into a fixed routine, but rather a plea for mercy and grace before the Omnipresent" (Avot 2:18).

The conclusion that follows from this premise is clear. Despite the fact that the actual text of the prayers is the same for everyone, prayer itself was never standardized. Everyone recites the same words [in the *Shemoneh Esreh*], bows at *Modim,* faces the Land of Israel, recites *mashiv haruaḥ* during the winter and *ya'aleh veyavo* on the first day of a new Jewish month—but every heart worships the Master of the Universe in its own individualized, unique way.

Already at the beginning of the *Shemoneh Esreh,* when describing the Master of the Universe as "the great, mighty, and awe-inspiring God," everyone experiences those words differently.

One person might sense the eternity and omnipotence of God as He reveals Himself in the great mathematical-physical universe: the astronomical expanses extending before man on a clear, starry night, as well as the dynamics of nature—how it exerts itself in all phenomena, from the fall of a stone to the flight of the nebulae unto the edges of the cosmos—whisper of the *Ein Sof* [Infinite One] to the philosophically-attuned individual, who might experience all of this in the course of his *Shemoneh Esreh*: "When I behold Your heavens, the work of Your fingers, the moon and stars that You set in place..." (Ps. 8:4).

Another, more aesthetically-inclined person perceives the breath of the *Ein Sof,* of the great, mighty, and awe-inspiring God, in the splendor and colorfulness of nature, in the majesty of the sea, in the setting and rising of the sun, in the play of light and shadow: "O Lord, my God, You are very great; You are clothed in glory and majesty, wrapped in a robe of light..." (Ps. 104:1–2).

An ethical-moral personality finds the Master of the Universe, the great, mighty, and awe-inspiring God, in the spiritual world order, in the human drive toward the good, in moral consciousness, and so on.

The mystical-religious soul encounters the great, mighty, and awe-inspiring God in its own yearnings for Him, in its striving toward endlessness and eternity, in its having fallen in love with the *Shekhina,* and in its constant searching after God: "Upon my couch at night I sought the one I love..." (Song 3:1).

And the simple Jew stumbles upon the great, mighty, and awe-inspiring God in the course of his humble, mundane life and in the fulfillment of his own private needs, like making a living, finding good careers for his children, and so forth.

Yes, everyone prays, everyone recites the same *Shemoneh Esreh*; the technical religious behavior is identical—but how very distinct is the *avoda shebalev*! It is an intimate, individualized, unique experience, one which refuses to be forced into the confines of conventional religiosity. It is, as is the spiritual-religious personality itself, lonely and alone; it cannot join the rest of the congregation.

If the fixed prayer rite is meant to serve as nothing more than a means of giving voice to the individualized, tender, and passionate *avoda shebalev*, one must always remain vigilant that the medium through which these remarkable feelings express themselves not entirely obscure the inner prayer; that the body, together with its clothing, not suffocate the soul; and that the form not supplant the living substance. That is why Judaism so tenaciously protected prayer, so that it not buckle under the aesthetic load that some attempt from time to time to impose upon it. Overdone singing, organ music, mixed choirs, and other decorous elements undermine the foundations of *avoda shebalev*. It is true that Judaism has always preferred that religious practice be observed in an aesthetically pleasing way—"This is my God and I will glorify Him" (Ex. 15:2). But Judaism has also always been careful—with respect to all commandments, and especially regarding prayer—that the glamour of the technique used to fulfill the law should never deaden that which is tied to, and sincerely felt by, the soul; that the mouth should never replace the heart.

Let us not forget that although the religious and aesthetic sensibilities share much in common—both seek out the sublime, mysterious, and unattainable—there is, nevertheless, a fundamental difference between them. The person looking for beauty finds his satisfaction in the harmonious form, in the fusion of colors, sounds, words, and phrases. Formal uniformity and consistency are the principle features of aesthetic achievement. As a result, form becomes primary and content secondary. By way of contrast, the splendor of the religious experience consists specifically in the influence of content on medium, in the irregularity of expression, in the inner storm that smashes to pieces all forms and all rules of external beauty.

The God-thirsty personality is very much removed from comfortable complacency. It is tattered and torn. It undergoes many metamorphoses. It springs from one state of mind/disposition to the next—from ecstatic joy to boundless fear, from equanimity to wild unrest. At times, it enthusiastically sings, "The Lord is my shepherd; I lack nothing. He makes me lie down in green pastures; He leads me to water in places of repose" (Ps. 23:1–2). At other times, it cries out in terror, "Where can I escape from Your spirit? Where can I flee from Your presence?" (Ps. 139:7). It is full of emotional caprice, its path snakes in a zigzag. For this reason, it cannot be constrained by the rigid formalities of artistic creation and refuses to reckon with the rules of external effect.

Were prayer to consist solely of externals, it might have been possible to accompany it with music, with stiff, decorous garb, the cadences of an organ, the rhetoric of a "rabbi," the singing of *Aleinu* in a churchly-ceremonial tone, and synchronized bowing at *va'anaḥnu kore'im*. "Unfortunately," though, Judaism conceived of prayer as an *avoda shebalev*, as a form of worship of the heart: a heart pulsing rapidly and irregularly; a heart overflowing with passion for the Divine; a heart that searches, seeks, and thirsts; a heart full of dissonances; a heart so "mad," so "wild," and so "primitive" that it recoils from the prospect of crossing the threshold of a temple, for there, everything is normal, civilized, and logical. It is this same remarkable Jewish heart that has been praying and petitioning ever since the times of our forefather Abraham.

For this reason, the traditional Jewish rite (the liturgical melodies) is rather imperfect from a musical standpoint. The Jewish melodic repertoire is often distinguished by its formlessness and sudden jumps; those seeking harmonious arrangements of notes in Jewish liturgical melodies will be disappointed. Instead, what one finds in them is an elemental outburst of feeling—for instance, of hope and anticipation when reciting [on Yom Kippur] *uvekhen ten paḥdekha*, silent joy and yearning during *vehakohanim veha'am*, resignation and sadness while saying *ashamnu* or *anna Hashem ḥate'u*, melancholy and simultaneous encouragement during the *Kaddish* of *Ne'ilah*, solemnity and anxiety when reciting *Kol Nidrei*. These melodies do not resound with an abundance of beautiful notes, but rather with a wealth of sincerity and soulfulness, the sounds of "In distress I called" (Ps. 118:5), of "Out of the depths I call You, O Lord" (Ps. 130:1), of "A prayer of the lowly man when he is faint and pours forth his plea before the Lord" (Ps. 102:1). *This* is the melodiousness of *avoda shebalev*, wherein the form is steeped in content, the prose in feeling, and the outward in the inward. Here, the heart, the truth, is at work.

I envision a *Kol Nidrei* eve in the study house of the Baal Shem Tov or of the Baal HaTanya, of blessed memory. Their services certainly did not feature music, choirs, or decorum. They had no ostentatious platforms bedecked with rugs and flowers, with "rabbis" schooled in proper diction and refined manners standing above. There prayed simple, ordinary Jews, who knew nothing of "the beauty of Japheth." But precisely because of that, they were also inextricably connected with past generations, full of religious fire and awe: "For love is fierce as death, passion is mighty as Sheol..." (Song 8:6). Form was completely absent from those services. But precisely because of that, there raged among them an inferno of flaming belief, of great love and passion for the Creator of the Universe. All of the petitioners no doubt swayed like the trees of a forest blown about by a howling gale, and certainly shook out of themselves their *avoda shebalev*.

I have the right to imagine such a scene. For in memories of my youth, though half-blurred and half-romanticized, I can still see before me the image of a Chabad community rocking back and forth on the first night of Rosh HaShana, the "Night of Coronation" (as the old Hasidim used to call it), when the small, insignificant, helpless human being, who is here today and gone tomorrow, crowns the Ancient, Infinite, Eternal One and gives Him the epithet "the Holy King." I can still hear the murmuring of hundreds of enthused and spirited Jews, which would spread through the synagogue as the prayer leader finished the *Kaddish* and the congregation began reciting the *Shemoneh Esreh*—a hum of something momentous, sublime, buoyant, and alive, which had no need of a cantor, choir, or theatrical decorousness in order to reach the Gates of Heaven.

Does a spring, gushing up from the ground with elemental force, need to be confined to some sort of artistic mold in order to be experienced as magnificent and moving? Must lava, erupting from a fiery volcano, operate according to the rules of vacuous, icy decorum? It is precisely in their naturalness, primitivity, and spontaneity that their splendor, the *hod shebigevura*, manifests! And is not the man at prayer a kind of bubbling spring, or even a fire-spitting mountain?

It is obvious, then, that Jewish prayer stands in opposition to the ceremonial with respect to the relationship between content and form, heart and word; and so, all of the previously mentioned aesthetic reforms, rather than deepening the experience, would rob it of its substance and soul.

But the other two features of the ceremonial also prove themselves incompatible with *avoda shebalev*. If true prayer takes place in the heart, there is no need for a master of ceremonies to mediate between the congregation and the Creator of the Universe. Every individual is endowed with a heart that is, from the Jewish point of view, filled with love—consciously or unconsciously—for God. And that heart is just as close to the Gates of Heaven as is the heart of a "rabbi"—and, many times, perhaps even closer. The "rabbi" need not stand on a platform, dressed up in "*bigdei kehuna*" [lit., priestly vestments; i.e., canonicals], to conduct the prayer service. In the eyes of the Master of the Universe, he and the simple Jew are equals, and both of them must pray below, on the same level in the synagogue, without any barriers between them. Here is not the place to enter into a halakhic disquisition on the prohibition against standing on a platform while praying. But one thing I do know: that towering over the congregation during prayer contradicts the spirit of *avoda shebalev*, according to which man is meant to approach God from "out of the depths." The contemporary, inauthentic role of the "rabbi" as leader of services is the result of a false ceremonial-conception having infiltrated our understanding of Jewish prayer.

Lastly, and most importantly, *avoda shebalev* cannot be severed from real life. Standing before God in prayer, man must give a full accounting for his mundane activities outside of the synagogue. Prayer has to hold up a mirror to a person's behavior and must never become an instrument that enables him to escape from himself and from his moral responsibilities.

The Jewish synagogue, in contrast to the church, never developed any architectural or decorative means to charm man and lull him into a sense of supernaturalism. It never sought to delude man into thinking that he is standing before God when his heart, hard as stone, brutal and cynical, does not even seek Him out. In our synagogues, mood lighting was never employed and the white light of the sun was never obstructed by narrow, stained glass. In our synagogues, the echo of the soft, rich cadences of organ music and of the singing of a mixed choir, hidden from the view of the congregation in order to create an otherworldly, mystical ambiance, never reverberated.

At no point did we strive to remove the Jew from reality and instead lead him with rhapsodic enthusiasm. Just the opposite: we have always demanded of him that his prayer be contiguous with his life and that he use it as an opportunity to give a true accounting. That is why the entire Christian-Catholic dramatization of prayer is so incomprehensible within our religious consciousness, and it is for that reason that the halakha is so negatively disposed to the so-called modernization of the prayer service, which effaces the original, individualized character of *avoda shebalev*.

THE LANGUAGE AND FORM OF OUR PRAYERS

Avoda shebalev, which constitutes the essence of prayer, consists of the sublime experience a person has when he encounters the *Ein Sof*. To pray means to meet the Master of the Universe; better put, it connotes a conversation between man and God, just like prophecy. The only difference between prayer and prophecy is that while in the case of prophecy, the Master of the Universe beckons man unto Himself, and man answers Him, "Here I am" ("Abraham, Abraham" – "Here I am!" [Gen. 22:11]; "Moses, Moses" – "Here I am!" [Ex. 3:4]; "Samuel, Samuel" – "Here I am!" [see I Sam. 3:4–10]), in the case of prayer, man takes the initiative of calling out to the Master of the Universe, and the *Ein Sof* responds, "Here I am." But here, too, man speaks with God; he stands opposite Him and addresses Him in the second person (via "You"): "Blessed are You." This idea is a halakhic fact. From a legal perspective, a man at prayer must consider himself to be "like one standing before the *Shekhina*" (Maimonides, *Mishneh Torah, Hilkhot Tefilla* 4:16; see also Sanhedrin 22a).

Given the foregoing, the halakha could never comprehend the rationale of, or the justification for, the institution of prayer. One question has continually tormented the halakha: How can man, with all his limitations, dependency, and smallness, with his depravity and vulgarity, approach the Creator of the Universe, the absolute, unconditional, endless Reality? How, in general, can man, who is more *ayin* [absence] than *yesh* [substance], encounter the *Ein Sof* and yet endure?

How can he be so audacious as to permit himself to beg the Master of the Universe for his petty, foolish needs? How can he bring himself to laud the Creator of the Universe, the One about whom it is said "for Him is silence praise" (see Ps. 65:2), and to sing unto Him hymns and paeans? Is it not an absurdity that nothingness extols endlessness and eternity? Is not prayer entirely paradoxical, incomprehensible, and in conflict with the rule that "man may not see Me and live" (Ex. 33:20), the rule that man cannot come too close to the *Ein Sof*?

The halakha has not succeeded in resolving this conundrum; it has conceded that it does not understand the concept of worship and that prayer remains an insoluble riddle. The sages of the halakha innovated one thing only. They said: True, we do not understand the possibility of, or the sense behind, prayer. But, despite our incomprehension, we do know that the forefathers of the Jewish people and its prophets prayed; that they arrogated to themselves the right to draw closer to the Master of the Universe, to meet and converse with Him, to plead with, praise, and glorify Him, and to stand in His presence. The halakha made us all aware of the historical fact that prayer is as old as the *Knesset Yisrael* itself. Abraham prayed, Isaac prayed, and Jacob prayed (Berakhot 26b). Moses petitioned on behalf of the nation in the passage "He implored" (Ex. 32:11–13), on behalf of his brother Aaron (Deut. 9:20), on behalf of his sister Miriam (Num. 12:13), and finally on his own behalf, too, in the tragic portion "I pleaded" (Deut. 3:23–25). Hannah poured out her heart before the Master of the Universe in Shiloh (I Sam. 1:10–13). David's Psalms is an entire book of prayer and supplication. Solomon prayed at the inauguration of the First Temple (I Kings 8). Jonah called out to God from the depths of the sea (Jon. 2:2–10). Hezekiah secluded himself with his Maker in an hour of fear and despair (Isa. 38:2–3). Daniel prayed three times a day facing Jerusalem (Dan. 6:11). And along with the forefathers, kings, and prophets, the entire *Knesset Yisrael* prayed; generations upon generations of Jews have prayed at all times and in all places.

We, say the sages of the halakha, cannot justify prayer *de jure*—but we also obviously cannot doubt its *de facto* existence, or the historical reality that Jews have always prayed. Thus, it is clear that man may and must pray to God; that he has permission to pour out his heart, to sing unto Him hymns and paeans, and to cling to Him like a child who nestles his head in his mother's lap or in his father's shoulder. The famous statement in the Talmud that "the forefathers instituted the prayers" (Berakhot 26b) expresses the idea that the precedent for prayer was established during the dawn of our history, and therefore we take it for granted. We have no other explanation for how we can pray. Our forefathers and prophets set an example that we simply emulate.

As a result, we must see to it that our worship—whether in regard to its structure and form, whether concerning the number and times of prayers, whether with respect to its content and formulas of praise—should accord with the prayers of the forefathers, prophets, and great leaders of the nation, whose model we imitate; we ourselves may not add anything to, subtract from, change, or embellish the prayers. Were we to grasp the essence of prayer and understand the "why" of worship, we could, perhaps, author our own supplications. However, since prayer remains an unsolved mystery, we cannot involve ourselves in literary-liturgical compositions, but must rather hold ourselves strictly to the sanctioned, traditional rite. Even concerning the Men of the Great Assembly, about whom tradition tells us that they set the text of the prayers, the Talmud relates the following: "One hundred twenty elders, including a number of prophets, established the Eighteen Benedictions in order" (Megilla 17b). Among the authors of the prayers were many prophets, because without their assistance even the Men of the Great Assembly themselves would not have dared introduce a fixed text for man to use in his dialogue with the Creator of the Universe.

It is worth noting that when the sages in Yavneh added to the *Shemoneh Esreh* the nineteenth blessing, *VeLaMalshinim*, Rabban Gamaliel himself did not wish to compose it. Instead, he instructed Shmuel HaKatan, whom the *Baraita* attests was fit to be a prophet (see Sotah 48b, Sanhedrin 11a), to do so. It is also interesting that the majority of our prayers are composed of words, and oftentimes even of complete formulas, taken directly from the Bible. The sages of Israel avoided, as far as possible, using their own words, because one must adopt a very cautious and careful approach toward something that one does not understand. Had Moses not described the Master of the Universe as "the great, mighty, and awe-inspiring God" (Deut. 10:17), we would have had no right to address Him as such in the *Shemoneh Esreh*.

Proceeding from this point of view, the halakha ruled that whoever changes anything about the text of the blessings acts improperly: "Anyone who alters the form in which the sages coined the blessings is naught but mistaken" (Maimonides, *Mishneh Torah, Hilkhot Berakhot* 1:5). Certain modifications actually disqualify the prayer, so that one must repeat it. The halakha goes on to establish that one must pray three times a day, and no more (a *tefillat nedava,* an additional, voluntary prayer, must satisfy many halakhic conditions, and Jews historically very rarely put it into practice) [see *Shulḥan Arukh, Oraḥ Ḥayyim* 107]. Twice a day, before we stand in prayer, we read the *Shema* together with its benedictions, and in the morning, we recite verses and chapters from Psalms. Even during the day at *Minḥa,* one first says *Ashrei,* because it is forbidden for man to simply stand up and approach the Master of the Universe in prayer straight away. The preamble to prayer is Psalms, that Godly book of confession, supplication, petition, praise, and song, in which every being who longs for, dreams about, and has fallen in love with God can find the echo of his thoughts, feelings, and yearnings. By delving into that wonderful book, man strengthens his resolve and commitment to encountering the *Ein Sof* and to entering into conversation with Him. David constantly argued with and complained to God, conversed and spent time with Him, cried and consoled himself before Him, and sang praise and thanksgiving to Him—so muses the man at prayer, and that thought gives him the courage he needs to knock at the Gates of Heaven.

Despite this, when all is said and done, the petitioner still begins his *Shemoneh Esreh* with "O Lord, open my lips, and let my mouth declare Your praise" (Ps. 51:17), with the plea that God help him open his lips, for he himself has neither the strength nor the audacity to do so. The feeling of unworthiness in drawing close to the Creator of the Universe has not been eliminated, regardless of all the preparations. After the *Shemoneh Esreh,* that same petitioner falls on his face for *Taḥanun,* in which he again expresses his worthlessness and lowliness and begs forgiveness and pardon even for the very act of praying itself.

The halakha did not view favorably the organization of special prayer gatherings or the arrangement of one's own order of prayers. All pleas must fit into the framework of the *Shemoneh Esreh,* whether in the middle benedictions, in *Shome'a Tefilla,* or immediately after the conclusion of the *Shemoneh Esreh.* Only at those points may the individual petition the Master of the Universe for his needs and cast himself before Him in supplication to his heart's content, because then his words and the ancient, traditional *Shemoneh Esreh* blend together. In times of peril for the collective or for the individual, Jews would indeed come together in their synagogues and storm the Throne of Glory, but their tempestuous plea would express itself in the recitation of psalms, not in new prayers. The only extra prayer gathering to which the halakha gave its imprimatur is the *seliḥot* service during the Ten Days of Repentance and before Rosh HaShana (*seliḥot* on fast days are recited immediately following the *Shemoneh Esreh,* like other supplications). But even regarding this exception, the sages of the tradition relied upon a special dispensation contained in the verse, "The Lord descended in a cloud; He stood with him there, and proclaimed the name of the Lord" (Ex. 34:5; see Rosh HaShana 17b); and when all is said and done, the original *seliḥot* consist of collections of verses, the Thirteen Attributes, confessions, and very short prayers like *Avinu Malkeinu, Aneinu,* and *Mi SheAna,* which are of ancient provenance.

The halakha was so extreme in its aversion to the composition of new prayers that it legislated a rather remarkable law: if a person traveling on a journey finds himself in a dangerous location where he cannot pray the entire *Shemoneh Esreh* (and not even *Havineinu* [an abridged version of *Shemoneh Esreh* prescribed by the Talmud]), he may request almost nothing of the Master of the Universe, because his petition would not conform to the structure of prayer as instituted by the Men of the Great Assembly. Rabbi Eliezer maintains, for instance, that a wayfaring Jew may only recite the following prayer: "Do as You will in the heavens above, grant contentment to those who fear You below, and act as You see fit. Blessed are You, O Lord, who listens to prayer" (Berakhot 29b). If he adds so much as a single word or wish to this short formula, he is considered to have breached normative practice; he must satisfy himself with this brief entreaty.

Even *piyyut* [liturgical poetry]—about which a great debate raged among the sages of the halakha, and which is itself, for the most part, more *midrash* than entreaty, more study material than supplication—was only permitted within the framework of the *Shemoneh Esreh* and of the blessings associated with the reading of the *Shema. Piyyut* was never recited on its own.

If here and there a plea or a *Yehi Ratzon* spontaneously emerged, it burst forth from the depths of the *Volksgeist,* from the inspiration of hallowed generations, from the hearts of Jews who sacrificed daily for the sake of Judaism and whose faith was as fresh and vibrant as the early-morning dew. Nevertheless, the great religious leaders of Israel did not recite such things; they strictly adhered to the text established by the sages of the Talmud. When one stands before the King of Kings, they would note, he must be careful with every word, every sound, every syllable.

The Jewish liturgy was composed and recited with the awareness of both the great mystery and incomprehensibility of the concept of prayer in general, on the one hand, and of its absolute indispensability and ancient historical existence, on the other hand. It consists of two components: the inner feeling, which is individualized, intimate, and fluid—every person experiences his own specific, unique *avoda sheba-lev*—and the technical realization of prayer, which occurs in the context of a rigorously fixed rite. We may not deviate from that rite, since all of prayer remains an inscrutable enigma over which we have no right to act as masters.

Despite the immutability of the text, however, the *Knesset Yisrael* succeeded in doing something extraordinary: it infused the set, stabilized order of prayer with torrents of feeling. With that liturgy, it ignited flames of Godly passion and ecstasy, wept, wiped away the tears, consoled itself, rejoiced, and triumphed. Every sentiment found its echo; every aspiration, its expression; and every need, its articulation in the text. That is how generations of Jews prayed in all places and at all times, each one, with its own moods and specific necessities, unburdening itself before the Creator of the Universe using none other than the old rite. No one felt uncomfortable. "No one said to his fellow: The place is too constricted for me to lodge overnight in Jerusalem" (Avot 5:7).

The fonts used in this book are from the Arno family

OU Press
Books that educate, inspire, enrich and enlighten

Maggid Books
The best of contemporary Jewish thought from
Koren Publishers Jerusalem Ltd.